62 - 10314

7-28-62

BRITISH FOREIGN POLICY SINCE
THE SECOND WORLD WAR

THE AUTHOR

The Honourable C. M. Woodhouse, the present Conservative M.P. for Oxford, has had a most distinguished career as a scholar and man of action. At Oxford he obtained a double first and won the Lord Justice Holker Scholarship at Gray's Inn. At the outbreak of the last war he was commissioned into the Royal Artillery and in 1943 commanded the Allied Military Mission in German-occupied Greece. His work with the Resistance won him the D.S.O. After the war he worked in industry from 1946 to 1948 and then became Secretary of the Nuffield Foundation. Before entering Parliament after the last election, he was Director General of the Royal Institute of International Affairs.

C. M. WOODHOUSE

British Foreign Policy Since the Second World War

FREDERICK A. PRAEGER, *Publisher*

New York

BOOKS THAT MATTER

Published in the United States of America in 1962
by Frederick A. Praeger, Inc., Publisher
64 University Place, New York 3. N.Y.

All rights reserved
© C. M. Woodhouse, 1960
Library of Congress Catalog Card Number: 62–10314

Printed in Great Britain

Contents

CONTENTS

PART II (*continued*)

PART III

THE QUEST FOR NEW RELATIONSHIPS

Introduction

LET me save reviewers the trouble of saying that this book is superficial by saying it myself at the beginning. It deals with the surface of events, which is all that a contemporary book on foreign policy can do. Ideally a study of foreign policy should take account of what was done, what were the intentions with which it was done, and what were the motives that lay behind those intentions. What was done is entirely public knowledge, and it is on this that I have concentrated in the present book. Much of the rest could only be guesswork.

Intentions are sometimes known in part from what ministers said when they did what they did, and also from their later memoirs, such as Sir Anthony Eden's.[1] But they cannot be fully known without access to official sources. I do not share A. J. P. Taylor's view that 'the Foreign Office knows no secrets', because I know it to be untrue from my own experience. In one or two instances where I happen by the accident of government service to have specialized knowledge that is not public, I have suppressed it for the sake of uniformity. This book should therefore be read as based entirely on published sources. It consequently also leaves out of account any consideration of the influence upon foreign policy of permanent officials, though I believe this to be greater than is generally appreciated.[2]

There is nevertheless a sense in which intentions and motives in British foreign policy are fully as public as actions. No government can escape the basic, objective facts of international politics. The purpose of British foreign policy is to protect British interests abroad. (Much confusion can be averted by thinking of it in terms of 'protecting interests' rather than 'pursuing objectives'.) British interests abroad are dictated by Britain's circumstances at home. These are that Britain is a small overcrowded island, which cannot feed more than half of its population from its own resources; which has practically no major industrial raw materials except coal; and which is practically indefen-

---

[1] Sir Anthony Eden, *Full Circle* (Cassell, 1960).
[2] For some indications, see especially Lord Strang, *The Foreign Office* (Allen & Unwin, 1955), pp. 151–4.

sible against nuclear attack. In these circumstances the essentials of British foreign policy are bound to be basically two: trade and defence, particularly the defence of trade. It also follows that there is no hard and fast line between foreign policy and other aspects of policy: domestic, economic, scientific, colonial and so on. They can be separated for the purposes of analysis, but only on the understanding that they are all aspects of one policy.

In any situation, therefore, the intentions of any British government will be governed by the overriding consideration of promoting and protecting the national interest as defined above. But there are also other general considerations, particularly the motives of humanity and ethics. British policies have never been governed solely by self-interest, not even when self-interest is also a mutual interest with others. Disraeli said of the Abyssinian expedition in 1868 that it was undertaken 'not to obtain territory, not to secure commercial advantages, but for high moral causes and for high moral causes alone'. Such arguments are often used by British statesmen. Whether they are valid or not, the fact that they are so often used shows that they appeal to a real instinct in the British make-up. The British public will not tolerate seeing people oppressed or left in poverty and misery, least of all when they think, however mistakenly, that their own government is responsible.

There are thus limitations on any government's freedom of action in any field of policy. Most of all is that true of foreign policy, a field in which no government is exclusively sovereign as it is in domestic policy. What happens in international affairs consists not merely of what is done or intended by the British Government, but of what is done or intended by many others as well. The British Government is not even free in reacting to what is done by a hostile power, because Britain has allies to consult and neutrals to consider and internal pressures to resist, as well as hostile actions to react against. This book is an attempt to examine all these forces separately and in combination.

Part I is concerned with what was going on in the world generally between 1945 and 1959, without particular regard to what Britain was seeking to do about it. The British role is not ignored, but the main object is to sketch the background created by larger forces outside Britain's control, against which successive governments had to conduct a policy aimed at safeguarding British interests. Part II is concerned with the British reaction to the course of events described in Part I; but more particularly it is concerned with the limitations imposed by a variety of factors, each of which has a chapter to itself, on the Government's freedom of action. Both the first two parts are based on a more or less chronological study of the course of events, day by day and year by year, in their several contexts. Part III is an attempt to summarize the British intention, achievement and prospects in a longer and larger perspective.

It will be seen at once that this is not a history of British foreign policy in the fifteen years under review, but a critical examination of it. None of the major episodes is recorded *seriatim* because the most important of them are already on record elsewhere, so far as contemporary record is possible at all; and the necessary references are given. Many episodes crop up again and again in this book, because they have many relevant aspects: the Suez Canal crisis, for instance, naturally has a place in almost every chapter, because it was relevant to the cold war, to defence, to the national economy, to Anglo-American relations, to party politics, and so on. But in each context I have mentioned only those aspects of it that are relevant to that context, leaving those who want to study it as a whole to read specialized works like *Middle East Crisis*, by Guy Wint and Peter Calvocoressi (Penguin Books, 1957).

The book is therefore kaleidoscopic as well as superficial. But that is not to say that it is formless or disordered. On the contrary, a kaleidoscope is a device for producing patterns out of a disorganized jumble of colours. I mention this point because it expresses metaphorically the one real anxiety which I feel about the book. That anxiety is concerned with the danger of creating patterns in the mere process of seeking a principle for analysing the events: the danger of imposing significance on the material studied instead of just finding it. If this has happened, it has happened in spite of my best intentions.

Certain other intentions, however, I would claim to have fulfilled. This book contains no moral judgements and no recommendations. I wish I could say also that it contains no predictions, but they seem in fact to be unavoidable, at least by implication. The most definite of them are in the final section, which can be easily skipped by those who dislike that sort of thing. Apart from such inadvertent crystal-gazing, the book ends chronologically with the General Election of October 1959. I chose this date in advance, because if the Labour Party had won, there would have been a new foreign policy; since the Conservative Party won, there is not; and in either case October 1959 was likely to make a natural terminus.

Of course, much that is important has happened since then, and goes on happening. To name only a few examples, there have been the famous speech by Macmillan on 'the wind of change' in Africa; the subsequent events in all parts of that continent; the frustration of the Summit Conference in May 1960; the breakdown of the ten-power Disarmament Conference a few weeks later. But these events do not alter the fact that, up to the chosen date – and there had to be some date chosen – British foreign policy was what it was. And I suspect that, fundamentally, it still is.

C.M.W.

PART I

The Cold War

1

The Deterioration in Europe (1945–50)

THE cold war, which is the general name for the relation between the Communist and the non-Communist powers since 1947, did not begin overnight. Thoughtful people – most of them thoughtful only after the event, however – could trace its origins back into the Second World War, or even earlier: perhaps as early as the Munich Agreement in September 1938. The lines were in any case clearly drawn before the end of the war. Churchill's agreement with Stalin in Moscow, during October 1944, upon certain rough proportions of influence in the liberated countries of Eastern Europe, may be regarded either as a last desperate attempt to avert the division of Europe into blocs, or as a tacit recognition that it was already happening. The treatment of Poland a few months later, at and after the Yalta Conference of February 1945, can fairly be regarded as a crucial indication of the future pattern of relationship between the Western Powers and the Soviet Union. It may not have been the first conflict in the cold war, but it was the first to become public, when it led to the resignation of a junior minister from Churchill's Coalition Government after the debate in the House of Commons on the Yalta Agreements.

The lines were not yet, of course, firmly drawn, even over the tragic case of Poland. After the Soviet Government had recognized the Communist Polish Government, established at Lublin in August 1944, and had refused to help the rising in Warsaw initiated by the rival Polish Government in exile during the same month, the Western Allies still continued to press their Polish Allies to compromise. Churchill urged the Polish Prime Minister in London to go to Moscow to negotiate, and criticized the Polish Government's obstinacy in the House of Commons. In the debate on the Yalta Agreements he stressed the folly of the London Poles in not following his advice. He had agreed at Yalta to withdraw recognition from the London Polish Government if democratic elections were guaranteed in liberated Poland, a condition on which the British and American leaders conducted the sternest of all their debates with the Soviet leaders at Yalta. If a satisfactory formula could not have been found, it was hinted that the U.S. Government might not come into the United Nations Organization, which was then about to be founded at San Francisco. The formula was found, though it was never fulfilled; and it was the Poles who were unrepresented at San Francisco when the national delegations assembled in April 1945, since neither of the rival governments could command general recognition. It was thus the tragedy of the Poles to have provided the *casus belli* both of the Second World War and of the cold war that followed it.

The Western Allies did not quickly despair over Poland. They still hoped to soften Stalin's heart. One of Roosevelt's last acts was to write a puzzled, critical letter to Stalin about his treatment of Poland. British and American representatives combined to impress their disappointment on Molotov in Washington in April 1945. Harry Hopkins was sent to Moscow in May expressly to make a last effort at persuasion. Ominously, Stalin used this opportunity to try to divide the British and the Americans, emphasizing to the latter that what the former still wanted was a *cordon sanitaire* across Europe. Poland remained undisturbed under its Soviet-sponsored Government. In July 1945 Britain and the U.S.A. gave up the struggle, and formally recognized it.

Poland was not the only indication of Stalin's determination in the last year of the war. In March 1945 the Soviet Government demanded a revision in its favour of the existing treaty of friendship with Turkey, and denounced the treaty when the Turks refused. Further pressures were brought to bear on Turkey by the Soviet Government during the course of the year, which were percipiently described by Forrestal, the U.S. Secretary of the Navy, as an attempt 'to detach Turkey from the orbit of British influence'. The same intention to extend Soviet freedom of action southwards, into the Mediterranean, the Middle East and ultimately Africa, seemed to be suggested by a request presented at the Potsdam Conference in July 1945 for Soviet trusteeship over one or more of the ex-Italian colonies. Specific Soviet claims were later made on Libya and the Dodecanese. The long delay of the Soviet evacuation of northern Iran (Azerbaijan), which was not completed until May 1946, pointed in the same direction. In Europe, which was the main arena of the cold war in its earliest phase, the steady consolidation of Soviet-sponsored governments in the minor ex-enemy countries, especially Rumania, Bulgaria and Hungary, had already begun. These were not yet wholly Communist, but they were criticized as unrepresentative by Bevin in the House of Commons as early as 20 August 1945. Even before the surrender of Germany, the Soviet Government declared its refusal to allow U.N.R.R.A. to operate in Eastern Germany. It is ironic to reflect that only two years earlier the Foreign Office had feared 'a Soviet decision not to cross the German frontier' at all.[1]

More serious than any particular event of 1945 was the deteriorating atmosphere in which events took place. It was not yet fully evident at the Potsdam Conference in July, since that conference took place before the war had ended in the Far East and was abnormal because two of the principal participants (Truman and Attlee) were new to the highest office. It was rather at the conference of Soviet, American and British Foreign Ministers, which followed in London in September, that the deterioration became painfully marked. On that occasion, after some progress had been made on secondary matters, such as a draft peace treaty with Italy, the conference was brought to a halt by a sharp denunciation of its procedure from Molotov, the Soviet Foreign Minister, with the result that no agreement could be reported even on matters that had already been agreed. A further meeting of the three Foreign Ministers in Moscow in December was less completely fruitless, for it resulted in some agreement on co-operation in the Far East. But when the first General Assembly of the United Nations met in London in January 1946, the danger of a head-on clash between the Soviet Union and the Western Powers (more particularly, at this stage, Great Britain) was disturbingly apparent.

The clash came in the Security Council, which met for the first time concurrently with the first General Assembly. There were two significant things in common about all the issues on which the powers clashed. One was that all of them ranged the Soviet Union, with a few automatic supporters, on one side against one or more of the Western Powers, whose support for each other probably looked no less automatic to the Soviet representatives. The other was that each issue concerned the relations between a major power and one of the minor or newly emergent states whose role in international affairs was to become increasingly important in the next decade. The main matters of dispute were three: firstly, Soviet troops in Azerbaijan (on an Iranian motion); secondly, British troops in Greece and Indonesia (on Soviet and Ukrainian[2] motions respectively); thirdly, French and British troops in Syria and the Lebanon (on the motion of the latter two states). All these issues, long since defunct, created great bitterness at the time, and it is doubtful

---

[1] Lord Strang, *Home and Abroad* (Deutsch, 1956), p. 200.
[2] Ukraine and Byelorussia, republics within the U.S.S.R., had been separately admitted to membership of the United Nations.

how much the reference to the United Nations did to improve any of them.

The Soviet reaction to criticism of the continued presence of the Red Army in Iran, from which American troops had already withdrawn and British troops were in the process of withdrawing, eventually took the extreme form of walking out of the debate on 26 March. The criticisms of the British intervention in Greece, where British troops had helped to suppress a Communist rising in December 1944, and in Indonesia, where they were engaged, most uneasily, in restoring Dutch control over Indonesian Nationalists, both caused Bevin to react with some intemperateness, for which he was later criticized by his colleagues and by neutral observers.[1] In both debates the British case was supported by the European governments principally concerned, the Greek and the Dutch, though of course the Greek Communists and the Indonesian Nationalists, neither of whom were represented, would have been in opposition.

In the case of Syria and the Lebanon, on the other hand, there was a division of interest between the two European governments concerned, the French and the British, as well as between both of them and the Soviet Government. There were British troops as well as French in the two Levant states, whose independence had been recognized in name as long ago as 1941, though still not fully conceded in practice by the French. The Syrians and Lebanese wished the French troops to leave, but had less objection to the British. Their discrimination added to the French chagrin an element of inter-allied resentment, such as has been familiar ever since the fall of France in 1940 and is still not wholly eliminated. But the dispute was aggravated not by the two Western Allies, who both agreed to negotiate with the Levant states for the withdrawal of their troops, but by the Soviet Government, which voted against the Security Council's decision to that effect, thereby using the so-called 'veto' for the first time.[2]

Up to that point the brunt of the growing tension between the Western Powers and the Soviet Government had been borne by the British. The United States was not under attack at all at the United Nations in its early days, nor did American representatives take the

[1] e.g. Trygve Lie (the first Secretary General of the United Nations), *In the Cause of Peace* (Macmillan, 1954), p. 31.

[2] Article 27(3) of the U.N. Charter requires 'an affirmative vote of seven members including the concurring votes of the permanent members' (i.e. the five great powers) for any but procedural matters in the Security Council. This article constitutes the 'veto', though the word is not used in the Charter.

lead in criticizing others. When, for instance, the Soviet Government pressed its claims for a revision of the Montreux Convention of 1936 on the Turkish Straits, it was Bevin who resisted them. It was Attlee who first publicly criticized the Soviet use of the veto at the Security Council in October 1946. At the Foreign Ministers' conferences in the summer of 1946, Bevin again took the lead on the Western side, as was natural since the matters under discussion were specifically European: for instance, the Danube Commission, the frontier between Italy and Yugoslavia, the Austrian Peace Treaty. The one major initiative by the American Secretary of State, James F. Byrnes, was the offer in April of a four-power treaty for twenty-five years, which Molotov rebuffed.

When incidents occurred characteristic of what later came to be called the cold war, it was the British interest that was primarily involved. A notorious example was the attack on vessels of the Royal Navy by mines in the Corfu Strait off the coast of Albania in May and October. Among the non-Communist countries, Britain's special position was particularly recognized in S.E. Europe. A new Turkish Prime Minister referred in August 1946 to the Anglo-Turkish Alliance as the principal basis of Turkey's foreign policy. Greece was economically, militarily and politically almost a dependency of Britain. Both these countries were to become within two years part of the United States' sphere of interest; but no such sphere existed in Europe in 1946.

Up to the end of that year, the main American object in Europe was to withdraw from it as soon as possible. But the shadow of future commitments was already being cast ahead. In March 1946 American observers took part with the British and French in the Allied Mission for Observing the Greek Elections (A.M.F.O.G.E.), in which the Soviet Government refused to co-operate on the ground that it constituted an interference in Greece's internal affairs. This small event was something of a landmark in the process of American involvement in Europe. It was followed by a much more important example in Germany.

The division of Germany into four zones of occupation (Soviet, American, French and British) had not been designed to disrupt the country's economy; but such had been its effect for reasons which the Western Governments laid at the door of the Soviet occupation authorities. In July 1946 a British investigating committee reported that the cost of the British Zone for the year 1946–7 would be over £80,000,000, and that this estimate could only be reduced by the

B

economic reintegration of the zones. British and American policy had not been undivided in Germany; but they were at one on this issue, and also in criticizing the Soviet policy of dismantling German industry to secure payment of reparations. The outcome was an agreement on the economic fusion of the British and American Zones, forming the so-called Bi-zone, from 1 January 1947.

It is perhaps from that date that the Soviet Government would date the start of the cold war, or at least of the United States' share in it. During the next twelve months the American commitment to Europe grew in the sort of way that breathless allies call typically American. Once again the Eastern Mediterranean, and specifically Greece, was the scene of the first act. The security of Greece had been constantly under threat since the end of the war, because the Greek Communist forces of the wartime resistance, although defeated in their attempt on Athens in December 1944, had continued to exist in a skeleton form. They enjoyed the physical and moral support of the Communist-controlled states along Greece's northern border (Albania, Yugoslavia and Bulgaria).

Sporadic guerrilla activity in the late summer of 1946 led the Greek Government to complain to the Security Council against the country's northern neighbours. A frontier commission was appointed by the United Nations on the motion of the United States, which thus took a further step towards more active involvement. It is interesting that at almost the same date Bevin was at pains to argue, in a radio broadcast on 22 December 1946, that Britain's position in world affairs was an intermediate one between the U.S.A. and the U.S.S.R. The Anglo-American Alliance, which Churchill had foreshadowed as a 'fraternal association' in his famous speech at Fulton, Missouri, on 5 March 1946, was still far from being an accepted fact.

In the new year relations grew more bitter on many fronts. The Soviet-sponsored Polish Government held a general election in January 1947 which was the cause of acrimonious exchanges between it and both the British and American Governments. By the end of March the British Ambassador to Poland had been expelled as *persona non grata* and the American Ambassador had resigned. The British Government lodged a complaint against Albania before the Security Council for the mining of the Corfu Channel, and in due course secured judgement against Albania in the International Court (April 1949), but no compensation was ever paid. Peace treaties were grudgingly signed in February with the minor ex-enemy states, Rumania. Bulgaria and Hungary, now almost entirely under Soviet control; and in each case arrests and purges soon followed, of those antagonistic to the new régimes.

There were also the first signs of deterioration between the Western Powers and the Communists in the Far East. In Indo-China, the French had reluctantly signed an agreement with the Communist leader of the Vietminh Nationalists, Ho Chi Minh, in order to secure an unopposed landing in March 1946; but by December hostilities had broken out between French and Vietminh forces, and the latter were attacking Hanoi. In China the Americans withdrew in January 1947 from the truce organization which was trying to keep the peace between Communist and Kuomintang forces; and in the following month the Kuomintang Government ordered the Communist delegation to leave Nanking. Although it is not to be supposed that all these manifestations of tension around the world were consciously co-ordinated, they nevertheless combined to create a hostile atmosphere, from which more such incidents were bound to flow.

The crucial event in the crystallization of the cold war took place again in the Eastern Mediterranean. In February 1947 the British Government informed the American Government that it could no longer afford the cost of its commitments in Greece. On 12 March President Truman announced that the United States would take over this commitment, as part of a policy of maintaining the security of the 'free peoples of the world' against the threat of totalitarianism. The Truman Doctrine, as it was called, also covered Turkey, which was equally threatened, though in a different form. It was the beginning of a new era in American foreign policy, and inevitably also of a more acrimonious phase in Western relations with the Soviet Bloc. On the one side, before the end of the month the Soviet Government had vetoed a resolution of the Security Council blaming Albania for the attacks on British ships in the Corfu Strait, and Tito attacked the United States for trying to interfere in the internal affairs of Yugoslavia as well as Greece. On the other side, during the course of May both the French and the Italian Governments rid themselves of the Communists and their sympathizers who had been included in the post-war coalitions. Not surprisingly, the Foreign Ministers' conference, which met in Moscow two days before the Truman Doctrine was announced, ended without result in April. What was perhaps surprising was that it lasted for six weeks. Even the process of conferring was itself becoming a means for conducting the cold war.

The Americans were so firmly and so rapidly committed to their new

line of policy that it is difficult in retrospect to disentangle the motives
of their next major initiative, which was made in the famous speech of
General George C. Marshall (Secretary of State since January) at
Harvard University on 5 June. The purpose of the speech was to offer
American aid for the economic recovery of Europe provided that the
European states would collaborate to plan the best use of it on an inter-
national rather than on a national basis. Thanks largely to the quick
and imaginative reaction of Ernest Bevin, the European Recovery Pro-
gramme with all its immeasurable consequences developed out of the
Americans' generous initiative. For this Western Europe regards itself
as eternally in America's debt; but Soviet opinion regards the Marshall
Plan as an act of cold war.

There is some basis for the Soviet view in the well-authenticated story
that Marshall only put forward the plan after being assured by George
F. Kennan, then a senior official of the State Department, that the
Soviet Government would rebuff it, and would refuse to allow the
Communist-dominated states (Poland, Rumania, Bulgaria, Hungary,
Yugoslavia, Albania and eventually Czechoslovakia)[1] to participate in
it. It is true that that was what actually happened: Molotov came to the
first conference on the Marshall Plan in Paris, but only to frustrate it.
Yet no one compelled the Soviet Government to oppose the economic
unification of Europe or to deny themselves a role in it; and but for
Molotov's intransigence the thaw in economic relations for which
Europe had to wait more than a decade might have been associated
instead with the Marshall Plan in 1947. Such was certainly Bevin's
hope. If it was not Marshall's, that only shows how early the British
and American conceptions of their relation with the Soviet Union had
begun to diverge.

The cold war had by now acquired a name. In July 1947 an article
appeared in the American quarterly *Foreign Affairs* entitled 'The
Sources of Soviet Conduct'. It was anonymous but the author was soon
known to have been the same Kennan referred to in the previous
paragraph, who became even better known ten years later as the author
of the B.B.C.'s Reith Lectures in 1957. His article in 1947 defined the
doctrine of 'containment', which became (or already had become) the
official policy of the Truman Government. The policy was penetratingly
attacked, on the grounds of its rigidity and sterility, by the American
political columnist Walter Lippmann, in a series of articles in the *New*

[1] Finland, though not a Communist state, also refused, no doubt under Soviet
pressure.

York Herald Tribune. The articles were later published as a booklet under the title *The Cold War.*[1] Thus the name was born; though presumably it was a name that was already understood, since the phrase 'cold war' does not occur in Lippmann's book elsewhere than in its title, and the situation which it describes was also no longer new.

From the summer of 1947 onwards the initiative on the Western side had passed decisively into American hands, though it was still a very tentative and qualified initiative. The policy of 'containment' meant what it said. It did not mean extending or intensifying the cold war. There was no intention of launching a crusade against Communism, as a crusade had been launched against Nazism. In Western Europe the object was only to stiffen the United States' potential allies against passing under the Communist system voluntarily or from apathy, as Czechoslovakia was about to do and France and Italy might also be on the way to doing. In Western Europe it was to encourage hope among the populations of the 'satellites', as the Peoples' Democracies were coming to be called, but not to incite them to revolt. Outside Europe the cold war did not yet exist, nor did the Americans want to call it into existence. In the Middle East and the Far East it was a time of withdrawal and relative quiescence – a quiescence which seemed to be directly related to withdrawal. Latin America was too remote from the Soviet Union, and Africa too remote from both America and the Soviet Union, to be regarded yet as arenas of the cold war at all.

In retrospect the American policy devised in 1947 may appear in some ways deficient. 'Containment' was like the Maginot Line of the 1930s in two respects: it was a static policy, and it did not extend the whole way along the front to be covered. The importance of maintaining control of the whole periphery of the Soviet Bloc from Norway round to Japan was fully appreciated only later. In 1947 the Americans' traditional dislike of colonialism or the dominance of one people by another was still uppermost. The British had lost their imperial instinct. During the first two post-war years the trend in Asia and the Middle East was towards independence and the reduction of great-power influence. 'Containment' was not facilitated by this trend, which affected all the great powers.

The French withdrew under pressure from the Levant. The British withdrew from Iraq (except certain aerodromes) and from the Egyptian delta into the Suez Canal Zone; and Bevin intended to move the

[1] Walter Lippmann, *The Cold War* (Hamish Hamilton, 1947).

Middle East base eventually from there to Kenya.[1] Both the British and the Americans withdrew their troops from Iran, and so did the Russians eventually, in May 1946, though they left a subservient government behind in Azerbaijan. In the Far East the Americans relinquished their sovereignty over the Philippine Islands, and withdrew their troops from China as part of a policy of quiet disengagement. They also offered, though in vain, to discuss with the Soviet Union the formation of a provisional government for the whole of Korea. The British were engaged in an even more important withdrawal from the Indian sub-continent, Burma and Ceylon. Their troops were out of Indo-China and Indonesia in the course of 1946, and only the French and the Dutch anachronistically held on.

The general trend naturally met with American approval at the time. Only where the European Powers could not or would not yet withdraw did they meet with American disfavour: the British in Palestine, Malaya, Singapore and Hong Kong, the French in Indo-China, the Dutch in Indonesia. All of these areas were soon to be involved in the conflict between Communism and the Western Powers, and the American judgements were then retrospectively revised; but this had not yet become apparent in 1947. Latin America and Africa were in a different category – the former being regarded as a natural sphere of influence for the U.S.A., the latter still barely on the threshold of contemporary history. But all four great areas outside Europe – the Far East, the Middle East, Africa and Latin America – had this in common in 1947: they were still outside the area of the cold war, though some were less remote from it than others.

When the U.S. Government committed itself to the struggle in Europe, it still wished to keep the rest of the world disengaged. Outside Europe, U.S. policy was most truly represented by programmes like Point Four, which grew out of President Truman's inaugural speech in January 1949, and the Technical Aid Programme of the United Nations. At that date the Americans had no designs to play power politics in Asia or to involve underdeveloped countries in the cold war. It is doubtful whether the same can be said of the Soviet Government, although Soviet control over Communist leaders in Asia (particularly Mao Tse-Tung in China and Ho Chi Minh in Indo-China) cannot be considered certain and absolute.

To this extent the responsibility for hardening the division of the

---

[1] 'The word "Mombasa" was often on his lips.' (Lord Strang, *Home and Abroad* p. 291.)

world rests with the Soviet Union. The Iron Curtain was Stalin's creation. To this extent also there is truth in the implications of the first serious attempt to define the cold war from the Western viewpoint, which was made in 1950 in the following words:[1]

> '. . . the cold war may be defined as the policy of making mischief by all methods short of war – that is to say, short of war involving the Soviet Union in open hostilities.'

The implication is – since no one would use the term 'mischief-making' to describe their own side's activities – that the cold war was something practised exclusively by the Soviet Union against the West. In Stalin's lifetime at least this was almost wholly true. 'Containment', if not a purely passive doctrine, was a doctrine of reaction, not of initiative. And although it was an American doctrine, it was one which the allies of the United States, particularly the British Government and Opposition of the day, wholeheartedly accepted and supported.

The Soviet interpretation of this period was quite different, and there were not a few voices in Britain as well, even from supporters of the Labour Government, raised in sympathy with it. Discounting for the moment the grim personality of Stalin, we can easily see the clue to Soviet foreign policy from the map. The clue lies in Russia's geographical position, almost entirely locked in by land and inland seas, or by seas frozen for half the year. Russia's traditional foreign policy, described by her antagonists as the quest for an outlet to the sea, could also be described as the quest for a secure frontier. Geography has denied her a natural frontier in almost every direction, particularly to the west. Mackinder's celebrated theory of the Eurasian Heartland rests on this fact, of which every Russian and German leader must be conscious. 'Containment' seemed to the Russians to be a policy of denying them the security which they needed: therefore it was aggressive. Stalin's morbid and tyrannical imagination worked to aggravate the suspicions which every Soviet leader shared.

The Soviet Government therefore did not believe in the Americans' disinterestedness, nor in their unwillingness to extend the area of the cold war. They noted with resentment the continual barrage of recrimination addressed to the new governments of Eastern Europe on account of their treatment of political opponents sympathetic to the West. They regarded the Marshall Plan as a means of resuscitating Germany; and

[1] *Defence in the Cold War* (R.I.I.A., 1950), p. 12,

although Bevin refuted this misconception in August 1947, there was no reason to doubt that the Soviet leaders sincerely believed it. They observed the American Ambassador in Tehran encouraging the Iranian Government to refuse them an oil concession in September, followed a month later by the signature of an agreement for a U.S. military mission to Iran. They saw the American Government sending a fact-finding mission to China under General Wedemeyer in July, three months after announcing the withdrawal of U.S. troops; though the open quarrel which ensued between the General and Chiang Kai-Shek cannot have been regarded as a deliberate act of American policy. Having disagreed over the handling of divided Korea, the Soviet leaders then saw the Americans secure the appointment of a United Nations Temporary Commission there, against their own objections. The Americans' power to influence the majority of votes at the United Nations also resulted in a succession of votes blaming Albania, Yugoslavia and Bulgaria for facilitating the growing Communist rebellion in Greece; and in the creation of the United Nations Special Committee on the Balkans (U.N.S.C.O.B.) to watch the frontiers which had now become part of the Iron Curtain.

Thus the United Nations Organization itself came to be regarded by the Soviet leaders as an American tool to be used against them. In November 1947 American initiative succeeded in creating the so-called 'Little Assembly' (the Interim Committee of the General Assembly), a transparent device for evading the frustration which the Soviet veto could impose on the Security Council. Debates at the United Nations became in many cases slanging matches between Soviet and American (or British) representatives. More than half the applications of the veto by the Soviet Government in the first decade of the Security Council were made to prevent new elections to the United Nations, chiefly of countries which were expected to increase the American majority. From 1947 onwards, the fact that mattered most in international relations between the great powers was not what the intentions of each side really were, but what the other side believed them to be. A tragic cycle of action and reaction was set in motion, to which it was increasingly difficult to trace an origin or foresee an end.

The succession of events speaks for itself. The Soviet reaction to the Truman Doctrine and the condemnation of Greece's northern neighbours by the U.N. can be seen in the proclamation of a Communist government in the northern Greek mountains on Christmas Eve, 1947. The reaction to the Marshall Plan was the creation in October of the

Cominform (the Information Bureau of the Communist and Workers' Parties) with its headquarters in Belgrade, and later in Bucharest. The members of this organization, whose chief function was to churn out propaganda of unexampled dreariness, were the Communist Parties of Yugoslavia, Poland, Rumania, Bulgaria, Hungary, the Soviet Union, Czechoslovakia, France and Italy. None of the last three was yet under Communist rule, though Czechoslovakia was very near to it, and the implication was unmistakable – that France and Italy were not much farther off. On the other hand, neither the Albanian Communist Party, which was already in full control, nor the Greek, which was certainly nearer to success than most in Europe at the time, ever belonged to the Cominform. Although it inspired great fear and hostility in the West, it is perhaps doubtful whether Stalin had a clear and determined purpose in mind in creating the Cominform; and his successors had no qualms about liquidating it in 1955.

It is still more doubtful whether the Cominform played any significant part in the next major event of the cycle, the *coup d'état* which brought the Communists to full power in Czechoslovakia in February 1948. Of Soviet support for this *coup* there can be no doubt: it cannot have been accidental that a Soviet Deputy Foreign Minister, Zorin, who had been Ambassador to Czechoslovakia, arrived in Prague only a day or two before it took place. But the reaction in the West perhaps underrated the acquiescence of non-Communist Czechs in this decisive change of course, which probably owed as much to memories of Munich and fears (however mistaken) of Germany's revival as it did to Communist subversion. A public denunciation of the *coup* by the United States, French and British Governments on 26 February was at any rate an unusual step, since ostensibly no foreign interference had taken place. It was perhaps partly prompted by irritation at Tito's complaints earlier in the same month of aggressive Western militarism, with reference to the establishment of bases in Spain, Portugal and Greece and to the flights of U.S. aircraft over Yugoslavia.

The rival powers were by this time scarcely on speaking terms, at least in diplomatic language. Even before the Czech *coup*, Herbert Morrison had accused the Soviet Government of aiming at 'triumph through chaos' and Bevin had accused it of aiming to dominate Western as well as Eastern Europe. In Berlin a few weeks earlier Marshal Sokolovsky had denounced the Western Powers for infringing the Potsdam Agreement; and earlier still a notable exchange of abuse had taken place between Vyshinsky and Hector McNeil at the United

Nations. It was not surprising that the fifth post-war conference of Foreign Ministers, which met in London in November 1947, adjourned *sine die* three weeks later. No further conference of the great-power Foreign Ministers took place until May 1949. A principal casualty of the breakdown was the draft Austrian peace treaty, which had reached the top of their agenda but remained unsigned until 1955, although the Foreign Ministers' deputies met to discuss it intermittently throughout the intervening years. Austria therefore remained, like Germany, divided into four zones, though nominally ruled by a single Austrian Government; and this partition helped to consolidate the dividing line which split Europe between East and West.

Definitive positions were now taken up on each side of the line. Each step led automatically to a counter-step. In February 1948 the British, French and U.S. Governments began separate discussions on the future of Germany. On 17 March the British, French, Belgian and Dutch Governments signed a treaty in Brussels which was nominally directed against German aggression but could equally be used as an instrument against Soviet aggression; and such in fact it became in 1954 when it was revised and enlarged to include Italy and Western Germany. On 18 March a Peoples' Congress met in the Soviet Zone of Germany as a preliminary to the preparation of an East German constitution. Two days later Marshal Sokolovsky walked out of the Allied Control Commission in Berlin. In April a conference of six Western Powers met in Frankfurt to plan a constitution for Western Germany. In June the U.S. Senate passed the so-called 'Vandenberg Resolution' authorizing military aid to allied defence pacts – a natural sequel to the Brussels Treaty and a harbinger of the North Atlantic Treaty. In the same month the eight Communist Foreign Ministers met in Warsaw to discuss their own future policy towards Germany. The blockade of Berlin against traffic with the West also began in June. The Western Governments declared their intention to break the blockade, which they did by means of a massive airborne operation lasting until May 1949. This co-operative effort created the Western Alliance in action even before it existed on paper.

Meanwhile the arena of the cold war was extending willy-nilly. In February Stalin invited the Finnish President to Moscow, and a Soviet-Finnish treaty was signed on 6 April. In the same month a South-East Asian Youth Conference opened in Calcutta sponsored by the World Federation of Democratic Youth (W.F.D.Y.) and the International Union of Students (I.U.S.), both already Communist-dominated bodies. The conference has been generally considered to have given the signal for Communist risings in S.E. Asia. It was followed within two months by the outbreak of an emergency in Malaya, and of a multilateral civil war in Burma involving two rival brands of Communists; and within six months by an abortive rising of the Communist Party of Indonesia. The Americans took warning that peace could not long be counted on in the Far East. In the early summer the Johnson Report on Japan recommended the end of reparation payments and the encouragement of industrial recovery; in June the Republican Party declared itself in favour of greater support for Chiang Kai-Shek; in August an anti-Communist government was formally inaugurated in South Korea. Many responsible British voices were raised in support of the new Western policy, or at least in denunciation of Soviet policy. They included those of Churchill and Eden and the General Council of the Trade Union Congress as well as Labour ministers. In September 1948 Morrison spoke of the need for precautionary measures, including the slowing down of demobilization.

Among the many points along the dividing line which needed clarification on one side or the other as it hardened was the Free Territory of Trieste. Claimed by both Italy and Yugoslavia, it was under Anglo-American military occupation. The Western Powers naturally wished to see it secured on their side of the Iron Curtain, just as the Soviet Government wished to acquire complete possession of Berlin. Since Italy was already looked upon as a future ally of the West, it was natural that the Western Powers should propose the return of the Free Territory to Italy, and equally natural that the proposal should aggravate the hostility of Yugoslavia. This hostility persisted for a considerable time: for instance, at a conference on the Danube in Belgrade during July, when an open breach took place between the Soviet Union and the three Western Powers, the Yugoslavs sided automatically with the former. There would normally have been no reason why the Western Governments should be surprised by this Yugoslav reaction; but in the meantime remarkable things had been happening.

On 18 March – the day after the signature of the Brussels Treaty – a bitter correspondence began between the Soviet and Yugoslav leaders, which culminated on 28 June in the expulsion of Yugoslavia from the Cominform.[1] This event was greeted with amazement and satisfaction by the Western Governments, though it is doubtful whether

[1] The texts of the letters exchanged are given in *The Soviet-Yugoslav Dispute* (R.I.I.A., 1948).

they appreciated the depth of the shock felt in Eastern Europe at the time. The quarrel between the Soviet Union and Yugoslavia, which lasted for the rest of Stalin's lifetime and was only partially healed by Khrushchev after he came to power in 1955, did nothing to diminish the acuteness of the cold war, but it altered the course of the dividing line. It gave Stalin a new enemy – the bitterest he had known since Trotsky – and it offered the Western Powers the opportunity of a new ally and the knowledge that the Soviet Bloc was neither monolithic nor impenetrable.

The chief immediate advantage was felt in Greece. Within the year Tito closed the frontier between Yugoslavia and Greece, across which the Greek Communist forces had hitherto been passing at will, and by September 1949 the Greek civil war was at an end. There followed a *rapprochement* between the two Balkan countries which, although imperfectly consummated in the Balkan Pact of 1954, did at least serve to show the possibility of a new relation between Communist and non-Communist states. Meanwhile the cold war continued unabated, with Yugoslavia in the unexpected position of undergoing a Communist blockade and enjoying financial and other support from the American and British Governments.

While the five powers which had signed the Brussels Treaty prepared to enlarge their alliance by taking advantage of the Americans' obvious willingness to join in, the Soviet Government ingeniously extended the conflict into the arena of mass propaganda. In August 1948 a congress was held in Wroclaw (formerly Breslau, in Polish territory acquired from Germany) from which sprang an international organization called the 'Partisans of Peace'. For the next few years the Partisans of Peace became the Communists' main instrument to frustrate the growing unity of the West. In April 1949, the month in which the Western Powers signed the North Atlantic Treaty, they held a World Congress in Paris; in March 1950 they launched a deceptively simple 'Peace Appeal' from another World Conference in Stockholm; in November 1950 they were prevented from holding yet another World Congress in Sheffield by action of the British Government. Thereafter their prominence in the public eye receded.

There were other 'front organizations' serving the same purpose of uniting people of common interests under Communist leadership across national frontiers: for instance, the World Federation of Democratic Youth, the World Federation of Trade Unions, the World Federation of Scientific Workers, Women's International Democratic

Federation, and so on. None of them was ever much more than a nuisance, though some were probably a cover for subversive activities. But the Partisans of Peace in particular gained some credit for the Communists in the eyes of the uncommitted peoples of Asia and Africa, since it seemed unnatural to be opposed to anything so straightforward as peace, and it was difficult to explain in simple terms why an organization dedicated to such a cause should be regarded as a menace.

The Americans wisely took the point. In January 1949 the State Department issued a policy statement under the title 'Building the Peace', to prepare American opinion for the North Atlantic Treaty. The Treaty itself was signed by the United States, Canada and ten West European powers on 4 April. It was rightly stressed from the first that the purpose was solely to preserve peace by resisting aggression. The peaceful purpose was emphasized by a provision (Article II) for non-military co-operation to which much importance was attached by Canada and the Scandinavian members of N.A.T.O., although little came of it in practice. It might also seem unreasonable to label as aggressive an organization in which one member (Iceland) had no armed forces, two others (Norway and Denmark) would not allow foreign troops to be stationed on their soil in peacetime, and others besides these contributed few or no forces under the central allied command.

If it was true, as Churchill more than once argued, that before N.A.T.O. only the American monopoly of the atomic bomb stood between Western Europe and Soviet conquest, then it was hardly less true immediately after the North Atlantic Treaty was signed. Possibly the Red Army's capacity for direct aggression in Europe in 1949 was overestimated. At any rate, the balance of force, whatever it had been, was upset again within a few months by the announcement on 23 September that the Soviet Union also possessed the atomic bomb, which had been successfully tested in July. The crucial fact at that date was that each side declared its conviction of the other side's aggressive intentions. It was only prudent to assume that each believed what it said, and was intending to act accordingly.

The actual consequences of the creation of N.A.T.O. are not to be measured merely by the course of events that followed it. The threat of war appeared to recede temporarily in Europe and certainly became more real in the Far East; but it does not follow that the creation of N.A.T.O. caused a redirection of Communist policy in that sense. In Europe Soviet tactics were determined more by Tito than by N.A.T.O. It was his defection that caused the collapse of the Communist guerrilla war in Greece. If there was a danger of Soviet aggression in the years immediately following 1949, it was against Yugoslavia rather than Western Europe; and this was recognized by the British Government when it was declared in the House of Commons in February 1951 that any threat to Yugoslavia was 'naturally of concern to His Majesty's Government'. In fact, however, the main Soviet effort in Europe was one of consolidation in the Peoples' Democracies, using the charge of 'Titoism' as an additional excuse for purges.

The years 1949–51 were those in which Rajk was executed in Hungary, Kostov in Bulgaria, Xoxe in Albania; Gomulka was dismissed and arrested in Poland, Slansky in Czechoslovakia; and Markos Vaphiadhis disappeared from the leadership of the Greek rebellion. All these were prominent Communists, none of them in sympathy with the West. Simultaneously the East European churches were attacked through their leaders: Cardinal Mindszenty in Hungary, Cardinal Wyszynski in Poland, Archbishop Beran in Czechoslovakia, and a group of evangelical pastors in Bulgaria. Stalinism was at its apogee. If Stalin had intended war against Europe – an unproved but not improbable hypothesis – then the one new deterrent was the unreliability of his satellites, symbolized by Tito, rather than the growing strength of the Western Alliance. Even in July 1950 Churchill quoted figures to show how weak the Western Alliance was; and the Government did not contradict him.

It is hardly more probable that the creation of N.A.T.O. caused the diversion of Communist initiative from Europe to the Far East. By 1949 in the Far East the initiative was largely in Chinese hands, and neither then nor since has the Chinese Communist Party shown itself subservient to Moscow. The Malayan rebellion rested on the Chinese population; the Vietminh rebellion enjoyed strong support from Communist China. Both became more confident and aggressive after the Communist successes in China. These were heralded in January 1949 by Chiang Kai-Shek's request for peace terms. They culminated in the eviction of the Kuomintang Government and forces from the Chinese mainland and the proclamation of the Chinese People's Republic in September. There is good reason to believe that Stalin neither encouraged nor welcomed the lightning campaign which brought Mao Tse-Tung to power. The eventual American reaction to it may also have caused disquiet to the Soviet Government, even though it had the partial advantage of distracting some of the U.S. Government's attention and resources away from Europe.

The Americans did not react rapidly at first to the dramatic change in the Far East. For an unexpectedly long time their policy continued as before. They recognized the new South Korean Government in January 1949, but they completed the withdrawal of their forces from Korea in June. There was little enthusiasm in their response to Chiang Kai-Shek's request for more military aid in November 1948, or to his appeal for mediation with the Communists two months later. No other power would respond to that appeal either: the general policy was to wait and see. In the immediate train of Communist successes, the British seemed at first to suffer most. In a celebrated incident, H.M.S. *Amethyst* was trapped under fire in the Yangtse River in April 1949, and later escaped. More prosaically, the change of régime severely hit British business firms in China. The Americans' turn for rebuffs and humiliations was to come later.

U.S. policy remained non-committal for the rest of 1949. In response to rumours, the Secretary of State denied any intention of taking part in any Pacific defence pact in May. In August the U.S. Government published a White Paper on the Chinese situation, placing the blame principally on the Kuomintang. Others, nearer to the scene of action, reacted less academically. President Quirino of the Philippines addressed a warning to the U.S. Senate of the threat to Asia a few days later. But even in December 1949, the month in which Mao-Tse-Tung first visited Moscow as head of the Chinese People's Government, the State Department circulated a confidential memorandum discounting the importance of Formosa, the island to which Chiang Kai-Shek had transferred his Government and forces.

In January 1950, after the British Government had recognized the Communist Government of China and the latter had demanded China's seat at the United Nations, Acheson made a statement to the Senate Foreign Relations Committee which clearly implied that both Formosa and Korea lay outside the United States' essential defence perimeter. There was still even a possibility that the United States might recognize the new Chinese Government. Some American business interests urged the Government to do so, for the same reason that British businessmen had successfully urged the British Government to do so, in order to promote trade and to avert a definitive alignment of policy between China and the Soviet Union. All these hopes proved illusory, but at least they were not yet regarded in the U.S.A. as treasonable, as later came to be the case in the heyday of Senator McCarthy. Nor had the Americans yet begun to think of strategy in global terms. Had they done so, they might have been inclined to infer that the upsurge of Communist activity in the Far East was the direct outcome of the frustration of Communist plans in Europe. It would, nevertheless, probably have been an error to attribute so much consequence to the creation of N.A.T.O.

The one certain achievement of N.A.T.O. in its first year was simply to restore the confidence of the Western European peoples. Their confidence showed itself in two forms. One was the determination to press on with the reconstruction of Western Germany in their own image. The other was a willingness to renew negotiations with the Soviet Government. Germany was itself naturally the first subject of negotiation, since the occasion for a renewal of the interrupted series of Foreign Ministers' conferences was the Soviet decision to end the blockade of Berlin, which lasted from 18 June 1948 to 12 May 1949. The four Foreign Ministers then met in Paris from 23 May to 20 June, to discuss the status of Berlin and the reunification of Germany, among other questions. The conference, though inconclusive, produced one significant new development, which was the withdrawal of Soviet support for the Yugoslav territorial claims against Austria. No further meeting of the great-power Foreign Ministers was held until March 1951, when they met in a marathon series of seventy-four fruitless sessions lasting three and a half months. By then it was evident that such conferences were themselves a means of conducting operations in the cold war. But the technique of propaganda by conference, which had been invented by the Soviet representatives, was also being mastered by the Western Governments in their new-found confidence.

The use of conferences for staking positions and influencing world opinion, instead of for agreeing about matters on the agenda, was well illustrated whenever Germany was discussed, which was often. For on each side of the dividing line a new Germany was coming into existence in conformity with the prevailing system: a West European German Federal Republic with its capital at Bonn, and an East European German Democratic Republic (D.D.R.) with its capital at Pankow, a suburb of Berlin. Berlin was itself similarly divided, though still deeply embedded in the Soviet Zone. Each time the powers met in conference on the reunification of these two political units, they had already taken further steps to make reunification more difficult. On the Western side the decisive steps were the promulgation of an Occupation Statute for their united zones in April 1949; the adoption of a Basic Law creating the German Federal Republic by the local parliaments of the *Länder* in May; and the holding of the first federal elections, which were rather narrowly won by Dr. Adenauer's Christian Democratic Union (C.D.U.) in August 1949. On 19 September 1950 the Western Foreign Ministers took the decisive step of agreeing to end the state of war with Germany. On the Eastern side, a constitution for the D.D.R. was voted by referendum in May 1949; a Provisional Government was set up under Grotewohl on 7 October; and three days later the Soviet Government transferred to it the military administration of its zone of occupation. Each side refused to recognize the legitimacy of the other's Government, and each accused the other of being the first to re-employ former Nazis in high positions and to put arms into the hands of organized German forces.

Neither side was entirely free from the fear of future German aggression. The Soviet Union, and particularly its allies, Poland and Czechoslovakia, feared that the Germans might try to recover the former German territories east of the Oder-Neisse line and in the Sudetenland. This fear was indeed one of the principal factors which kept the Poles and the Czechs loyal to the Communist alliance. So far as Eastern Germany was concerned, the fear was said to be kept down by two forces. One was the transformation of the social system to eliminate the big landlords and businessmen, who were reputed to have been the source of German aggressiveness in the past. The other was the loyalty of Grotewohl's Government and the Socialist Unity Party (S.E.D.) in recognizing the post-war frontiers and educating their people to accept them as final. The fear of aggression could therefore be directed by the Soviet Bloc exclusively against Western Germany, which had had to absorb several million refugees[1] from Eastern Germany and the lost territories.

In Western Europe, the fear of German aggression naturally took a different form. The French, the Dutch and the Belgians wanted safeguards against renewed aggression westwards, rather than eastwards. But they recognized that Germany must be allowed to recover economically and encouraged to develop democratically. The fear of Soviet aggression, which was now greater than that of German aggression, appeared to require that eventually German forces must be admitted to the Western defence system. Distasteful though it was to many former victims of the Germans, it was to be made acceptable by the principle of creating supranational institutions in Western Europe, embodying a German component under European control.

[1] Nine million by 1959, i.e. about 20 per cent of the population.

The Council of Europe, created in 1948, admitted Western Germany in November 1949. The Schuman Plan of May 1950, which led to the creation of the European Coal and Steel Community, and the Pleven Plan of October 1950, which sought unsuccessfully to create a European Defence Community, were both intended to achieve the simultaneous feat of rehabilitating Germany while rendering her harmless to her neighbours. So far as her Western neighbours were concerned, this feat was eventually achieved, at the price of admitting the German Federal Republic into N.A.T.O. in 1954. But from the East European point of view the interpretation was different. The Federal Republic was seen as a Frankenstein's monster destined to dominate Western policy; and its creators were seen to be trying to divert its appetites eastwards.

2

The Involvement of Asia (1950–5)

THE fears felt in Europe were for the time being illusory and somewhat theatrical, since the stakes and the risks were too high. They would have had more substance where they were less felt, in the Far East. A process similar to that in Germany was taking place in Japan, with the important difference that the Americans there had a position of strength which they shared not at all with the Soviet Union and hardly even with their allies. Their reaction to the disappointment of their hopes of China, the traditional American sphere of friendly influence in the Far East, was to adopt Japan as a substitute. More slowly than Germany, but nevertheless perceptibly, Japan was brought back to a position of respectability. In July 1949 the Military Government Section of the U.S. Army of Occupation was disbanded. In February 1950 the Supreme Commander, General MacArthur, was authorized to allow Japan to take part in international conferences. The urgency of signing a Japanese peace treaty was widely canvassed. The Soviet Government reacted in ways that were also familiar by boycotting the Allied Council in Japan and the Far Eastern Commission.

The lines began to be hardly less clearly drawn in the Far East than in the West. A Sino-Soviet Treaty was signed in February 1950, followed by a trade agreement in April. Belatedly, the Americans began to increase their aid to the Kuomintang Chinese, who held only Formosa and a number of islands off the coast of the mainland. An Aid to China Bill was passed in February 1950, and a Supplementary Bill in May. Korea was still regarded as a doubtful risk: it was only at the second attempt, after revision, that a Korean Aid Bill became law. The view that Korea lay outside the United States' defence perimeter had not yet been revised, even by the summer. It was a coincidence, though it was not so interpreted in the Soviet Bloc, that early in June the Republican Party's chief expert on foreign affairs and future Secretary of State, John Foster Dulles, was in Seoul and visited the neighbourhood of the 38th parallel, which separated Korea between north and south. Both the Americans and the Russians had almost entirely withdrawn from Korea but it was on the 38th parallel that their spheres of influence met in the Far East. On that line the last war to engage the forces of the great powers openly against each other broke out on 25 June.

The details of the Korean War, which lasted for twelve months of continuous fighting and twenty-four more of intermittent fighting and armistice negotiation, are relevant only in so far as they illustrate the hardening of the division between the two sides engaged in the cold war. It may seem at first sight paradoxical to speak of the Korean War as a continuation of the cold war at all, since the fighting was unmistakeably hot. But it is no more paradoxical, and no less accurate, than Clausewitz's celebrated definition of war as the continuation of policy by other means. A definition of the cold war was quoted earlier[1] which excluded not the use of force but the use of the armed forces of the country conducting the cold war, specifically, in that context, the Soviet Union. The Korean War is an illustration of that definition, not an exception to it, since the Red Army was never engaged. On the other hand the Sino-Soviet Alliance was drawn much closer, as was the American *rapprochement* with Japan. The other principal result of the war was to commit the United Nations, and particularly its Secretary General, to outright participation in the cold war on the Western side.

These results were closely related to each other. The Soviet representative had withdrawn from the Security Council early in 1950 as a protest against its refusal to give China's seat to the representative of Peking instead of Formosa. As a consequence, when the fighting began in Korea the Security Council was able to approve military aid to the South Korean Government without frustration by a Soviet veto. The Secretary General, Trygve Lie, on his own testimony, took the initiative both in naming the North Koreans as aggressors and in maintaining that the mere non-attendance of the Soviet representative did not constitute a veto.[2] The Soviet Government declared the U.N. decision to help the South Koreans illegal, but also instructed its representative soon afterwards to return to the Security Council, of which he became chairman by rotation in August. Although this enabled him to reduce the Security Council's proceedings to a nullity, it was already too late. The Americans were in action in Korea with the United Nations' formal approval by the end of June; the British Government announced the dispatch of a self-contained force to Korea in July; and fourteen other governments added their contributions in due course. On a

[1] See p. 23.
[2] *In the Cause of Peace*, pp. 330, 432.

British motion, the United Nations created a unified command under General MacArthur.

The Communist Chinese Government naturally supported the Soviet view that the United Nations' action was illegal, but gave no immediate sign of intervention. At the end of September, however, they indicated that China would not stand aside 'should the imperialists wantonly invade the territory of its neighbours'. The words evidently referred to the possibility that the U.N. forces, having held and driven back the North Koreans with some difficulty, would cross the 38th parallel in their turn. General MacArthur was determined to do so for military reasons. In the House of Commons Bevin spoke apparently in favour of crossing the parallel and reuniting Korea. Eden, for the opposition, advocated establishing a line across the 'wasp-waist' of Korea, which approximated to the parallel. Nehru urged an end to the military operations and the admission of Communist China to the United Nations. On 8 October U.S. troops crossed the parallel, and within three weeks they stood on the Chinese border along the Yalu River.

The Peking Government declared the crossing of the parallel a threat to China's security, and Peking radio referred to 'Chinese volunteers' in Korea early in November. On a British motion, the Chinese Communists were invited to send representatives to the Security Council. The invitation was at first refused, but on 24 November Chinese representatives arrived in New York. Two days later large Chinese forces counter-attacked in Korea, and drove General MacArthur's forces back. The U.N. General Assembly appointed a Cease-Fire Committee on 14 December, on an Indian motion, but the Communist Chinese refused to co-operate with it. On 26 December they crossed the 38th parallel in their turn, and in January 1951 they rejected the United Nations' proposals for a cease-fire. Before the end of the month, the United States Government had presented to the United Nations a resolution declaring Communist China an aggressor, which was adopted by the Political Committee on 30 January and by the General Assembly on 1 February, not without grave misgivings among the allies, including Great Britain. The Chinese Foreign Minister declared that this motion had ruined the chances of a peaceful settlement.

The hardening of the lines in the Far East had its repercussions far beyond Korea. Japan, S.E. Asia and Tibet all felt the effect of it. A draft Japanese Peace Treaty was prepared by the U.S. Government, which circulated the main heads in October 1950. In July 1951, before the treaty was signed, the Japanese were conceded the right to establish an armed National Police Reserve of up to 75,000 men. The Chinese Communists accused the Burmese Government of allowing the Americans to use airfields in Burma. The Vietminh increased their operations to the scale of massive and open assaults in Indo-China at the end of 1950. The Malayan emergency also took a grave turn for the worse. The Chinese invaded Tibet almost simultaneously with the American crossing of the 38th parallel. The peoples of the Far East were under increasing pressure to take their stand on one side or other of the line which was becoming an extension of the Iron Curtain in Europe. Many of them were anxious to avoid doing so, but only Nehru, the Indian Prime Minister, was in a strong enough position to take an independent stand, which was neutral but not detached. He agreed to send a medical team to Korea; and he publicly criticized the Peking Government's subservience to Moscow. But he equally criticized many of the actions taken by the United Nations, particularly the crossing of the 38th parallel and naming Communist China as an aggressor. India thus put herself in a position to play a mediating part in eventually bringing the armed conflict to a close.

As a result of a hint of compromise by the Soviet representative in New York on 23 June 1951, the fighting was halted, though not finally, on a line not far from where it had begun. This was only the beginning of a protracted series of negotiations, punctuated by renewed fighting, which lasted until July 1953. In the meantime the Americans' attitude towards Communist China had grown increasingly hard, while some of their allies became increasingly uneasy and inclined to share the Indians' qualms about the division of Asia. The British attitude was noteworthy in this respect. The Labour Government believed that the right way to deal with Asia was through economic and social development, such as had been set in motion on Bevin's initiative by the Colombo Plan in May 1950, rather than by extending the area of war. In December 1950, when it was feared that the Americans intended to attack the Chinese mainland, possibly with atomic weapons, Attlee flew to Washington to dissuade President Truman. There was undisguised relief in Britain when Truman relieved General MacArthur of his command in April 1951. Nevertheless, the leadership in allied policy-making continued to rest with the Americans, who made by far the largest contribution to the war in money, materials, and (apart from the South Koreans) in manpower.

The principal Western Allies were in no position to take over the initiative from the Americans, even if they had wanted to do so. The French were heavily committed to the war in Indo-China; and in Europe they were deeply and even passionately engaged in the problems of creating a supranational authority. The British were similarly committed in Malaya and, in addition, were distracted in the Middle East by concurrent disputes with the Egyptian and Iranian Governments.

British foreign policy in particular was going through an unlucky period in 1951. Morrison took over as Foreign Secretary from Bevin early in the year, but never had time to grapple successfully with his problems before the Labour Government fell in October. The defection of two Foreign Service officials, Burgess and Maclean, at the end of May had a demoralizing effect and was particularly damaging to Anglo-American relations for years to come. Apart from other troubles in the Middle East, the year was also marked by the humiliating rebuff by Egypt of the British attempt, in conjunction with the U.S.A., France and Turkey, to create a Middle East Defence Organization. Despite the participation of the U.S.A. and Turkey, the Egyptian refusal was essentially a snub to the two former great powers in the Middle East; and there was no alternative but to accept it, and to drop the plan.

Neither Britain nor France was thus in a position, or in a mood, to elaborate a distinctive foreign policy in 1951. Both countries were also handicapped by a precarious economic situation and by political weakness at home. However reluctantly, both followed the lead of the U.S.A. because they had no alternative, especially in the Far Eastern area, where the United States carried overwhelming responsibility. They supported the U.N. condemnation of Communist China as an aggressor in February 1951, and the U.N. embargo on trade with China and North Korea in strategic materials in May, both on American initiative. They agreed to vote for the postponement of the question of admitting Communist China to the United Nations. They joined the United States in signing a peace treaty with Japan in September, although not only the Soviet Union but also India and Burma declined to do so, and both Chinese Governments were excluded.

The United States Government at the same time took a further step towards consolidating the division of Asia by signing a defence treaty with the Philippines on 30 August and a security pact with Japan on 8 September, concurrently with the peace treaty. American relations with the Kuomintang Chinese were already regulated by a defence agreement, which was made public in April; and a defence treaty with South Korea eventually followed. Although none of these engagements involved Britain formally, it would have been difficult to insulate British policy from their consequences.

The one ray of hope lay in the fact that armistice talks did in fact begin in Korea in July 1951, and by the end of November a demarcation line had been provisionally agreed. But real peace was still a long way off, and in the meantime the words and actions of the great powers continued to be acrimonious. Vyshinsky attacked the United States at the United Nations for helping and encouraging Kuomintang troops to establish themselves in Northern Burma. Broadcasts from Moscow and Peking began to accuse the Americans of conducting bacteriological warfare in Korea. Churchill, who became Prime Minister as a result of the general election in October 1951, visited Washington to discuss the Far East, among other matters, early in 1952, and declared after his return that 'prompt, resolute, effective' action would be taken if the Korean truce were broken. Eden, who accompanied Churchill to Washington as Foreign Secretary, declared in the U.S.A. that the French and British positions in S.E. Asia must be held. Both were in jeopardy; and Ho Chi Minh was threatening to extend the Vietminh revolution to Laos and Cambodia. The delivery of U.S. bombers to the French in Indo-China was said to have 'tripled their air-power' in March 1952.

In Korea itself the infinitely slow negotiations were still accompanied by outbreaks of violence on both sides. The Communists organized a serious and bloody revolt in a U.N. prison camp in February 1952, which underlined the fact that the most awkward of the unsettled points of negotiation concerned the repatriation of prisoners. In June the U.N. command launched a bombing raid against Chinese installations north of the Yalu River, an American initiative taken without consulting the other allies. The negotiations nevertheless continued, despite long interruptions. The Indians made helpful proposals for a compromise in November 1952, which the British and American Governments accepted but the Soviet Government sharply criticized and the Chinese Communists rejected. A new urgency was injected into the negotiations by an undertaking given by General Eisenhower, in his campaign for election to the presidency of the U.S.A., to go to Korea at once and to liquidate the war. On 4 November he was elected President and in December he duly went to Korea.

Early in the new year, after his return from Korea and his inauguration as President, he announced the withdrawal of the 7th U.S. Fleet from the Formosa Strait, where it had served to prevent the invasion of the mainland from Formosa or vice versa since 1950. This was interpreted, and indeed represented, as 'unleashing Chiang Kai-Shek', and there were fears of an American blockade of mainland China which would have brought war near again. But the decision remained no more than a gesture. Whether by good luck, or because of President Eisenhower's intervention, or even conceivably as a by-product of the death of Stalin on 5 March 1953, the Korean armistice negotiations were renewed on 6 April, after an interval of six months. Agreement was reached a month later on the outstanding issues, in particular that there should be no compulsory repatriation of prisoners. The armistice was formally signed after further anxious delays, at Panmunjom on 27 July. The political future of divided Korea was left over for a future conference.

The intended composition of the political conference was left vague at the time, and was a matter of some disagreement among the sixteen allied powers who had furnished armed forces in Korea. There was also uncertainty about what would happen if the armistice was broken. The sixteen powers signed a declaration at the time of the armistice, from which the British Labour Party in opposition dissociated itself, to the effect that if hostilities were to be renewed it might prove impossible to confine them to Korea. Fifteen of the sixteen presented a draft resolution to the U.N., from which the British Government dissented, proposing that only those countries which had fought in Korea should be represented at the political conference. The British Government wished that both India and the Soviet Union should take part also, although neither had fought in the war, because both were clearly interested: the Soviet Union had a common frontier with Korea, albeit a very short one, and the Indians were carrying the main burden of supervising the repatriation of prisoners.

The U.S. Government was willing to accept Soviet participation, since it regarded the U.S.S.R. as a belligerent, but objected to the Indians. Eventually the United Nations voted to include both, but as the majority was small in the case of India, the Indian Government withdrew its claim to be represented. The Chinese Communists in any case rejected the U.N. resolution and rebuffed all attempts to organize the political conference. As a result it was never held in the form intended, but Korea was discussed, without fruitful result, at the Geneva Conference in 1954. By that date the problems of the cold war in three major theatres – Europe, S.E. Asia and the Far East – had become inextricably merged; so that the Foreign Ministers' conferences on their respective problems in 1954, which took place at Berlin in January and Geneva from May to June, were something like successive sessions of a single conference.

The chance that the war which had been expected in Europe broke out instead in the Far East was seen by the Western European powers as giving them a respite but not a relief. To the French and to other continental Europeans the best use of the respite seemed to be to push on with the unification of Europe, including Western Germany. To the British it seemed to be more urgent to strengthen the military alliance while at the same time looking out for the possibility of new relationships which were best left undefined until they evolved. The Americans sympathized in part with both attitudes. They had a theoretical faith in the unity of Europe and a conviction that military alliances were an essential pre-condition of security; but in particular they desired the restoration of Germany and the use of German troops for the defence of Europe. Although American generosity was immense in all directions and for many purposes, a larger proportion of it now tended to be earmarked for military purposes or directed towards reliable allies. In this context Germany, like Japan, had the advantage of being an industrious and efficient country which could make the best use of American aid and give the best return for it.

Germany was therefore a beneficiary of the differently oriented policies of all three principal Western Powers. There were also other beneficiaries in Europe. Yugoslavia received substantial aid, including American arms, so long as her quarrel with the Soviet Union persisted; and Tito was received on an official visit to Britain in the month of Stalin's death. Greece and Turkey, both of whom contributed contingents to the U.N. force in Korea, were admitted to N.A.T.O. in 1952. They were also encouraged to form a new relation with Yugoslavia, which took the form first of a Treaty of Friendship in February 1953 and eventually of a Balkan Alliance in August 1954. There were thus four additional countries that could be regarded as standing opposed to Soviet aggression since the signature of the North Atlantic Treaty.

To these the U.S. military leaders were anxious to add Spain as a fifth. While Truman was President and Attlee Prime Minister, there was strong opposition on both sides of the Atlantic to any gesture of reconciliation towards Spain, from which most members of the United Nations had, after a formal decision by vote, either severed diplomatic relations or at least withdrawn Ambassadors in 1946. Of the N.A.T.O. powers, Portugal steadily pressed for Spain's admission and the

Scandinavians firmly opposed it. Britain and France had no cause for affection towards Franco, but agreed to the restoration of full diplomatic relations with Spain at the end of 1951. The Americans came increasingly to favour the admission of Spain to N.A.T.O. on strategic grounds. But although they established air bases on Spanish territory and gave substantial economic and military aid to Spain, this proved to be the limit of what they could achieve. The slow rehabilitation of Spain reached no further, in the period under review, than admission to O.E.E.C. and the International Monetary Fund; though these steps, taken in 1959, looked likely to be the forerunners of others.

N.A.T.O. was thus gradually strengthened, but not so completely as purely military considerations would have required. French attempts to strengthen the West by unification were also only incompletely successful, partly no doubt because successive British Governments were not able to support them to the extent the French desired. The exercise which the French called *faire l'Europe* proceeded jerkily. It began (mistakenly, in the British official view) on the political level with the creation of the Council of Europe as a result of a series of conferences in 1947–8, to which the British official contribution was lukewarm at best. There followed an effort on the economic level, initiated by the Schuman Plan in May 1950, which led to the creation of the six-power European Coal and Steel Community in April 1951. Later, on the same economic plane but with an equally definite political purpose, came the European Economic Community (the 'Common Market') and Euratom in 1957.

In the meantime an attempt to achieve the same result on the military plane proved to be a fiasco. The intention was to form a European Defence Community (E.D.C.) which the French initiated as the Pleven Plan in October 1950. Although the same six powers (France, Germany, Belgium, the Netherlands, Luxembourg, Italy) all signed the E.D.C. Treaty in May 1952, the French finally refused to ratify it in August 1954. The outcome of all these endeavours was a patchwork European union, limited in extent and incomplete in scope, in which Western Germany, vigorously reviving, played an unexpectedly important role and France, down on her luck, a relatively less dominant one, at least until the return to power of de Gaulle in 1958. The various acts of fusion of the Six contributed much to Europe's economic recovery, but little to its defence.

It had still to be admitted that Europe depended for its defence overwhelmingly on the U.S.A. The American contribution in money, materials and manpower was far greater than that of any other power, though not disproportionately so in relation to population and national income. Their predominance was emphasized in three ways in the early 1950s. First, when a Supreme Commander was appointed to organize N.A.T.O.'s military headquarters (S.H.A.P.E.) it was never questioned that he should be an American, nor has it been questioned since: Eisenhower, Ridgway, Gruenther, Norstad held the appointment in unbroken succession. Secondly, to render the process of decision rapid and effective in N.A.T.O., a 'standing group' of the three principal military powers (the United States, Britain and France) was established in Washington, with the result that before long the smaller allies began to assume regretfully that it was in Washington, not in Europe, that the real decisions were taken. Thirdly, the Americans formed a Strategic Air Command, which (like the R.A.F.'s Bomber Command) was not under N.A.T.O. control, but had independent bases, not only in N.A.T.O. countries (for instance, in Britain and France) but also on other territories, such as Spain and Morocco. By the middle 1950s some Europeans were beginning to be more nervous of their great ally than of their potential enemy. Certainly their defence was sure; but was it so necessary as it had once seemed to be?

In this atmosphere, the year 1953 came to seem curiously one of *détente* between the rival blocs. Obviously the death of Stalin on 5 March was a prime cause. His immediate successor, Malenkov, addressed the West in more friendly tones. When, for instance, a British aircraft flying to Berlin was shot down by Soviet fighters a week after Stalin's death, the Soviet authorities set a precedent by apologizing for the mishap and proposing a conference to prevent its recurrence. Adenauer declared that there had been no change of Soviet policy; and the new American régime under Eisenhower, with Dulles as his Secretary of State, reacted with cold caution. But Churchill struck a note which appealed to a wider public when he looked forward in April, and again in a notable speech on 11 May, to a conference with the new Soviet régime 'at the highest level'. His idea was to attempt a piecemeal settlement, taking the problems one by one at a meeting 'not overhung by a ponderous or rigid agenda'. But the American reception of the idea was lukewarm. Although some steps were taken to bring about Churchill's desire, they were taken cautiously, and more than two years passed before anything like it was realized. By that time Churchill had retired, and so had Malenkov.

Nevertheless, the habit of communication across the Iron Curtain was restored. At least things became no worse. In some parts of Europe they even seemed momentarily to become better. Malenkov promised the Soviet people a rise in their standard of living; and he overthrew and executed Beria, the much-feared head of the secret police and Minister of Internal Affairs and State Security. A new, milder government came to power in Hungary under Imre Nagy, though not for long. The Bulgarian Government made overtures to Greece for a settlement of their disputes. The East German Government first raised and then lowered the 'norms' of work on which wages were calculated in the D.D.R. This had the unexpected result of provoking an uprising in Eastern Berlin and elsewhere in the D.D.R. on 17 June, which the Red Army forcibly suppressed. Relaxation did not appear to pay, and it did not last. Although the professed willingness to meet in conference persisted, each side insisted on its own terms.

Churchill's proposal of 11 May for a Summit Conference fell by the wayside. The Americans disliked it; the French were without a Government to pronounce upon it for several weeks; Churchill himself was taken ill. It was typical of the use of what may be called the 'conference gambit' to influence events rather than to reach agreements that in August the Soviet Government sent a note agreeing to a Summit Conference, on condition that specific subjects were on the agenda, such as banning bases on foreign territory. In other words, they accepted Churchill's proposal when it was clear that the Western Governments would not and could not carry it out, and they did so on conditions which Churchill had expressly excluded. The Western Governments, which had been about to hold a 'summit meeting' of their own heads of Government in Bermuda, could not allow themselves to be entirely robbed of the initiative by Churchill's illness. After a meeting of the three Western Foreign Ministers in Washington in July, they proposed a four-power meeting of Foreign Ministers to discuss the Austrian peace treaty and the future of Germany, the latter with particular reference to reunification and free elections. A protracted correspondence between the Soviet and Western Governments followed, before it was finally agreed to meet in Berlin on 25 January, 1954. Both sides naturally had an eye on the elections in Western Germany, which Adenauer duly won with an increased majority in September 1953.

It was hardly possible that either side should expect the other to agree to the proposals which it put forward for discussion. Such was no longer the point of conferences. Conferences were held not to settle problems but to influence them: they thus became themselves part of the process of events known as the cold war. The purpose of going to conferences, on both sides, was to take up positions in the eyes of the world, to register facts and changes, to make one's opponents appear foolish and obstructive, or even to trap them. Consequently the initiative in convening conferences often rested with the side which had temporarily lost the initiative in influencing and controlling the events which were nominally to be discussed. All these characteristics of great-power conferences were illustrated by the series which began in 1954.

A long-drawn-out example, which stood rather apart from the main stream of events, was the series of conferences on disarmament. The subject of disarmament had been discussed intermittently ever since the creation of the United Nations, though originally the organization was charged only with the task of 'regulating', not of reducing, armaments. It is unnecessary to recount here the whole course of the discussions,[1] which were almost entirely barren. But it deserves mention that they were reactivated early in 1954, partly because of the pressure of world opinion, to which neither side could show itself indifferent, and partly because by the spring of that year both the Soviet Union and the U.S.A. had successfully exploded hydrogen-bombs, so that what was called 'nuclear parity' was virtually an accomplished fact. These things made it seem necessary to confer again without making agreement in the least more probable. It was a harsh and ironic fact that in the ensuing years each side appeared to put forward proposals which the other was unlikely to accept, and to withdraw them if in fact they looked likely to be accepted. One of those who took part in the negotiations for a time on the British side has recorded his belief that real agreement was never a practical possibility.[2] But each side knew that it would court international reprobation by breaking them off.

In the same way the negotiations over Germany and Austria, which began again in Berlin in January 1954, were conducted presumably without any real expectation of agreement. The Soviet Government's objects at this time were evidently to prevent the rearmament of Germany and the establishment of the European Defence Community. The two objects were related, since the E.D.C. without German rearmament would have had no substance, and German rearmament except in the context of the E.D.C. was still unacceptable to the French.

[1] This has been done by Anthony Nutting, *Disarmament – an Outline of the Negotiations* (O.U.P. for R.I.I.A., 1959).

[2] Nutting, *op. cit.*, p. xi.

The Berlin Conference was seemingly just as much intended by the Soviet leaders to achieve these two objects as were the rest of their diplomatic activities in 1954. When Molotov put forward on 1 February a draft peace treaty providing for the neutralization of Germany and her exclusion from the Western defence system, he cannot have supposed that it would be accepted: he was speaking for the record. Similarly the Western proposals for the reunification of Germany on the basis of free elections were known to be unacceptable to the Soviet Government, especially since the uprising in Eastern Germany in June 1953. The only immediate result of the Berlin Conference, which ended on 18 February, was an agreement to hold a further conference on Far Eastern questions, particularly Korea and Indo-China, in the early summer.

The second conference of 1954, which was the first attended by Communist China as a great power, met in Geneva from 26 April to 21 July. It reproduced the familiar pattern in two respects. On the political future of Korea nothing was agreed, and the subject was simply allowed to drop from sight. On Indo-China, the result was not so much to produce an agreement, since both the American and the Vietnamese Governments strongly dissented from the rest, as to register a decisive change in the balance of power in S.E. Asia and a grave set-back for France. These were facts, which would have been facts none the less if the Geneva Conference had never met. Ironically, the crowning disaster to French arms, which was the capture of Dien Bien Phu by the Vietminh, occurred on 7 May, the day before the discussion of Indo-China began at Geneva.

Yet there were redeeming features from the Western point of view. One was the vigour and courage with which a new French Prime Minister, Mendès-France, coming to power on 12 May, set about liquidating the tragedy of Indo-China by agreeing to the partition of Vietnam and the final independence of the other two Associated States, Laos and Cambodia. Another was that the French, and hence their allies, were disencumbered of an expensive and embarrassing commitment; and that was done without in fact sacrificing the whole of S.E. Asia to Communism, as had often been gloomily predicted. A third was that the Western Powers at last came to agree on a common policy for S.E. Asia, which eventually took shape in the Collective Treaty usually known as S.E.A.T.O. (the South-East Asian Treaty Organization).

None of it was achieved cheaply. In March it was feared that the

U.S. Government was about to intervene openly in the Indo-China war, possibly with atomic weapons. Dulles had already made America's allies uneasy with talk of 'massive and instant retaliation . . . by means and at places of our own choosing', and it was not considered impossible that he would choose Dien Bien Phu. Later he spoke of having 'gone to the brink of war' on this occasion. In April he visited London and Paris, evidently with the intention of persuading the British Government to support an intervention in Indo-China.[1] But this purpose failed, for Churchill and Eden both stated before the end of the month that Britain had undertaken no new commitment in S.E. Asia. What is certain is that serious friction between the British and American Governments became apparent at this time. The essential cause of it seems to have been a disagreement on the timing of the steps to be taken to create a S.E. Asian defence organization, which the British Government wished to postpone until after the Geneva Conference. An accumulation of such frustrations caused Dulles to adopt an attitude of frigid disinterest in the Geneva Conference, from which he absented himself completely for several weeks.

Yet Dulles's attitude to Geneva should not be regarded merely as a display of ill-temper. It showed a realistic appreciation of the facts in more than one respect. In the first place, the conference could not be expected to produce any result except to recognize what was already the case; and there were advantages for the U.S. Government in not being committed in the eyes of the world to approval of what it could not change. In the second place, a prominent role at Geneva was being played by representatives of a Chinese Government which the U.S.A. did not recognize. To the Communist side there were advantages in forcing U.S. representatives to sit at the same table as Communist China, just as there were five years later in the case of the Communist Government of Eastern Germany. It was to the U.S.A.'s advantage to avoid giving the implicit degree of recognition which this would carry, for unlike full diplomatic recognition it would be irreversible. Finally, the American Secretary of State had other preoccupations in the summer of 1954, some of them even more urgent that those of a situation which could not be saved. One, for instance, was the apparent intrusion of a Communist Government on the United States' own doorstep, in Guatemala. (It was overthrown, evidently not without American connivance, at the end of June.) Another was the fate of the E.D.C. which depended upon a decision of the French Government in August.

[1] Sir Anthony Eden, *Full Circle*, chapter V, especially pp. 102–3.

The Soviet Government and the American Secretary of State were probably at one in believing that the security of Europe was a matter deserving more of their attention than the Geneva Conference. The struggle in S.E. Asia had for the moment settled itself in a Communist victory, but the struggle in Europe was still open. The common factor in both cases was the role of the French, to whom the defeat in Indo-China was a moral blow which could not fail to affect their attitude to problems elsewhere. Mendès-France had to deal simultaneously not only with Indo-China and the ratification of E.D.C., but also with the long-frustrated claims to independence of Tunisia and Morocco. He settled Indo-China, and he went some way towards settling Tunisia, with ruthless and realistic simplicity; but his application of the same qualities to the problem of the E.D.C. resulted only – perhaps intentionally – in destroying the treaty. After a last-minute attempt to persuade the other five partners (all of whom had already ratified the treaty) to revise it, he put it to the French Assembly at the end of August and acquiesced without a struggle in the vote 'to pass to other business'.

Thus was achieved at least one of the major objects of Soviet policy in 1954. But the other, which was to prevent German rearmament, did not follow. The British and American Governments had already agreed, and declared their agreement, that Germany must resume her full place in Western Europe whether or not E.D.C. came into existence. On 11 September Eden began a rapid tour of the Western capitals to devise a way of making this outcome acceptable, and at the end of the month a conference was held in London of the six countries involved in E.D.C. together with Britain, the United States and Canada. At the price of a promise by the British Government to maintain their existing forces in Europe (four divisions and a tactical Air Force) or whatever the Supreme Commander deemed equivalent, it was unanimously agreed to form a new organization, West European Union, including Britain as well as the six continental allies. It was also agreed to recommend the admission of Western Germany to N.A.T.O., the Federal Republic having agreed unilaterally at the same time not to manufacture atomic and certain other weapons. On 22 October the North Atlantic Council invited the German Federal Republic to join N.A.T.O., and on the following day the agreement creating W.E.U. was signed.

There were no further setbacks, despite strenuous Soviet efforts and even threats. In February 1955 the Soviet Government warned Western

D

Germany that the creation of W.E.U. would prevent reunification; and in March, two days before the French Assembly debated ratification, they threatened to denounce the Franco-Soviet Treaty of 1944 and to form an East European military pact. W.E.U. was nevertheless ratified, and on 5 May the occupation of Germany was formally ended. The Warsaw Pact was duly signed by the powers of the Soviet Bloc on 14 May, and there were some other signs of a hardening line. For instance, Malenkov, who had become identified with a policy of relaxation, was removed from office by Khrushchev and Bulganin in February 1955, and Nagy similarly fell from power in Hungary.

But on balance the signs were more favourable. A peace treaty with Austria was at last agreed upon in April with startling suddenness; and almost simultaneously a *rapprochement* took place between Tito and the new Soviet leaders, who visited Belgrade in May. In June Adenauer was invited to Moscow – an invitation which was accepted after a cautious delay, and led eventually to the establishment of diplomatic relations. Meanwhile Churchill revived his proposal of a meeting at the summit, and found a more cordial reception from Eisenhower than before. A formal invitation to meet at Geneva was addressed to the Soviet Government on 10 May, almost exactly two years after Churchill's first initiative, but a little over a month after his retirement. It was accepted for 18 July.

The two new Soviet leaders, Bulganin and Khrushchev (respectively the Prime Minister and the Secretary of the Communist Party), presented something of an enigma. They had not been in power long, and it was difficult to foresee if they had come to stay: one of them in fact had not. It was also difficult to see which was the senior. They claimed to represent a 'collective leadership', but they were readier than Malenkov to act on their own initiative, more forthcoming and willing to make international contacts. Willingness to meet and travel, however, did not entail willingness to compromise or even really to negotiate. The Geneva Conference of July 1955 quickly revealed diametrically opposite views on the essential points, especially the future of Germany and the security of Europe.

Some interesting ideas nevertheless emerged. One was Eisenhower's 'Open Skies' plan for aerial inspection by the great powers of each other's territory, which disquieted American defence chiefs. Another was Eden's proposal for a progressive limitation of forces in Central Europe as part of a plan for the reunification of Germany, together with a simple system of inspection of the forces confronting each other.

On the Soviet side the proposals were for a European security treaty and a programme of disarmament which had, in its essentials, already been put before the U.N. Disarmament Sub-Committee in May. None of these proposals proved mutually acceptable. The Geneva Conference ended in an atmosphere of some disappointment, which was increased by the failure of a subsequent meeting of the four Foreign Ministers, also held at Geneva, in October. The public disappointment perhaps arose from a misconception of the current function of great-power conferences in international relations.

A fragment of hope which seemed to be salvaged from the failure was an invitation to Bulganin and Khrushchev to visit England in 1956. The visit was made, but was no more than a qualified success. It followed closely upon an important revision of Soviet policy, of which the immediately visible part was more spectacular but perhaps less substantial than the parts which became apparent more gradually. In February 1956 the Twentieth Party Congress of the Soviet Communist Party heard a startling, perhaps unpremeditated, attack on Stalin by Khrushchev. This occasion launched a period known as 'de-Staliniza-tion' which had great and tragic results in Eastern Europe later in the year. But no less important was the evidence that Khrushchev was looking beyond Europe to the countries of Asia and Africa and even Latin America as a future sphere of Soviet influence.

The new emphasis was placed on peaceful economic competition with the other great powers, who were warned nevertheless that Soviet influence was backed by immense military, material and technological power. In November and December 1955 Bulganin and Khrushchev made a spectacular tour of India and Burma, scattering promises of aid. China was already heavily dependent on the Soviet Union. S.E. Asia and beyond also came within the Soviet leaders' purview. Broadcasting to Africa was developed on a vast scale. Early in 1956 Bulganin initiated a correspondence with Eisenhower on the Middle East, in which he insisted on the Soviet Government's right to take part in any settlement of the area. This claim was publicly repeated before and after the Soviet leaders' visit to London in April, though they were warned by Eden that the British Government would resent and resist Soviet interference in the area.[1] But the warning was in vain, for such interference had in fact already begun with the purchase of Soviet arms by President Nasser, nominally from Czechoslovakia, in September 1955.

[1] Sir Anthony Eden, *Full Circle*, p. 358.

3

The World at Stake (1955–9)

WITH the involvement of the Middle East, the entire periphery of the Soviet Bloc except the Indian sub-continent became engaged in the cold war. The responsibility for extending the area of conflict from Europe out to the Far East and then back through S.E. Asia and the Middle East has been laid, naturally and inevitably, by each side at the door of the other. Soviet apologists point to the creation of S.E.A.T.O. in 1954 and the Baghdad Pact in 1955, along with numerous bilateral American military pacts, as the decisive cause. In this argument they enjoy some support even from the West and its friends. The French, for instance, were sharply critical of the Baghdad Pact, as also was the Labour Party in Britain. The Indians regarded both the Baghdad Pact and S.E.A.T.O. as unjustifiable, although they were prepared to accept the need for N.A.T.O. Several of the countries which signed bilateral treaties with the U.S.A. (notably Pakistan, which also joined both the Baghdad Pact and S.E.A.T.O.) wondered in retrospect whether they had done wisely. The Western answer to such strictures is that circumstances left them with no alternative but to establish such military alliances, and that the circumstances were largely, though perhaps not wholly, of Communist creation.

Perhaps the most fateful step on the Western side was taken by the Americans alone when they signed a Mutual Defence Treaty with the Chinese Government of Chiang Kai-Shek on Formosa early in 1955. The treaty was approved by the Senate Foreign Relations Committee only on three provisos: firstly, that it did not settle the question of sovereignty over Formosa; secondly, that it was not to be extended to cover other territories without the Senate's consent; thirdly, that no military operations were to be launched from Formosa without the joint agreement of both the Governments concerned. One group of islands close to Formosa, the Pescadores, was covered by the treaty, but the so-called 'offshore islands' close to the Chinese mainland were not. All alike were claimed by the Chinese Communists, and some of the offshore islands were under intermittent fire from mainland batteries which might well be, as was to be feared again in 1958, the preliminary to armed attack. To reduce the risk, two small groups of the offshore islands were evacuated of Chiang Kai-Shek's troops under U.S. naval cover in February 1955, but the more important, including Quemoy and Matsu, remained in the hands of the Kuomintang Government. The situation disquieted the British Government, which regarded the offshore islands, unlike Formosa, as falling properly under the sovereignty of Peking; but it could certainly not be argued that the U.S. treaty with Chiang Kai-Shek was aggressive.

Elsewhere in Asia the Western Allies were taking similar measures collectively for the same defensive purposes. In S.E. Asia the creation of S.E.A.T.O. was seen by them as the only immediate way to stem the tide of Communism after the collapse of the French position in Indo-China in 1954. The treaty was based on the presumption of Chinese aggressiveness, for which there seemed at the time to be several undeniable motives: the nationalist impulse to extend Chinese influence, a missionary zeal to extend the Communist ideology, a desire to control the S.E. Asian supplies of rice and other raw materials, and a desire to ensure China's own security against counter-attack. From the Western point of view the primary need was to prevent a Communist conquest of Siam, which would have had as probable consequence the loss of Malaya by Britain. Longer-term objectives were to promote the stability and prosperity of the S.E. Asian countries, but these could only be promoted if their frontiers were first made secure. Soon after the Geneva Conference of 1954, therefore, the powers concerned set about convening a conference on S.E. Asian defence, which met in Manila in September. The Manila Treaty was signed on 9 September 1954 by Australia, France, New Zealand, Pakistan, the Philippines, Siam, Britain and the U.S.A. Certain other states which did not sign the treaty were offered protection by it (Cambodia, Laos and South Vietnam) but others whose participation would have been valuable (such as India, Burma and Indonesia) looked at it with disfavour.

The treaty thus had an unfortunate appearance of being dominated by non-Asian powers (the U.S.A., Britain, France, Australia and New Zealand). It has been said of it[1] that 'the Western powers are in the invidious position of wishing to defend countries, which do not wish to be defended, from dangers the existence of which their governments deny in public'. Nevertheless, despite its political disadvantages, the treaty gave to the area some assurance of military security; and the probability of a successive collapse of the existing S.E. Asian régimes,

[1] *Collective Defence in S.E. Asia* (R.I.I.A., 1956), p. 166.

beginning with South Vietnam, which was expected almost daily in 1954, did not materialize.

One reaction of the S.E. Asian countries had unexpectedly important consequences. There was organized in April 1955 at Bandung, in Indonesia, what was called an 'Afro-Asian Conference', which gave a confused but emphatic expression to the point of view of twenty-four Asian and African countries, many of them new to the international stage. Since the conference included among others Communist China, which was at least potentially a great power, and Turkey, which was wholeheartedly committed to the Western Alliance, it was an exaggeration to say that it created an Afro-Asian neutralist bloc speaking with one voice. But there was a clear consensus of the majority against becoming involved in the struggle of the great powers; and this was an important new phenomenon.

The Bandung Conference also included most of the states of the Middle East, which were simultaneously going through a crisis similar to that of the S.E. Asians as the Baghdad Pact began to take shape in 1955. The Baghdad Pact differed from S.E.A.T.O. in two ways, apart from the absence from it of the U.S.A. and France. It did not result from a war between Western and Communist Powers, but was intended only to forestall one; and it did not emerge all at once from a single act of negotiation, but came together piecemeal. The first suggestion of such a pact came, despite the Americans' later reluctance to take part in it, from Dulles himself after his first tour of the area in 1953. In a sense, however, it was also a successor to the abortive attempt of Britain, France and Turkey to form a Middle East Defence Organization in 1951; but it differed from that earlier attempt not only in the absence of the Americans and the disapproval of the French in 1955, but also in the omission of any attempt to include Egypt. A new Anglo-Egyptian Treaty had been signed in October 1954, but it was impossible to create a collective organization that would accommodate both Egypt and Iraq; and the latter was regarded by the British as more dependable. In fact Iraq was the only Arab state ever to join the treaty which was named from her capital (the others being Turkey, Pakistan, Iran and Britain); and even Iraq seceded in 1959, after which the name was changed from 'Baghdad Pact' to 'Central Treaty Organization'.

The Baghdad Pact was thus even less like N.A.T.O. in its conception and structure than was S.E.A.T.O. It was not designed: it just grew. The first step was taken as early as February 1954, when Turkey and Pakistan made a defence pact, which was criticized both in Egypt and

India as well as by the Soviet Union. At the end of the year the Iraqi Prime Minister, Nuri es-Said, announced his intention to terminate the current Anglo-Iraqi Treaty before it expired in 1957. This made it necessary for the British Government to seek some new arrangement, which it was thought would be more acceptable to Iraq if it were placed on a multilateral instead of a bilateral basis. In January 1955 the Iraqi Government announced its intention to make a treaty with Turkey, which was already tied to Pakistan. This step was welcomed in Britain, though not in a number of other countries, including France, Israel, Egypt, India and the Soviet Union.

There was thus created the opportunity for a multilateral pact, though one necessarily limited in scope. It came into being with Britain's adhesion at the end of March 1955, followed by Pakistan's in September. The obvious gap between Turkey and Pakistan was closed by the adherence of Iran, despite sharp warnings from the Soviet Union, in October. The Egyptian Government showed its resentment by forming a closer alliance with Syria, which was later joined by Saudi Arabia and Yemen. Egypt also played a vigorous part in discouraging other countries from joining the Baghdad Pact: for instance, ¹he Lebanon, and particularly Jordan, whose adherence was frustrated in December 1955 by a political crisis which led instead to the dismissal of the British commander of the Arab Legion, General Glubb, a few months later. Egypt's opposition was thus effectual though not decisive. What effect the Baghdad Pact had on Soviet policy, on the other hand, is more difficult to say.

The Soviet Government had shown little interest, at least publicly, in the Middle East since the withdrawal of the Red Army from Northern Iran in May 1946. They had left behind a pro-Soviet Government in Azerbaijan, and another in Kurdistan, but both were easily overthrown by the Iranian authorities in December of the same year. For ten years thereafter little was heard of the Russians in the Middle East. During the troubles in Palestine, they consistently took a line hostile to British interests, but this was part of the great-power struggle rather than an incursion into Middle Eastern politics. They were among the first Governments to recognize Israel in May 1948, but thereafter pursued a capricious policy towards the new state: for instance, severing diplomatic relations on a trivial pretext just before Stalin's death in 1953, and renewing them a few months later. Towards the Arab states, before the Egyptian revolution of 1952, the Soviet attitude was indifferent or hostile. During the protracted Anglo-Iranian dispute of 1951–3, there were fears that the Tudeh Party of Iran, under Communist leadership though not Communist in origin, would seize power with Soviet help, or that Iran would become 'another Korea', partitioned between warring great powers. None of these fears was realized, and in fact few people in the Middle East were conscious of a Soviet danger at all, except those who lived in the immediate vicinity of the U.S.S.R.

The Western Powers, particularly Britain, were nevertheless constantly alert to the possibilities of Soviet aggression in the Middle East, whether they were real or not. Their first effort to organize its regional security was the proposal of a Middle East Defence Organization, put forward by Britain, France, the U.S.A. and Turkey in October 1951. The proposal was scornfully rejected by Egypt, which was trying to break the Anglo-Egyptian Treaty of 1936 at the time; nor would the other Arab states, with the possible exception of Iraq, have found it acceptable. To all of them, the first enemy of the day was not the Soviet Union but Israel; and the second enemy was what they called 'Western imperialism' – that is, the very powers which were proposing the new treaty. The subject was therefore allowed to drop for several years. When it was revived by Britain, in the new form of the Baghdad Pact, it was no less true than before that most of the peoples of the Middle East, particularly the Arabs, were unconscious of any threat from the Soviet Union. Many critics of the Pact, particularly the French, were inclined to argue that it created the very danger which it was intended to forestall, by challenging the Soviet leaders to enter Middle Eastern politics. This they did in 1955–6 with a vengeance; but it cannot be certain that they were not already committed to doing so, and therefore it cannot be certain whether the Baghdad Pact provoked or mitigated the shock of Soviet intervention.

The first overt move on the Soviet side was an invitation to President Nasser to visit Moscow in August 1955. A month later the Egyptian Government announced the purchase of arms from Czechoslovakia, which were later admitted to be of Soviet origin. Payment was to be made by means of Egypt's one major export, cotton, for which the demand had declined in recent years in its normal markets. There followed in October a general offer of Soviet economic aid to the Middle East, and early in 1956 a specific offer to Egypt of Soviet aid for an atomic power-station. All these offers illustrated the increasingly familiar pattern of Soviet foreign economic policy, which was to obtain the maximum propaganda advantage from the minimum actual contribution. The crucial test was to come over President Nasser's long-cherished ambition to transform Egypt's economy by building the so-called High Dam at Assouan, for which he had conditional offers of financial help from the U.S.A., Britain and the World Bank (the International Bank for Reconstruction and Development).

It was clear early in 1956 that the Western Powers were uneasy about President Nasser's capacity to fulfil the conditions of the loans for the High Dam after committing the cotton crop for several years ahead to pay for Soviet arms. It was also clear that President Nasser was becoming impatient with the uncertainties and reservations on the Western side. No doubt he sought assurances of Soviet help if the Western offers were withdrawn, particularly when Shepilov, the Soviet Foreign Minister, visited Cairo in June 1956. But although there had been 'tempting overtures' at an earlier stage,[1] it seems probable that he received no such assurances; and even the possibility of obtaining partial help from the Soviet Union to supplement a Western loan was scotched by Dulles's statement on 22 May that the U.S.A. was 'unlikely' to help Egypt with the High Dam if the Soviet Union also did so. From this point onwards each Government concerned seems to have miscalculated the consequences of its actions. Since so much is still unknown about the Suez Canal crisis, however, the following are no more than presumptions.

The Soviet Government acted as if it assumed that President Nasser could be made into a dependable satellite by the supply of arms, economic aid and technicians. But he proved to be more like a Middle Eastern Tito. (By an ironic chance, Nasser was visiting Tito at Brioni, together with Nehru, when the moment of crisis came in July 1956.) Nasser seems to have assumed that he could extract advantages from both sides, as Tito and Nehru had done, by skilful diplomacy. But he carried the gambit too far, at least in his dealings with the Americans, when he agreed to recognize the Communist Chinese government on 16 May. The British Government, on the other hand, had based its policy since 1954 on two assumptions about President Nasser: firstly, that his position was insecure; and secondly, that it was more advantageous than otherwise to British interests that he should remain in control.

The second assumption was upset by President Nasser's dealings with the Communist Powers, leaving only the first assumption intact. It was on this remaining assumption, that Nasser's Government could fairly easily be toppled over, that the British Government seemed to act

[1] Sir Anthony Eden, *Full Circle*, p. 420.

for the rest of 1956. The American view was less extreme: it was rather that Nasser could and should be 'cut down to size', in the current phrase. On this principle, the U.S. government withdrew its offer of financial help for the High Dam on 19 July; the British Government did so also on the following day, in spite of having had no prior consultation; and the World Bank's conditional offer automatically lapsed. President Nasser retaliated on 26 July by nationalizing the Suez Canal Company, ostensibly to provide the revenue necessary for building the High Dam.

The detailed study of the Suez Canal crisis[1] does not, except intermittently, belong to the history of relations between the Soviet Union and the Western Powers, though the occasional interaction of events was crucial. The Soviet Union gave President Nasser its moral support at every stage; for instance, by encouraging his resistance to the proposals of the London Conference on the Suez Canal in August, and by denouncing the Suez Canal Users' Association which the Western Powers formed in September. When the French and British intervened by force after the Israeli attack on Egypt at the end of October, the Soviet Union continued to give moral support to Egypt, but no more.

Soviet aircraft based on Egyptian aerodromes, if they were not destroyed on the ground, were flown away to safety. The Soviet radio talked of sending 'volunteers' to fight against the French, British and Israelis, but none were sent. The Soviet Government sent notes to the British and French Governments on 5 November threatening to use rockets against their countries if they did not halt their operations, but only after it could be calculated as likely that they would halt in any case. This calculation, which was correct if it was made, suggests one reason for the inadequate physical support given to Egypt by the Soviet Union. Another reason was presumably that the Soviet Union was itself deeply committed to military action in Hungary.

The rising in Budapest in October 1956 was the climax of a process which Khrushchev had started by his attack on Stalin at the Twentieth Party Congress in February. 'De-stalinization' led to what was called 'the new course' and even to the belief that Peoples' Democracies were free to pursue 'separate roads to Socialism'. Relaxation and change took place everywhere (except perhaps in the German Democratic Republic, which had learned its lesson in June 1953), and particularly in Poland

[1] It can be read in detail in Guy Wint's and Peter Calvocoressi's *Middle East Crisis* (Penguin Books, 1957). Sir Anthony Eden's account is given in Book III of *Full Circle* (Cassell, 1960).

and Hungary. In Poland serious riots at Poznan in June led the Government to admit that much of its economic policy had been wrong, or at least needed drastic revision. The anti-Stalinist Communist leader Gomulka, whose release from gaol was announced in February, was re-elected First Secretary of the Party on 20 October. A new *Politburo* was announced, and a general election was promised.

In Hungary the revolution began, by comparison less violently, with the anti-Stalinist agitation of a group of writers and intellectuals. The movement gained such strength that on 18 July Rakosi, the First Secretary of the Hungarian Workers' Party, was forced to resign. The fall of Rakosi was tolerated by the Soviet Government, but by the middle of October the Hungarian revolution was felt to have gone too far, no doubt in part because the Polish revolution had already been so successful. The climax came when Imre Nagy, who had been Prime Minister for a short time in 1953 and later overthrown and expelled from the Party, was invited to take office again on 24 October. Soviet forces then began to close in on Budapest. They had already been in position to do so for several days beforehand; and this seems to weaken the argument that they acted only as a consequence of the Anglo-French action in the Middle East, which can be dated only from after the ultimatum of 30 October.

It appears (though this is uncertain and has been denied) that Nagy began his brief tenure of office by invoking the Warsaw Pact and appealing for the help of Soviet troops. Although he certainly reversed these decisions later, and actually denounced the Warsaw Pact on 1 November, the fact that he was believed to have made them was a fatality for which he later paid with his life. The Soviet Government was able to argue a legitimate pretext for acts of repression in Budapest which shocked world opinion. With intermissions, the suppression of the Hungarian revolution went on until well into November, long after the Anglo-French operation in Egypt had been brought to a halt during the night of 6–7 November. The intervention of the United Nations, which was eventually successful in the Middle East, was entirely ineffective in Hungary. Soviet control was completely re-established under a new Communist Government. On the other hand, the Poles were able to maintain their new position as a kind of licensed heretics within the Soviet camp, under a régime which conformed to Soviet principles in most of the essentials but managed to remain at least as distinctively nationalist as Tito's in Yugoslavia.

The immediate result of the combined crises of Hungary and the

Middle East was a state of startled disarray, certainly to the west of the
Iron Curtain and probably to the east of it as well. The Anglo-French
action severely shook the Anglo-American alliance, N.A.T.O., the
Baghdad Pact and the Commonwealth. There is less evidence of the
reaction in the Soviet Bloc, but the events in Poland and Hungary at
least cannot have had a negligible impact on the Soviet leaders. The
number of them who fell from office or whose disgrace was completed
in the next two years – Malenkov, Molotov, Shepilov, Kaganovich,
Bulganin and Zhukov – was abnormal. But in both East and West
the disarray appears to have been short-lived, and the recovery was
practically complete.

On the Western side there were no defections from the alliances,
though both in India and in Pakistan there was talk of leaving the
Commonwealth; and the Moslem members of the Baghdad Pact
pointedly held a meeting without Britain's participation. The U.S.
Government, which found itself held much to blame for inadequate
leadership, began to treat its allies with greater consideration than
before, and the habit of political consultation within N.A.T.O. was
strengthened. An ostentatious meeting of the N.A.T.O. Council,
attended by fourteen of the fifteen heads of Government, was held in
December 1957 to emphasize the resuscitation of the Alliance. In the
Soviet camp, though less publicly, a similar process of rallying the
ranks may well have taken place; and their policy of 'peaceful co-existence' and economic competition among the underdeveloped and
uncommitted nations was pursued, if anything, more vigorously than
before.

The long-term effects were more important. The first to become
apparent was that both the U.S.A. and the U.S.S.R. were now Middle
Eastern Powers, not less so than France and Britain had been, though
in different ways. Both played prominent parts in the debates at the
United Nations on the Anglo-French action, and did their best, short of
active hostilities, to frustrate it. Their interest in the area came to be
taken for granted from 1956 onwards, so that formal declarations of it,
although made, were obviously superfluous. The Soviet interest was
made evident, though not precise, both in Bulganin's correspondence
with Eisenhower early in 1956 and in the communiqué issued at the
end of the visit to England by Bulganin and Khrushchev in April. The
American Government declared in November its interest in the integrity and political independence of the Baghdad Pact Powers; and
without actually adhering to the Pact, the U.S.A. joined its Military

Committee (being already a member of its Economic Committee) during 1957.

The most explicit declaration was the so-called Eisenhower Doctrine, made in January and approved by the Senate on 5 March, by which the President was empowered, among other things, to use American forces to protect Middle Eastern States against 'overt armed aggression from any nation controlled by international Communism'. There were also provisions for military and economic aid. The Eisenhower Doctrine was accepted in principle by some states in the Middle East and repudiated, at least partially, by others. Its principles were naturally disapproved by the Soviet Government, which in February proposed as an alternative a joint four-power declaration on the Middle East, consisting of six points, one of which was a cessation of arms supply. Such declarations had in fact little impact on the course of events, except to register the undoubted fact that the U.S.A. and the U.S.S.R. were irrevocably engaged in the area.

Another long-term conclusion that could be drawn from the crisis of 1956 was of a more momentous, because world-wide, importance. The double crisis appeared to show that a war between the great powers was unlikely, and that a war between the small powers could fairly easily be stopped. The clarity of these lessons was obscured by the fact that the two crises coincided, but it is not hard to disentangle them in retrospect. Either the U.S.A. or the U.S.S.R. could easily have gone to war in 1956 with sufficient justification to satisfy themselves, but clearly neither of them wanted to do so, nor did they want to allow lesser powers to drag them into it. In Hungary it was painfully apparent that the U.S.A. could do nothing whatever to support a ready-made revolution, spontaneously set off by her natural friends, without being willing to risk war with the Soviet Union. If she had been ready to take that risk, she could never have had a better justification in the eyes of the world. The problem was certainly complicated by the embarrassment felt in the U.S.A. at her allies' conduct in the Middle East, and by the fact that in October 1956 Dulles was incapacitated and Eisenhower was in the middle of his second election campaign. But these embarrassments pale into insignificance compared with the fact, which would have been a fact in any case, that the U.S.A. was not prepared to go to war with the Soviet Union to liberate Hungary.

In the Middle East the facts are more obscure, but it was certainly the belief of the British Government that if they did not act vigorously a major war would follow the conflict between Egypt and Israel, and that no other power, least of all the United Nations, would act effectively in time. For their belief in the danger that the war would spread they had the justification of knowing that Egypt contained substantial quantities of Soviet equipment, some of it accompanied by Soviet technicians. There was also the fact that Egypt had rejected the Anglo-French ultimatum of 30 October, although Israel had conditionally accepted it. In other words, President Nasser had declared his intention to go on fighting, and no one could tell where the fighting would stop. What was not known at the time was the extent to which Egypt was incapacitated for further fighting; nor was it known how determined the Soviet Government was not to be drawn into the fighting – a determination belied by bellicose words.

In retrospect it may be argued that even without the Anglo-French intervention the war between Israel and Egypt would have been stopped and the *status quo ante* would have been restored by the collective action of the powers. To say this is to speak without certainty and with the wisdom of hindsight. But the general proposition of which this argument, whether right or wrong, is an illustration – that the powers intended at all costs to avoid war with each other and to prevent lesser powers from dragging them into war – remains apparently valid, and has been further confirmed by every subsequent great-power crisis since 1956, in every part of the world. Such crises occurred in the Middle East (1957–8), in the Far East (1958) and in Europe (1958–9).

In the Middle East, after the alarms of 1956 had died down, they were sounded again by the King of Jordan in April 1957. Believing his régime to be endangered by Egyptian intrigue, he declared martial law on 25 April and later closed his Embassy in Cairo. There was no apparent threat from the Soviet Union, and although Communist intrigue was spoken of, the term could only be applied to Egypt by a long stretch of the imagination, so it was technically impossible to invoke the Eisenhower Doctrine. Nevertheless the American 6th Fleet was moved to the Eastern Mediterranean as a precaution, and considerable U.S. aid was sent to Jordan, which had ceased to enjoy British aid since the termination of the Anglo-Jordanian Treaty in March. The bold reaction of the young King, with the clear indication of American support, brought the crisis temporarily to a close. Before it was re-opened (in 1958), another crisis came near to involving the great powers against each other in the Middle East, when the Syrians accused Turkey in September 1957 of aggressive intentions.

The Syrian Government had already, apparently not without reason, accused the Americans of intriguing against it. The Soviet Government warmly took up the Syrian complaint against Turkey, the U.S.A.'s ally, at the United Nations. Turkey made counter-charges against Soviet policy in the Middle East; Egyptian forces were shipped to Syria; and a state of emergency was proclaimed there. During this period the Syrians moved increasingly close to the Egyptians, with whom they eventually coalesced to form the United Arab Republic in February 1958. Both also were thought to be moving close to the Soviet Bloc; but appearances were deceptive. The crisis between Turkey and Syria was dissipated as quickly as it had gathered, and was seen to be as good as over when Khrushchev ostentatiously presented himself at a Turkish Embassy reception in Moscow on 29 October. On the other hand, from the turn of the year, if not earlier, relations between the Soviet Government and President Nasser actually deteriorated. It was even arguable that the Syrian motive for joining the United Arab Republic was to solicit Egyptian protection against the threat of Communism.

Conditions returned more or less to normal in the Middle East – which is not to say that they were not confused and unsettled – until the early summer of 1958, when disorders broke out in the Lebanon in connexion with an impending presidential election. It was believed in Britain and the U.S.A. that the trouble was deliberately fomented from across the border in Syria, from which it followed that President Nasser was assumed to be responsible. A team of U.N. observers was sent to the Lebanese-Syrian frontier, but their coverage of it could not be adequate. For some weeks the trouble simmered unsteadily in the Lebanon, until matters were brought to a crisis throughout the Arab world by a revolution in Baghdad on 14 July, which overthrew and killed the King of Iraq and his Prime Minister, Nuri es-Said. The revolution was again assumed to have Egyptian support, though this support, if given at the time, was later reversed into a state of violent hostility between President Nasser and the new Iraqi Prime Minister, Brigadier Kassem. The Western reaction was to safeguard its interests elsewhere in the Middle East lest disorder should spread and serve the advantage of the U.S.S.R. American marines were landed in Beirut on 15 July at the invitation of the Lebanese President, and British air-borne forces in Jordan on 17 July at the invitation of the King.

On 19 July Khrushchev declared that the Middle East was on the brink of disaster. He demanded an immediate meeting 'at the summit' to discuss the Middle East, in advance of a general Summit Conference which was already under negotiation. The British Government agreed, provided that the meeting took place at the United Nations, which was already seized of the Middle East situation; and the U.S. Government agreed, though reluctantly, provided that the meeting took place under 'Security Council rules', which entailed the right of veto. Khrushchev, at the end of July, accused the Western Powers of deliberate delay and evasion; but in August he appeared to lose interest in the Middle East after a flying visit to Peking. The United Nations duly debated the crisis, with the surprising result that an innocuous resolution presented unanimously by all the Arab Powers was accepted, leaving the future initiative to the Secretary General. Once more the crisis quietly petered out. At the end of September the U.S. and British Governments announced their intention to withdraw their troops from the Lebanon and Jordan respectively, having achieved their object of restoring stability to the area. By early November the withdrawals were completed without further incident.

While the Middle East returned again to normal – normality being again interpreted in a local sense – the point of crisis shifted to the Far East. The shift cannot be wholly unconnected with Khrushchev's visit to Peking in August, but the presumption is that he was trying to mitigate the crisis, not to aggravate it. On 6 August the Nationalist Chinese Government on Formosa declared a state of emergency in the offshore islands, which were again under fire from the Chinese mainland. The British Government had long since acknowledged the Peking Government's legal right to these islands, but it supported the American Government in opposing any change by force. The Chinese Communists had repeatedly declared their intention to conquer, or liberate, the offshore islands, as well as Formosa itself. The American Government had suggested, though somewhat ambiguously, that possession of the offshore islands was necessary to the defence of Formosa; and they had made it more definitely clear that if a Chinese Communist attack on the offshore islands appeared to be a first step towards an attack on Formosa, U.S. forces might be committed to defending them.

Such an attack could be construed to be imminent in August 1958. A concentrated bombardment of the islands, particularly Quemoy, was begun from the mainland, and threatening speeches and broadcasts were made from Peking. Warnings against the risk of war were directed at the Chinese Communists by the U.S. Government, and less forcefully by the British Government, which felt obliged to support the American position though not to go to war for the offshore islands. The bombardment and the threats were both relaxed in September, but increased again in October, when Dulles visited Formosa. There cannot be any certainty what then took place either between the Americans and the Nationalists or between the Soviet and Chinese Communist Governments, but it is reasonable to suppose that Dulles urged restraint upon Chiang Kai-Shek and Khrushchev urged restraint on Mao Tse-Tung.

Certainly restraint eventually prevailed, and the crisis over the off-shore islands quietly petered out like the crisis in the Middle East. Both crises illustrated the principle that the great powers were determined not to let other powers drag them into war, and in both cases they were successful. The principle was plainly stated by Khrushchev to Vice-President Nixon in Moscow a year later, on 24 July 1959, in the following words:[1]

'We are the two most powerful countries, and if we live in friendship then other countries will also live in friendship. But if there is a country which is too war-minded, we could pull its ears a little and say, "Don't you dare: fighting is not allowed now".'

There is a strong presumption that both sides had already accepted this principle in practice.

The other aspect of the same principle, which was that the great powers were determined not to go to war with each other on their own account, was illustrated by the third of the crises of the years 1957–9, which began in Europe almost as soon as those in the Middle East and the Far East had ended. On 10 November 1958, during a visit to Moscow by Gomulka, Khrushchev declared that it would be 'correct' to hand over control of Berlin to the East German Government. Ten days later the Soviet Ambassador in Bonn foreshadowed the end of the occupation of Berlin. To the Western Powers, who occupied the Western sectors of Berlin on the basis of agreements made during the war and tacitly though not unwaveringly recognized ever since, the suggestion was unacceptable; and so was the later Soviet proposal, made on 27 November, that Berlin should become a 'free city', if only because the economy of West Berlin was inextricably linked to Western Germany. Khrushchev announced on 27 November that if the future of Berlin were not settled to his satisfaction in six months, he would sign a separate peace treaty with the East German Government – an action for which he had a precedent in the Japanese Peace Treaty signed by the

[1] *The Times*, 25 July 1959.

Western Powers alone in 1951. Mention of the specific period of six months gave an impression of coercion to the Soviet *démarche*, which was perhaps not intended and was later withdrawn; but it caused the gravest anxiety in the West, particularly in Germany, as the supposed deadline of 27 May 1959 drew near.

The problem of the future of Berlin naturally raised that of Germany as a whole, and that in turn raised the problem of European security. These were subjects which it was already intended to discuss at a Summit Conference, the preliminaries to which had been in motion – though extremely slow motion – since early in 1958. A protracted correspondence between Bulganin (later replaced by Khrushchev) and the Western heads of Government had been in progress since the middle of 1956. The subjects covered in it had included the Middle Eastern crises, disarmament, nuclear tests, European security, and (since January 1958) a Summit Conference. The Western side had been cautious: the Americans because they saw no point in such a conference, after the failure at Geneva in 1955, unless the Soviet Government were prepared to show its good will in deeds as well as words; and the British because they considered it necessary to prepare the ground first, for instance by means of a preliminary meeting of Foreign Ministers. It is possible that the Soviet *démarche* on Berlin was intended to do no more than accelerate the pace towards the Summit. If so, the American reaction must have come as a shock, for it included unmistakable preparations for war. The British reaction was still cautious, but not idle. The Prime Minister decided early in 1959 to visit the U.S.S.R. with the Foreign Secretary, on what he called a 'reconnaissance' to investigate the Soviet intentions.

Macmillan and Selwyn Lloyd were in the U.S.S.R. for ten days, from 21 February to 3 March, and subsequently spent most of the rest of March visiting Paris, Bonn, Ottawa and Washington. The later journeys were necessary not only to inform Britain's allies of the results of the 'reconnaissance', but also to calm the fears which had been expressed, particularly in Bonn and Washington, that the British had gone over to a policy of 'appeasement'. The West German Chancellor in particular spoke bitterly of British intentions, and it was clear that there were real divisions of approach among the Western Allies towards the problem of European security. For instance, the communiqué on Macmillan's visit to Moscow contained a reference to the possibility of arms limitation in Europe, which was well received in Eastern Europe, but not in Western Germany or the U.S.A. Later discussions among the

Western leaders restored a sufficient unity of policy to make possible a new round of negotiations with the Soviet Bloc. It was agreed by the end of March to hold a meeting of Foreign Ministers at Geneva on 11 May. The Soviet Government wished to include Poland and Czechoslovakia among the conferring powers; and although this was resisted on the Western side, both the East and the West German Governments were allowed to be represented by observers.

The conference lasted, with one intermission, until August without achieving any definite result. But it served to make clear once again that the great powers were not prepared to risk war with each other, even over so important a matter as the future of Berlin. By the middle of the summer the public opinion of the world had ceased to take the prolonged crisis seriously; and in the sense that war had become extremely unlikely, public opinion was right. There was a widespread feeling, which was officially repudiated in the West and to which only the Soviet leaders gave public expression, that the existing division of Europe, unsatisfactory and confusing though it was, was very much less risky and disadvantageous than anything likely to replace it. The main interest of the Foreign Ministers' discussions at Geneva was to see whether they would lead to a meeting at the Summit. This prospect still divided the British Government, which hoped for it, from the American Government, which was inclined to set firm conditions. The anxiety was interrupted, and largely superseded, when Vice-President Nixon visited the U.S.S.R. in July, officially returning earlier visits by Soviet Ministers to the U.S.A. It then became known on his return that Eisenhower and Khrushchev had agreed to visit each other's countries in the near future.

Rightly or wrongly, this *dénouement* appeared to the world to symbolize the impossibility of war between the two greatest powers. It further symbolized the fact, to which the remarks of Khrushchev quoted above[1] also pointed, that for the time being at least the ultimate issues were in the hands of two powers alone. That is not to say that other powers had no influence: there was probably never a time in history when more states had some influence on international relations. On the Western side Britain and France and Western Germany and Canada; on the Communist side China and Poland; among the uncommitted nations India and Yugoslavia – all these were important. Britain in particular carried great moral weight through the media of N.A.T.O. and the Commonwealth. But ultimate political power is the outcome of physical,

[1] See p. 65.

economic and technological power combined. Britain could assert a measure of physical equality when it came to nuclear weapons, having exploded her own hydrogen-bomb in 1956; and France was not outdistanced in the same field. Manpower and economic resources were another matter. And when the Soviet Union opened the 'space age' by launching the first *sputnik* in October 1957, it seemed that this was a field in which only the U.S.A. could compete on equal terms from her own unaided resources.

To say that the ultimate issues rested in the hands of two powers alone after 1957 is not to say that they could dispense with allies. On the contrary, both the U.S.A. and the Soviet Union needed allies as much as ever. The development of missiles implied in the *sputniks* was only one of many good reasons: the Americans needed bases in Europe to offset the fact that they were relatively behindhand in developing long-range missiles, and the Soviet Union needed the maximum geographical depth between the American bases and herself. These needs were reflections of the suspicion which each side had of the other's intentions upon its own security. They were reflected in their turn in the protracted debate on what came to be called 'disengagement', or the establishment of either a neutral or a 'denuclearized' zone between the two blocs in Europe, which was intimately linked with the question of German reunification from the end of 1956 onwards. The details of this debate[1] need not be elaborated, since it was clear that none of the major governments concerned was interested in the prospect of disengagement, any more than in that of disarmament or the reunification of Germany, except on terms unacceptable to the other side. But all these debates were symptomatic of an important phenomenon, which was the growing anxiety of the lesser powers to urge upon the two greatest of the great powers a sense of the overwhelming responsibility of their position.

Throughout the latest crises that have been described in the Middle East, the Far East and Europe from 1957 to 1959, the powers appeared to act as if with a reasonable sense of responsibility. Perhaps they did so only from fear: as Churchill had foreseen in 1955, safety was 'the sturdy child of terror'. But although the great powers recoiled regularly from the 'brink of war' whenever they reached it, they ran great risks in between the brinks. Neither the U.S. nor the Soviet Government hesitated to take steps that were certain to infuriate the other, and the air was loud with mutual recriminations. The Americans put atomic

---

[1] An account of it is given in Michael Howard's *Disengagement in Europe* (Penguin Books, 1958).

weapons at the disposal of N.A.T.O. (though retaining control of the war-heads) and established missile-bases of their own on the territory of several N.A.T.O. members. The Soviet Union continued to supply weapons, including submarines, to Egypt and others to Syria and Yemen. The Americans equipped their troops in Korea with what were called 'modern arms'. The Soviet Government warned Britain and other Western countries of their vulnerability to missiles, and protested to the United Nations at flights by U.S. aircraft carrying nuclear weapons over the Arctic.

In 1958 the competitive pace of nuclear tests increased. The Soviet Government announced a unilateral cessation of tests at the end of March, after an exceptionally crowded series, but began them again later in the year. The British and American Governments announced in September that they would suspend tests for a year from the end of October, provided that the Soviet Government would do the same; and provided also that the Soviet Government would send representatives to a conference on nuclear tests at Geneva in November, in succession to an earlier technical conference on the possibilities of control. The Soviet Union duly sent representatives to Geneva, but defiantly made two more nuclear explosions at the beginning of November. This was a characteristic way of indicating to the Western Powers that the Soviet Government did not care whether they approved of what it did or not. The same attitude was evident in may of Khrushchev's public speeches. (He made, for instance, an insulting anti-Western speech even while Macmillan was his guest in the Soviet Union in February 1959.) It was also shown again in the casual announcement from Moscow in June 1958 that Imre Nagy, who had been seized by Russian forces in breach of a safe-conduct at the end of the revolution in Budapest, had been tried and executed at an unspecified date.

The treatment of Nagy was looked on in the West as virtually a reversion to Stalinism. There were other similar signs, though less severe. Khrushchev, who had denounced the 'cult of personality' prevalent in Stalin's time, elevated himself to almost the same position of dominance by removing most of his senior colleagues from the 'collective leadership'; but none of them lost his life, as they would have done under Stalin. A harsher policy began also to be reintroduced in Eastern Europe, though again perhaps less merciless than under Stalin. The D.D.R. (Eastern Germany) had never experienced 'de-Staliniza-tion', so no change was needed; but in Hungary complete Party control was re-established. In Poland there was a partial relapse from the relaxa-

tions allowed after October 1956. Although there was not a full return
to the rigours of the past, freedom of speech was somewhat curtailed
again, and Gomulka's Government showed an increasing degree of
conformity with the Soviet line. While a kind of licensed heresy went on,
Poland was used as a channel by Soviet leaders for trying out new ideas.
For instance, the Rapacki Plans for reducing tension in Europe, put
forward by the Polish Foreign Minister in October 1957 and in a
revised form a year later, must presumably have enjoyed the acquiescence of Moscow even if they did not originate there.

On the periphery of the Soviet Bloc the signs were ambiguous.
Yugoslavia was alternately wooed and castigated. Tito in his turn
imprisoned his former Vice-President, Djilas, who had been one of the
staunchest of his anti-Stalinist colleagues. On the other hand, Yugoslavia's representatives alone refused to sign the communiqué issued in
Moscow at the end of the fortieth anniversary celebrations of the
Bolshevik Revolution in November 1957. In May 1959 Khrushchev
visited Albania for the first time, and used the occasion to warn Greece
of the dangers of allowing American missile-bases to be established on
her soil. Finland was sharply warned against entering the European Free
Trade Association in July 1959. In the same month Khrushchev cancelled a visit to Scandinavia which he had accepted some weeks earlier.

Among the uncommitted nations outside Europe, the Soviet Government pursued its established policy of making its influence felt regardless of Western reactions. The methods included the supply of arms to
the Middle East; trade agreements with Iraq and Guinea; aid to India
and Indonesia; a joint Soviet-Afghan survey for a dam on the River
Oxus; and similar ventures which achieved more publicity than material
result. There was sometimes a paradoxical and almost quixotic perti-
nacity about Khrushchev's quest for popularity abroad. For instance,
in December 1958 agreements were signed by the Soviet Government
with Egypt for a number of projects, including a contribution to the
first stage of building the High Dam at Assouan, almost simultaneously
with a violent attack on the Communists by President Nasser. Khrushchev was either exceptionally far-sighted and patient, or determined to
annoy the West regardless of the cost to himself.

A similar indifference, on all matters except those vital to national
security, was shown towards Soviet susceptibilities by the Americans
and by some at least of their allies, particularly Chancellor Adenauer.
The West German Government tolerated, or at least failed to prevent,
public demonstrations of irredentism directed towards the Sudetenland

and the western territories of Poland, although Adenauer himself had declared that the Federal Republic would never go to war to recover them. In May 1958 Dulles gave what appeared tantamount to a guarantee to fight for Berlin; and he gave it in Berlin itself. When the crisis over Berlin began in November 1958, the U.S. and West German Governments stood in the forefront in rallying allied resistance to the Soviet threat. In March and April 1959 American aircraft were deliberately flown to Berlin at heights exceeding 10,000 feet, which the Soviet authorities declared to be illegal and provocative. Allegations that American nuclear weapons had been put at the disposal of the West German Army passed without sufficiently effective contradiction, though in fact the war-heads remained under American control, as was the case in all allied countries. In many respects the Americans seemed to seek the reputation of being tough and uncompromising, just as the Soviet leaders did. Although American economic aid to the poorer countries of the world far exceeded that of the Soviet Union, much of this generosity passed unnoticed or was taken for granted. It was to bases, military pacts and weapons that attention was drawn, such as the agreement with Britain in July 1958 on co-operation in the development of nuclear weapons, or the bilateral defence agreements in March 1959 with Pakistan, Turkey and Iran. A striking case of disregard of Soviet reactions was the inauguration of a national week of prayer for 'captive peoples' in July 1959, immediately before Vice-President Nixon's visit to the U.S.S.R.

One or two other episodes of the period, particularly in Asia, illustrated not only the anxiety of the great powers to avoid conflicts, however local and small, which might involve them against each other, but also the extent to which that anxiety could be exploited. The Chinese Communists had never been subservient to the Russians, and after 1956 they were less so. Their own policy was hardened by the fiasco of their purported attempt at liberalization in 1957 under the slogan 'let a hundred flowers bloom' and by the failure of the intended 'great leap forward' in their economy in 1958. They were thus little inclined to tolerance. When in March 1959 a rising occurred in Tibet against the Chinese, it was put down with great severity. The Dalai Lama escaped to India, where he was given asylum. Chinese sovereignty over Tibet was not universally recognized, though it had been accepted by India in an agreement of 1954.[1] Nevertheless, although much indignation was

[1] The agreement is notable for having incorporated the first statement of the 'five principles (*panch shila*) of co-existence'.

expressed about the Chinese Communists' action, and it was even
brought before the United Nations, nothing was done or could be done
to restrain it. Legalistic arguments apart, the difference between Tibet
and the offshore islands was that no great power felt its own vital
interest to be involved, or likely to become involved, in the former as
they did in the latter.

For similar reasons, no serious consequences followed from a renewed
threat to the independence of Laos in August 1959, whether provoked
by the Vietminh from outside the country or merely by Laotian
Communists from within; though a U.N. mission was sent, despite
Soviet objections, to investigate the situation. Nor did any consequences immediately follow from the aggressive claims forcibly asserted
by the Chinese Communists to areas on the northern frontiers of India
at the same time, which were vigorously rebutted by Nehru. The motives
behind these probes were obscure. They could have been in either case
deliberately promoted by the Chinese Communist Government, or the
result of local adventurers taking matters into their own hands. It is
certain that when Khrushchev visited Peking after his tour of the U.S.A.
in the autumn of 1959, he urged the Chinese Communists to forgo and
restrain such risky ventures; but it is less certain what response he had
from the Chinese.

There were still a number of such marginal areas between the Soviet
Bloc and the rest of the world, over which a miscalculation was possible.
But a sufficient number of test-cases in the decade 1949–59 had made
such a miscalculation increasingly unlikely. It was then established that
cases comparable to Greece, Berlin, Korea or Vietnam, if pushed to
extremes, were likely to lead to war; cases comparable to Hungary or
Tibet were not. Central Europe, the Middle East and the Far East
generally were areas where there was very little margin for risky
experiment, and risks were therefore unlikely to be taken. On the
fringes of these areas there were uncommitted or neutral countries – for
instance, Finland, Afghanistan or Burma – which presented tempting
and dangerous uncertainties. But the evidence of experience suggested
that in all such areas of potential great-power conflict, not to mention
the wider and remoter worlds of Africa and Latin America, although
rivalry would continue, conflict would be kept within bounds.

This assumption no doubt partly accounts for the lack of urgency
with which the great powers pursued their approach to a new Summit
Conference, although the negotiations for it began early in 1958. The
slowness of the approach was due, on the surface, to many-sided dis-

agreements on procedure, but these were symptomatic of two real diffi-culties of substance. One was a doubt, reinforced by the experience at Geneva in 1955, whether the Summit Conference was still an appro-priate instrument of diplomacy, as it had been during the Second World War, when all the participants shared a common object. The other was a question about the conference's composition. The 'Big Four', a relic of the war, were manifestly an anachronism. Several new powers out-classed France, if not Britain also. What reality could there be about a Summit Conference which excluded the effective rulers of the two largest states in the world (Nehru and Mao Tse-Tung) as well as that of the most powerful state in continental Europe (Chancellor Adenauer), especially when all three were oustanding personalities in their own right?

As a consequence of these real uncertainties, the years 1958-9 were increasingly filled with bilateral and other interchanges at the highest governmental level but short of the true Summit. Khrushchev visited the U.S.A. and Peking, and even a number of satellite capitals, to prepare his mind for the main meeting. Similarly Eisenhower visited Bonn, Paris and London during the summer of 1959, and nearly a dozen other capitals in Europe, Asia and North Africa later in the year. (His return of Khrushchev's visit to Washington was conspicuously delayed and finally cancelled in 1960.) The Western leaders, many of whom also paid calls on each other, finally met in Paris in December and agreed to invite Khrushchev to meet them there in May 1960. Thus the actual Summit at last came into view only after the preliminaries had greatly reduced its predominant importance; and in the event it proved abortive.

The conclusion over the whole post-war period is therefore twofold. The possibility of a Third World War had greatly receded, perhaps almost to vanishing point; but the cold war as a relation between the two great-power blocs was likely to continue indefinitely. Things would probably get no worse, but they would also probably not get much better. Such was the background against which Britain's foreign policy had to be worked out: a background which was in large part, but not wholly, outside any British Government's control.

PART II

The British Reaction

4

Defence Policy

THE most succinct form in which the defensive reactions of British policy to the cold war can be studied is the annual series of Defence White Papers from 1946 to 1959.[1] These have the advantage of showing policy under all, or most of, its aspects: what was done as well as what was said; what was intended, why it was intended, how it was carried out; and in what ways it was modified from time to time because circumstances changed or the intentions proved to have been miscalculated or over-ambitious. It will also be seen from a study of the series as a whole what were the limitations on Britain's freedom of action in foreign policy, and what were the considerations other than the needs of defence that had to be taken into account.

The first White Paper in the series begins with a picture of Britain's situation in 1945. There were 5,000,000 men under arms in all parts of the world, and 4,000,000 civilians working on production and other tasks in support of them. The country was faced with a conflict of two necessary tasks: economic reconstruction at home and the maintenance of responsibilities overseas. The latter included the stationing of troops in Germany, Japan, Austria, Venezia Giulia (including Trieste), Greece, Palestine and S.E. Asia; the maintenance of 'internal security and settled conditions throughout the Empire'; 'the safeguarding of our communications and the upkeep of our bases'; together with temporary commitments such as troop-carrying and mine-sweeping. It was proposed to reduce the armed forces necessary for these commitments to less than 2,000,000 by mid-1946, and to 1,100,000 by the end of the year, while the supporting civilian manpower was to be reduced to half a million. The upshot was to be a tremendous feat of organized demobilization, bringing down the total manpower in the services or in support of them by more than 80 per cent. Call-up under the National Service Act was to continue, 'without prejudice to any final decision'. The cost for the year 1946–7 was estimated at £1,667,000,000. No

---

[1] Cmd. 6743 (1946); 7042 (1947); 7327 (1948); 7631 (1949); 7895 (1950); 8146 (1951); 8475 (1952); 8768 (1953); 9075 (1954); 9391 (1955); 9691 (1956); Cmnd. 124 (1957); 363 (1958); 662 (1959).

reference was made to allied powers, except that collaboration 'with the Dominions and India' was to be maintained. It was too early to assess post-war needs arising from technical changes and new commitments, among which the United Nations was specified.

In the following year, the situation had not greatly changed. There was still the basic dilemma of seeking 'healthy social and economic conditions' at home without 'ill-considered jettisoning of defence responsibilities' overseas. The commitments were slightly revised in definition. Current commitments included forces in Western Europe, the Middle East and Mediterranean, the Indian Ocean, the Far East, Africa and the West Indies. Long-term commitments included the security of the United Kingdom, the safeguarding of communications and a contribution to the forces of the United Nations (which had already created a Military Staff Committee to plan a U.N. defence force). One or two slightly ominous notes were also to be heard. The run-down of the armed forces was behind the estimates, having passed only a little below 1·5 million by the end of 1946, though the run-down of the supply services was ahead of schedule. This caused criticism, both from Churchill as leader of the Opposition and from Government supporters in the House of Commons, who feared that the Labour Government was inheriting too readily the imperialist policies of its predecessors. There was also a concluding paragraph about the policy of preventing war, in which the phrase 'to deter aggression' occurred for the first time. It had been announced[1] during 1946 that a permanent Ministry of Defence was to be created. National Service in peacetime was to continue. However, the numbers in the armed forces were to be reduced to a little over 1,000,000 by the end of March 1948; and the estimates for the year 1947–8 were only £899,000,000, not much over half those of the preceding year.

The 1948 White Paper began with the cheering news that the numbers in the armed forces at the end of March 1948 had dropped even lower than the estimate, being below 1,000,000. There had been accelerated reductions as a result of events in India and Burma, which had recently become independent countries, and Palestine, where the Mandate was about to be given up. Almost all British troops had also left Japan. There had been some offsetting delay in liquidating commitments in Europe (particularly Greece, Austria and Trieste); and there was a temporary unbalance of manpower. But on balance the recent trend, measured in men and money, had been favourable, and the estimates for

[1] In a supplementary White Paper, Cmd. 6923.

1948–9 were down to less than £700,000,000. There were also some interesting indications of the future patterns of strategy. Aircraft faster than sound were predicted; a 'new storeholding area for the Army' was to be created in Kenya; there was not to be an amalgamation of the administrative services of the forces, but co-ordinating committees were to be set up under chairmen supplied by the Ministry of Defence; liaison staffs were to be formed in the Dominions; and the outline of a new civil defence organization was presented separately to the House of Commons.

If that were all that the White Paper for 1948 had contained, it would have been an interesting though not particularly startling document. But there were other more disquieting paragraphs. There had been a severe dislocation of production by the fuel crisis early in 1947. Difficulties over the balance of payments were affecting works programmes overseas. New references to the importance of 'deterring aggression' reflected the growing tension between the Soviet Union and the Western Powers. There was a special emphasis on the 'defence of the Commonwealth' (no longer the Empire) in which 'control of communications and of strategic key-points' was essential. There was an ominous reference to 'the inescapable responsibilities of a Great Power intent on preserving peace'. The whole problem was set out in carefully selected and balanced detail in the following paragraph:

'The fulfilment of the main object of the United Nations – the maintenance of world peace – depends on the ability and readiness of the Great Powers to keep the peace. The United Kingdom, as a member of the British Commonwealth and a Great Power, must be prepared at all times to fulfil her responsibilities not only to the United Nations but also to herself. For this purpose, the first essential is a strong and sound economy, with a flourishing industry from which to draw the strength to defend our rights and fulfil our obligations.'

Here were all the key ideas of the time brought together: the importance of the U.N. and its weaknesses; the importance of the Commonwealth; the sense of being still a great power; the economic problem; the danger of aggression.

The White Paper published in 1949 re-emphasized the same ideas, and underlined them by announcing the first increase of the defence estimates since the war, to just under £760,000,000. Since the strength of the armed forces continued to be reduced – the target for the end of March 1950 being 750,000 – it was clear that the main incidence of the increased cost was on research and development of weapons and equipment. In retrospect there is no doubt that a reference to atomic weapons was concealed, among other things, in the paragraph which said that research and development 'for the most part must remain secret', and that they were being devoted 'to the production of unconventional weapons . . . on high priority'. At the same time there was a new emphasis on recruitment for the regular forces. The general appreciation of the world situation was summed up in a sentence referring to the United Nations:

'The degree of success realized has proved a grievous disappointment and the establishment of collective security on a world-wide basis under the United Nations has not been achieved.'

There was also the first post-war reference to a foreign alliance: 'Western Union', the creation of the Brussels Treaty of 17 March 1948, which had set up a joint headquarters at Fontainebleau. The participants, in addition to Britain, were France, Belgium, the Netherlands and Luxembourg.

By the following year all the foregoing implications had been carried a stage further, and the North Atlantic Treaty had been signed on 4 April 1949. The White Paper of 1950 declared that British policy was

'. . . to seek security through the development of collective self-defence, within the framework of the United Nations' Charter, in co-operation with the other members of the Commonwealth, the United States of America and other like-minded nations'.

This was the first mention of the U.S.A. in a Defence White Paper. Otherwise there was little strikingly new in it. The trend towards spending more on the research and development of weapons and less on manpower continued. The total numbers in the armed forces had fallen even below the estimate by the end of March 1950, and were to fall below 700,000 in the following twelve months. But the increased cost of defence, from £760,000,000 to £780,000,000, was more than accounted for by an increase of £35,000,000 on research and development. Air defence and anti-submarine research were receiving much attention. For so momentous a year, the White Paper was remarkably terse.

So was the White Paper of 1951, but it was even more momentous. It came out unusually early, in January 1951 instead of February or March, in the form of a statement by the Prime Minister on the new situation created by the outbreak of the Korean War on 25 June 1950. There was, said the statement, 'an urgent need to strengthen the defences of the free world' (the last expression being now introduced for the first time in such a document); and the purpose was 'to prevent war'. The target for manpower in the forces was to be raised from 682,000 to 800,000 at the end of March 1951, by calling up reservists, retaining time-expired regulars, and other methods. The estimated cost for the year 1951–2 was £1,300,000,000, an increase of two-thirds over the previous year, excluding stockpiling; and with stockpiling again excluded, the cost over the next three years 'might be as much as £4,700,000,000'. The programme was described a year later as 'the biggest the United Kingdom could undertake without going over to a war economy'. It was too big for some members of the Labour Government, three of whom, led by Aneurin Bevan, resigned on the ground that the cost was excessive and bound to impose cuts on the social services.

Some of the economic consequences of the programme were admitted in the 1951 White Paper itself. The intention was to meet the cost out of income without running into debt abroad or reducing the level of invest-ment. The expansion of defence production required a check on civilian demand and a switch in the engineering industries, which would inevitably reduce their exports. Some controls that had been relaxed would have to be reimposed. There would have to be a system of alloca-tion of raw materials and a limitation on supplies to the home market and on civil building. But there would be no 'overriding priority' for defence in all cases at the expense of exports. The sacrifices called for were considered bearable. It was essential not to 'imperil the future strength of our economy'. This was the last Defence White Paper produced by the post-war Labour Government, and of course by far the grimmest.

It was not to be expected that the next White Paper in the series, being produced by a Conservative Government, would give unstinted endorsement to its predecessor. It declared that the level of defence production foreseen in 1950 was unattainable, and that the three-year programme proposed would have to be spread over a longer period.

(In other words, it had not been either necessary or desirable for the Labour Government to take such drastic steps as those which led to Bevan's resignation.) There were still shortages of manpower, tools and materials in the defence industries, as a result of the competition of export trade. A number of adjustments had therefore to be made to the previous calculations, though comparatively little to the numbers in the armed services, which very slightly exceeded 800,000 at the end of March 1951. A great and unpredictable change in the situation had been brought about, however, by the initiation of substantial military aid from across the Atlantic, chiefly from the U.S.A. but also from Canada. The British share in the new U.S. programme for the year 1951–2 was $300,000,000 (less 5 per cent for American administrative expenses). This sum enabled the defence budget to be relieved by the sterling equivalent or 'counterpart'; but it also entailed responsibilities, such as the contribution to be made to the 'infrastructure' of N.A.T.O. (airfields, communications, headquarters, etc.) on the Continent of Europe. All these terms were new in the 1952 White Paper. So was the paragraph on 'steps to combat the risk of invasion', which included the re-establishment of the Home Guard. The White Paper bore the impress of Churchill's personality no less firmly than its immediate predecessor had borne that of Attlee's.

The 1953 White Paper was even more explicit than its predecessors about the nature of the danger. It divided the defence programme into two parts, firstly:

'. . . our overseas obligations and our commitments in resisting the Communist campaign known as the cold war';

and secondly:

'. . . the preparations which we must make together with our Commonwealth partners and our allies against the risk that Communist policy, whether by accident or design, might force us to defend ourselves against a direct attack'.

The reference to the cold war was an innovation. It was a term much more readily used by the Service Ministries than by the Foreign Office, where it was felt to be full of ambiguities, such as the notion that a cold war, like any other war, could be won or lost. Nevertheless, the distinction made was a valid one; and another useful distinction was that between accident (meaning miscalculation) and design on the part of the Communists, who were named for the first time as the potential enemy in this White Paper.

The cost of defence began to approach nearer to the figures customary at the end of the war, though rearmament was 'to be spread over a longer period and held to a lower peak'. The actual cost in 1952–3 had been over £1,513,000,000, and the estimated cost for 1953–4 was a little under £1,637,000,000, against which could be offset £140,000,000 of counterpart funds; but the cost of atomic energy research (now also for the first time explicitly mentioned) was not included in the above figures, nor was the British contribution to four 'infrastructure' programmes in Europe. Legislation was foreshadowed to prolong National Service, which would otherwise have ceased at the end of 1953. Co-operation with the Commonwealth and N.A.T.O. was again stressed, and also with the European Defence Community, which had been created on paper (though abortively, as it turned out) by an agreement signed on 27 May 1952. Britain had 'explained her inability to become a member of the Community', but had signed an agreement with it and a joint declaration with the U.S.A. and France promising close collaboration. All of this was superseded in 1954, when France failed to ratify the E.D.C. Treaty.

The White Paper of 1954 began on a note of cautious optimism, reporting 'some alleviation of international tension'. (Stalin was dead, and the Korean War was over.) But a series of qualifications followed:

'. . . the long-term aims of World Communism appear to be unaltered. In the Far East fighting continues in Malaya and Indo-China. It is clear that one of the principal Soviet aims is to weaken the strength and cohesion of the Atlantic Alliance.'

Later, it was added that 'in the Cold War, World Communism has great advantages'. The White Paper defined the intention as 'for the next few years to maintain our defence effort at the maximum which our economic capabilities permit', and emphasized 'the prime necessity of basing our defence policy upon the prevention of war'. This inference was drawn not merely from obvious theoretical considerations, but from a picture of the opening of an atomic war, in which a phase of 'broken-backed warfare' would follow what was ironically called at the time (not in the White Paper) the 'initial exchange of nuclear stockpiles'.

The White Paper went on to give the first explicit account of the theory of deterrence as adopted by the British Government:

'The primary deterrent remains the atomic bomb . . . We intend as soon as possible to build up in the Royal Air Force a force of modern bombers capable of using the atomic weapon to the fullest effect.'

'Atomic weapons are in production in this country and delivery to the forces has begun.'

It followed that the country's defences were going through an interim period of tactics and training. There was greater emphasis on the R.A.F.; expenditure on the Army would decline; the Navy's would remain steady; the importance of Civil Defence was marked by the Queen assuming the post of 'Head of the Civil Defence Corps'. The estimates for 1954–5 were just below £1,640,000,000, including over £85,000,000 of counterpart funds. There was emphasis on Britain's obligations to the Commonwealth, N.A.T.O. (including infrastructure) and E.D.C. (not yet quite defunct). But there was a necessary warning:

'Clearly, within a limited defence budget, we may not be able to afford both new weapons and conventional forces of the present size.'

There was the shadow of coming events.

The White Paper for 1955 began by announcing 'the emergence of the thermo-nuclear bomb', which was already well known as the 'hydrogen-bomb'. What was less well known, but was now declared, was Britain's intention to produce such weapons. Defence policy was thereby given a new direction, since it was argued that 'this deterrent has significantly reduced the risk of war on a major scale'. (Eden considered that it had been decisive in preventing a major war at the time of the Geneva Conference on the Far East in 1954.[1]) It was now paradoxically possible to 'strive for a practical scheme of disarmament'. Such disarmament must be 'real and comprehensive, and there must be secure and workable safeguards', including an agreed time-table and a machinery to supervise agreed prohibitions and reductions. All this was new matter in a Defence White Paper. Another example of the new direction was that although there was increasing emphasis on the

[1] Sir Anthony Eden, *Full Circle*, p. 123.

deterrent, it was admitted to be not enough by itself. Conventional forces were not outmoded; and the danger of 'infiltration and subversion' was, if anything, increased, at least relatively. Britain's alliances and friendships were as important as ever. These were specified as the Commonwealth, N.A.T.O., West European Union (which had replaced E.D.C.) and the South-East Asian Collective Defence Treaty (usually known as S.E.A.T.O.). There was also 'close collaboration with the U.S.A. in the guided weapon field'.

It was clear that in this, the last Defence White Paper issued under Churchill, a turning-point had been reached. Churchill believed that the hydrogen-bomb had made the stakes so high in a war between great powers that such a war would never break out. Malenkov evidently shared this belief; but he was rebuked by his colleagues for suggesting that a nuclear war would destroy both Communist and Capitalist civilization, and he later reverted to the orthodox view that only the latter would be destroyed. World opinion outside official circles, especially in Britain, became increasingly impressed, not by the relative safety assured by nuclear stalemate, but by the risks of accidents and the consequences of continuing nuclear tests. There was much discussion of 'fall-out', especially after the accidental contamination of a Japanese fishing-boat in the Pacific by an American hydrogen-bomb test in March 1954. Scientific opinion was inconclusive, and the paragraph on the subject in the 1955 White Paper was vague.

But the British Government had to pay increasing attention to a public opinion alerted by such statements on home defence as the following in three successive White Papers:

'We are not, nor shall we ever be, able to forecast the precise effect or the extent of any nuclear attack against this country.' (1955.)

'Whatever the preparations made, an attack on this country would involve loss of life and destruction on an unparalleled scale.' (1956.)

'It must be frankly recognized that there is at present no means of providing adequate protection for the people of this country against the consequences of an attack with nuclear weapons.' (1957.)

Admissions of the above kind were largely responsible for the strong public pressure in favour of meetings 'at the Summit', from which comprehensive settlements were over-optimistically expected.

The White Paper for 1956 analysed three sets of factors affecting the country's continuing task: political, strategic and economic. Under the political head, it said that the relaxation of tension was illusory, that Communists still believed in their 'ultimate triumph', and that co-existence was only a façade to disguise new offensives. Under the strategic head, it said that nuclear weapons had made global war 'more frightening and less likely', but it emphasized the danger of 'limited wars'. (Co-existence and limited war were new terms in this White Paper.) British forces had four tasks: to contribute to the allied deterrent; to play a part in the cold war 'by their mere presence'; to deal with limited wars; and to play a part in global war, if it came. Under the economic head, the White Paper emphasized that Britain's economic strength was part of her ability to resist. It stressed the high cost of defence (nearly £1,550,000,000 for 1956-7, including U.S. aid); the burden on the metal-using industries, which also supplied half Britain's exports; the effect on the balance of payments, especially of establishments overseas; the cost and claims of research; and the demands on manpower. Looking forward no doubt to the abolition of National Service, it argued that the smaller and better-equipped forces which were now needed 'place a premium on the highly-skilled long-service regular'.

The last point was to be ominously confirmed during the course of the year 1956. When the Suez Canal crisis began in July with the nationalization of the Canal by President Nasser, it was immediately clear in Britain that the situation might necessitate the use of force; but it was also clear that the services were not in a state of readiness to mount an immediate operation. In the case of the Army in particular, what was needed was the recall of certain key reservists, chiefly those with technical training. The call-up of reservists, which took place in August 1956, had an important bearing on the later evolution of the crisis, and even perhaps of British policy, especially when those called up began to become restless in inactivity during September and October. In effect, once they were called up, it was difficult not to use them, since to release them without using them would be tantamount to conceding victory to President Nasser. The restlessness and even mutiny which broke out among the troops held ready for action pointed to a further difficulty: to have held them beyond Christmas without action would have provoked even more disturbing reactions, and would perhaps have been politically impossible. Thus the necessity to call up reservists in August imposed some limitation on the Government's

freedom of manœuvre in the autumn. It was an embarrassment which
had to be avoided in the future.

In addition to analysing the country's defence problem at length,
the 1956 White Paper was marked by an interesting discussion of the
prospect of disarmament. It argued that

'. . . the ultimate goal remains the conclusion of a comprehensive
disarmament agreement, covering both conventional and nuclear
armaments'.

But it pointed out that there was no known method of

'. . . guaranteeing the elimination of stockpiles of nuclear weapons
or of controlling completely the future production of potentially
dangerous fissile material'.

Faced with this and other problems, the British Government favoured
a 'step-by-step approach' to disarmament. It was satisfied that 'the
likelihood of global war has decreased', but it continued to attach
great importance to 'Commonwealth and international co-operation'.
Under the last heading a new alliance, the Baghdad Pact (later the
Central Treaty Organization), made its first appearance.

The White Paper for 1957 was written in the aftermath of the Suez
Canal and Hungarian crises, and under the impact of a new Minister
of Defence with enlarged powers. It was said by the Minister himself to
embody 'the biggest change in military policy ever made in normal
times'. It began by admitting that a fresh appreciation was required,
but related the need for it not to the crises of 1956 so much as to scientific advances and economic considerations. Chief among the latter was
the fact that for the last five years defence had absorbed on average
10 per cent of the gross national product, 7 per cent of the working
population, and one-eighth of the output of the metal-using industries;
and that could not go on. The estimates were accordingly to be scaled
down.

In the previous year it had been calculated that the cost for 1957–8
would be £1,700,000,000: this would be reduced to £1,483,000,000
(including contributions from the U.S.A. and 'support costs' from
Western Germany for troops stationed there since the restoration of
German sovereignty). Forces stationed in Europe were to be reduced
from 77,000 to 64,000. Manpower was to be reduced generally and

there was to be no call-up for National Service after the end of 1960. But there were certain commitments which could not be shed. A British 'megaton' weapon (i.e. a bomb with an explosive power equal to a million tons of T.N.T.) had been developed; the defence of bomber airfields was an essential part of the deterrent; civil defence was still necessary; sea-power was still important; so was a central reserve in the British Isles. There were also responsibilities to allies outside Europe. In the Far East there were the S.E.A.T.O. and A.N.Z.A.M. (Australia, New Zealand and Malaya) defence systems to be supported. In the Middle East there was the Baghdad Pact: Cyprus had to be retained to support it, and also as a nuclear bomber base. Economies were therefore difficult to achieve.

The solution was found in the concept of what later became 'interdependence', but at present was merely called 'collective defence'. The White Paper declared that 'no country can any longer protect itself in isolation', and that 'the trend is towards the creation of integrated allied forces'. It was said to be not necessarily desirable to have 'national forces which are by themselves self-sufficient and balanced in all respects'. It was argued that Britain had hitherto borne a disproportionate share of the common burden. All this was theoretically justifiable, but the argument had two aspects which distressed Britain's allies. One was that it was put forward without consulting them, though the assent of the Supreme Commander at S.H.A.P.E. was later obtained to the reduction of forces in Europe. The other was that since Britain and the U.S.A. already had nuclear weapons, the implication was that the role of the other allies in an 'integrated force' was to provide the ground-troops. This invited a new variant of the old accusation that 'Britain would fight to the last Frenchman'.

The argument was carried a step farther in the White Paper for 1958, the longest and most copious in the series. It began with a reference to *sputniks* or earth-satellites, the first of which had been launched by the U.S.S.R. in the preceding October. It argued that these had not altered the balance of military power. On the contrary, the medium-range ballistic rocket increased the overall superiority of the West, since the U.S.S.R. with a similar weapon could not reach the U.S.A.; whereas it would be 'several years' before inter-continental rockets would be available, and then (it was apparently assumed) they would be available simultaneously to both sides. Meanwhile both sides were also developing submarines 'capable of firing nuclear missiles from under water', which accounts for the emphasis later put on the anti-submarine role of the Navy. It was further argued that 'balancing fears of mutual annihilation' might preserve peace indefinitely, but that the 'arms race' must not be allowed to continue. The ultimate British aim was therefore 'comprehensive inspection and control by a world authority', which could only be achieved 'by stages'. A considerable section of the White Paper was devoted to setting out the Western proposals for disarmament, which had been approved by the United Nations against Soviet objections.

Before proceeding to disarmament, however, the White Paper was at pains to rub in the deterrent. It estimated the Soviet forces at 200 divisions facing the West, about 20,000 aircraft, and a fleet including some 500 submarines. It argued that:

'If Russia were to launch a major attack (on the western nations), even with conventional forces only, they would have to hit back with strategic nuclear weapons.'

To this retaliation Britain would make an important contribution, since megaton bombs were already being delivered to the R.A.F. But once again, this alone was not enough. The success of the deterrent increased the danger of the other forms of attack, including subversion. A 'collective effort' was still needed, through N.A.T.O., the Baghdad Pact and S.E.A.T.O. Here followed the first introduction by name of 'the concept of interdependence'. Within N.A.T.O. in particular, it was argued:

'. . . it should be possible gradually to get away from the idea that each member nation must continue to maintain self-contained national forces, which by themselves are fully balanced'.

Stress was laid on joint research and planning within W.E.U., perhaps in the hope of dissuading the French from finding it necessary to develop their own nuclear weapons. (The same argument would apply to the West Germans, but they were debarred by the terms of the W.E.U. agreement from manufacturing nuclear weapons themselves.) There was another paragraph, however, which might seem even more persuasive to the French in a different sense. It revealed that the cost of the strategic bomber force and nuclear bombs would amount to less than 10 per cent of the 1958–9 estimates, and that even with the inclusion of fighters for the defence of the bomber airfields and the warning system and related research, the figure would still be only between 15 per cent and 20 per cent of the total. Moreover, the total estimates were themselves again reduced, to £1,465,000,000 (including 'support costs' in Germany). The White Paper concluded by stressing again the need for a stable economy, and claiming that the previous year's measures were already proving effective.

By contrast, the White Paper for 1959 was almost terse. It began with a preamble declaring that the aim was 'to promote peace and security through the settlement of international differences and comprehensive disarmament'. It described the 1957 White Paper as having contained a 'five-year defence plan' to produce 'compact, all-regular forces of the highest quality, armed and organized on the most up-to-date lines'. Thereafter the White Paper proceeded, without further elaboration of policy, to describe what was being done under various technical headings: modernization of the Fleet; re-equipment of the Army; air support and mobility; strategic bombers; ballistic rockets; air defence; civil defence; inter-service commands (a new post-war feature, though common in the Second World War); recruitment and terms of service; and so on. The White Paper contained almost no surprises, except the small one that the estimates were up again (to £1,514,000,000 for 1959-60, including the German contribution) after two successive years of reduction.[1]

Taking the series of fourteen White Papers as a whole, it is possible to see a clear reflection of the British reaction to the evolution of great-power relations as they moved from uneasy peace to near-war (1946–53) and back again to deadlock (1954–9). But what is almost more important is that equally clear indications can be seen of the other factors affecting the British reaction, and especially those limiting the British Government's freedom of action. They can be summed up under seven headings. There was, firstly, the need for allies and, secondly, the need to safeguard the country's economic position. Thirdly, a particular case of both the first two, there was the special but unequal relation with the U.S.A. Fourthly, there was the influence of international organizations, particularly the United Nations; and fifthly, closely related to the last, the emergence on the international scene of new countries. Newness in this context covers both those states which had not previously had an independent existence, such as Indonesia, Israel, Tunisia, and also those which existed but had never before

---

[1] The White Paper for 1960 (Cmnd. 925) showed a further increase; but that lies outside the scope of this chapter.

exercised any real impact on international relations, such as Greece, Siam and the Latin American states. Important examples of both classes are comprised within the Commonwealth, which is the sixth of the factors in the list. Seventhly and lastly, there was the effect of party politics in Britain, including relations both within and between the two major parties, both inside and outside parliament. All these factors affected the policy in successive Defence White Papers, and each of them deserves a chapter to itself.

5

The Need and the Cost of Alliances

THE first reference to an alliance in the annual series of Defence White Papers occurs in 1949. The reference then is to Western Union, as a sequel to the Brussels Treaty of 1948. An earlier treaty had been signed with France alone at Dunkirk in March 1947, but this was primarily a symbolic gesture in commemoration of the wartime association. There was also a treaty still in force with the Soviet Union, signed in June 1942, as Bevin was sharply reminded by the Soviet Government when he declared in December 1946 that Britain had no obligations to any other power except under the Charter of the United Nations. There was no question, as the Soviet Government chose to believe, of denouncing that treaty, which was reaffirmed by Bevin in January 1947. But the incident served to illustrate the traditional and almost subconscious dislike felt by British Governments for continuing engagements in peacetime. This was particularly true when a treaty was regarded as being of 'indefinite duration' – a phrase used by Eisenhower of the North Atlantic Treaty in March 1955, though it was open to any party to withdraw from it at one year's notice after twenty years.

Before the present century peacetime alliances were almost unknown to British foreign policy in modern times. The change seems to have come with the Boer War, which forced Britain to face the fact that a profound change had taken place in international relationships – that is to say, at that date, relationships in Europe. The change showed itself in the early twentieth century in the division of Europe into 'great armed camps'.[1] British policy had rested on principles which included certain traditional friendships (with France since 1815, with the U.S.A. and with Ottoman Turkey, for instance) but no formal alliances. The turn of the century brought a decision to abandon the concept of 'splendid isolation', and to enter into formal treaties of alliance, the first of which was signed with Japan in 1902, and soon followed by agreements with France and Russia.

[1] *Cambridge History of British Foreign Policy*, Vol. III, pp. 267–8.

Between the two world wars such commitments were again in disfavour, and were theoretically rendered unnecessary by the Covenant of the League of Nations; but the inadequacy of the policy of 'collective security' in practice and the growth of aggressive powers led the British Government reluctantly to undertake new engagements, which eventually had to be implemented in the Second World War. At the end of the war it was again hoped that 'collective security' would suffice, under the Charter of the United Nations; but as this began to appear inadequate in its turn, a new course had to be found. In the words of Lord Strang:[1]

'The United Kingdom has since 1945 evolved another foreign policy, very different from the old, but suited to our relative decline in terms of power; its main characteristic is the merging of our defences with those of like-minded governments in an intimate community of free peoples bound by mutual engagement.'

In other words, we cannot survive without allies, nor even perhaps without commitments going beyond mere alliances.

It is common ground among all political leaders in Britain that some alliances and similar relations, whether more or less formal than alliances, are necessary. But there are different views of the consequences that logically follow. Allies are in some ways more difficult to deal with than enemies: with an enemy you know where you are, and you do not have to consider his feelings. In the case of an ally it is necessary to consider all sorts of questions other than the specific purpose for which the alliance is formed. There is even a consequential danger of sometimes losing sight of that specific purpose, as happened with N.A.T.O. in 1955-6, between the Geneva Conference and the Suez Canal crisis. Attlee said in 1948 that when people enter an alliance, that 'does take away to a certain extent their absolute power to do as they will'. Conversely countries become involved even in each other's domestic and economic policies, and in their foreign and colonial policies outside the area of the alliance. They have to make new friends of old enemies, to support actions which they disapprove, and even to go back on their pledged word. This chapter is concerned with the irritations which result. Normally the irritations here described are those caused to Britain by her allies, since this is a book about British foreign policy. But it must not be forgotten that British foreign policy gives as good as

[1] *Home and Abroad*, p. 154.

it gets in this matter of mutual friction, and some instances will appear in which the boot is on the other leg.

France

Leaving aside the U.S.A. and the Commonwealth, which will be considered separately later,[1] the most indispensable of Britain's allies was clearly France. There is a long tradition of mutual admiration and incomprehension between France and Great Britain, of which the post-war period gave ample illustration. It began as the war was ending, with an armed intervention by British forces between the French and the Syrians in Damascus; and de Gaulle's recriminations in June 1945 were bitter. When the Syrian and Lebanese Governments appealed to the United Nations in March 1946 to remove the French and British forces from their territory, the situation was complicated by the fact that the Syrians at least were plainly more anxious to be rid of the French than of the British; and many Frenchmen believed that the British only wanted to take their place as the dominant power in the Levant.

The Middle East continued to be an area of bad relations between the two countries. For instance, the French authorities presumably connived at the escape of the Mufti of Jerusalem, an old enemy of the British, from Paris to Cairo in May 1946; and French opinion blamed British intrigue for the murder of the Syrian Prime Minister Zaim in August 1949. The one startling exception to the tradition of Anglo-French hostility in the area was the joint expedition against Egypt in November 1956, when the two countries succeeded instead in combining practically all their allies as well as their enemies against themselves.

In two other areas of the world the problem of Anglo-French relations lay not in mutual rivalry (except in a few French imaginations) but in the French need for unconditional support which the British could only give at the cost of alienating opinion among the 'new countries', including members of the Commonwealth. These areas were S.E. Asia and North Africa.

In the southern part of Indo-China, British forces had accepted the Japanese surrender in 1945, since no French forces were available. They duly handed over sovereignty to the French in January 1946, the very month, as it happened, in which de Gaulle resigned as Prime Minister and gave way to a succession of weak governments lasting in all over twelve years. The precarious hold of the French in Indo-China

[1] See chapters 7 and 8.

became apparent almost at once; for in Tonking the Communists, or Vietminh, established themselves in control, not without help from American units in China. The Communist leader, Ho Chi Minh, was at that time presenting himself rather as a Nationalist. He had even declared the Communist Party to be dissolved in November 1945, and formed a 'Government of National Unity'. But the successive agreements which he signed with the French did not lead to a settlement. By the end of 1946 the French and the Vietminh were engaged in open hostilities, which lasted intermittently until 1954. In this war the French repeatedly sought the moral support of their allies, and also the physical support of the U.S.A., but reserved to themselves the responsibility for matters of policy until it was too late.

French policy in the dependent territories had traditionally been one of assimilation to French culture, rather than the development of their own institutions. The resultant progress towards independence seemed by British standards too slow. British advice to the French therefore tended to press for faster progress, and this was naturally unwelcome. In the case of Vietnam, where the British Commissioner-General for S.E. Asia, Malcolm Macdonald, had formed an admiring opinion of the Emperor Bao Dai, the British Government urged the French in November 1949 to concede more independence to a Vietnamese Government in order to deprive the Vietminh of their main attraction. Such advice was unacceptable.

The French found more gratification in the declarations of solidarity occasionally made by allied leaders. For instance, in September 1951 President Truman equated the French stand in Indo-China with that of the United Nations in Korea; and in January 1952 Eden linked the French and British territories in S.E. Asia as positions which must be held. In May 1952 S.E. Asia, together with North Africa, was the subject of discussions between the French, British and U.S. Governments in Paris. At the end of the year a resolution of the North Atlantic Council supported the French stand in Indo-China, though in somewhat vague terms which perhaps revealed allied embarrassment without altogether satisfying French anxiety.

By the following year the situation in Indo-China had deteriorated so far that France's need of allied support was becoming desperate. In March 1953 a joint warning was issued from Washington by the French and U.S. Governments to the Chinese Communists, who were supporting the Vietminh, against new acts of aggression. American military equipment was sent to Indo-China in large quantities, including aircraft manned by American crews. Nehru refused landing rights for these aircraft on Indian airfields and criticized the use of British-controlled airfields in Ceylon. Here was an example of the conflicting claims on British good-will of old allies and new members of the Commonwealth.

In the event all was in vain. The French at last bowed to the inevitable, and joined the British Government in its cool reception of Dulles's proposal, in April 1954, to enlarge the war in Indo-China by the active intervention of the U.S.A., Britain and such Asian powers as could be so persuaded. At the Geneva Conference, a month later, France acknowledged defeat, and the former Associated States of Indo-China (Vietnam, Laos and Cambodia) became fully independent, with the loss of only Northern Vietnam to the Communists. This was not the end of the need for allies in S.E. Asia, however: on the contrary, it was the prelude to S.E.A.T.O. which was followed by five years of unexpected peace and stability. From the British point of view, the liquidation of the French commitment in S.E. Asia was a matter for scarcely qualified relief.

But no sooner were France's troubles over in Indo-China than they began in North Africa. After a long-drawn-out struggle, independence was conceded to both Tunisia and Morocco, and in both cases the process was formally completed in March 1956. But in Algeria, which was constitutionally a part of France (and therefore within N.A.T.O.) and which had a considerable French population, the situation was very different. The problems of North Africa were discussed with France's two principal allies at least as early as May 1952. They became increasingly grave with the accession to power in Egypt of President Nasser, who supported the anti-French North African nationalists both with propaganda and with weapons. In November 1954, less than six months after the end of the war in Indo-China, violence began in Algeria. A state of emergency was proclaimed in April 1955. From then until the end of the period under review, no way out of the Algerian tragedy ever became clearly visible. The gravity of it was even enhanced by the discovery of oil in the Sahara, which increased the French determination not to give way. Even the return to power of de Gaulle, in May 1958, inspired only a faint flutter of hope that a settlement might be found.

The French problem in Algeria naturally caused Britain and her other allies embarrassment. It imposed material handicaps: for instance, in May 1955 France announced the despatch of 20,000 troops from Germany to Algeria; and these were not the last to go. What was even more difficult was to defend French policy, and some questionable French conduct, against attack by the smaller and newer states, including members of the Commonwealth, whose good-will Britain also desired. As in Indo-China, the French insisted on an absolute control over the policy pursued, while expecting unqualified allied support. Such support was given so far as practicable: for instance, at the United Nations, and in public statements by ministers and officials; and the U.S. Government rejected the demand of the Arab states in 1957 that military aid to France should be stopped. Ironically, military aid was also the subject of an angry dispute between France and her two chief allies later in the same year, when Britain and the U.S.A. supplied small arms to Tunisia, after France had refused to do so, in order to forestall the probability that otherwise Tunisia would turn to the Soviet Bloc. There were almost unlimited possibilities of such trouble between France and her allies in the North African situation.

In many cases there were evident different conceptions of the nature of an alliance between the French and the British. The French considered the alliance total and world-wide: it should therefore entail automatic mutual support everywhere. The British had a more limited conception – limited, in fact, to the definitions of scope and extent given in the North Atlantic Treaty. They differed from the French again in taking a more limited view of the extent to which national policies should be merged. Bevin had said of the Brussels Treaty that it 'made us really a part of Europe', but he showed no enthusiasm for Bidault's plan in July 1948 to set up a European Assembly for the five partners of the treaty. The whole history of the movement to unite Europe was, from the French point of view, a record of Britain 'dragging her feet'. And this difference of attitude was related to another, in which again the British gave offence to the French. British governments attached particular importance to their 'special relation' with the U.S.A., from which they seemed to the French to wish to exclude all other powers. Strong efforts were made, particularly under Macmillan, to remove any grounds for such suspicion; but the suspicion still remained.

The French quest for parity as a great power was intensified after de Gaulle's return to office in 1958; and Britain was a principal victim of it. It underlay the determination of the French to develop nuclear weapons, which were expected to have the consequence of making American secrets available to them as well as to the British. It also explained much of their attitude towards N.A.T.O.: for instance, the removal of the French fleet in the Mediterranean from N.A.T.O. command, the removal of American strategic bombers from France, and the refusal to co-operate in an integrated system of air defence.

It was reasonable to suppose, however, that it was with Britain rather than with the U.S.A. that France was seeking parity. The conviction that the British Government was seeking to deny France what it sought was probably one of the psychological motives behind the hostility with which the French Government responded to the British attempt to create a Free Trade Area around the Common Market in 1958. There were other good reasons why that attempt failed, and Britain's consequent isolation from the main body of Western Europe was also largely her own Government's fault. But to say that there were faults on both sides, as there invariably have been in Anglo-French relations, is not to make those relations easier.

Other N.A.T.O. Allies

A case somewhat similar to that of the French in the difficulties and heart-searching it caused in Britain was that of the Dutch. The Netherlands were also close allies of long standing, and also a colonial power. The differences from the case of France were two: there was only one area of potential conflict of loyalties, in S.E. Asia; and over that area the British had an uneasy conscience, as they had not towards the French, because British and other allied pressure had been successful in coercing the Dutch to give up their colony in 1946. It is not necessary to tell in detail the story of the emergence of Indonesia to independence, but a few points in it are important to Anglo-Dutch relations.

In November 1945, while British troops were engaged against Indonesian Nationalists armed by the Japanese, Bevin said that the British Government felt itself under an obligation to restore the Netherlands East Indies to the Dutch Government in return for help given when the Japanese attacked in 1941–2. But it was desirable to extricate British troops from this predicament as soon as possible. This was achieved during 1946 at the price of persuading the Dutch, under considerable allied pressure (Australian as well as British and American), to sign agreements recognizing the Indonesian Republic. The new republic, which was formally recognized by Britain in 1949, proceeded to divest itself progressively of all remaining links with the Netherlands.

At the beginning of this process, British sympathies were decidedly against the Dutch. When the Dutch Government used force against the Indonesians in the first 'police action' of July 1947, Bevin not only expressed disapproval but announced the suspension of all military supplies and facilities to the Dutch in the Far East. On that occasion the British Government did not support the Indian and Australian initiative in referring the situation to the Security Council; but eighteen months later, when the Dutch launched a second 'police action' in December 1948, the British Government did support a series of resolutions at the Security Council calling for the end of hostilities, the release of political prisoners, and the resumption of negotiations. With the passage of time, however, as the threat of chaos and the probability of Communism in S.E. Asia grew, the Western Allies began to revise their judgement about Indonesia.

The Indonesian Government was not successful in imposing its authority throughout its vast territories. It discriminated vindictively against the Dutch, expelling or arresting their citizens and seizing their industries and businesses. It maintained a permanent feud both with the Dutch over the western half of New Guinea (West Irian), which had formed part of the Netherlands East Indies but had not passed to the Indonesian Republic; and on a lesser scale with the Australians, who administered the eastern half of New Guinea. In recent years, British, American and Australian sympathies turned increasingly towards their Dutch allies; but the potential importance of Indonesia, with its population of 80–90,000,000 and its dominant geographical position, is such that none of them, particularly the Australians, could discount its good-will.

There was no other European ally with which so many awkward questions were created by the alliance as with France or even with the Netherlands. But since all had their separate interests, difficulties were always liable to arise with any of them. These were spread over a very unequal range of importance, but their intensity was not always commensurate with their importance. There was a sharp dispute with Belgium in O.E.E.C. in 1949, over the transferability and convertibility of currencies in the European Payments Union; but this was fortunately an exception in Anglo-Belgian relations, which otherwise presented few problems. A conflict of British loyalties towards Portugal and India was brought out by the Indian claim to Goa in 1955. What might have been a similar problem involving France was removed by the cession of the French Indian settlements to India in 1956. The dispute over Cyprus,[1] which was acute from 1954 until the settlement of 1959, put

[1] See below pp. 160-1.

Britain in the painful position of having to choose between the friendship of Greece and that of Turkey. In that case Britain's own vital interests were directly engaged: in others they were only engaged at one remove through her allies, especially the U.S.A.

Differences involving the U.S.A. followed no general pattern. Sometimes Britain found herself bound to side with the U.S.A. against another ally, as for instance when Denmark earned American disfavour in 1956 by building ships for the U.S.S.R. outside the specifications permitted by the restrictions on strategic trade. Sometimes Britain's sympathies were against the U.S.A., as in the case of Canadian opposition to American tariff policy, or Dutch resentment of the American refusal to allow transit rights to foreign airlines. Sometimes British loyalties were torn both ways, as over the case of Spain, whose admission to N.A.T.O. was urged by American defence chiefs and bitterly opposed by the Scandinavians.

An example of the tensions that could be created within an alliance by even the smallest power was the case of Iceland. The role of Iceland in N.A.T.O. was to provide a base and a staging-post. The island depended for its balance of payments on the presence of the base and its American personnel; but one-third of Iceland's trade was with the U.S.S.R. Its divided status in the great-power rivalry was reflected in the fact that for some time (from 1956 to the end of 1958) it was the only member of N.A.T.O. to have Communist ministers in its Government. After the election in 1956 which produced that situation, the Government gave notice to the U.S.A. of its intention to demand the withdrawal of the American base. Wiser counsels eventually prevailed, but the potential threat remained.

Scarcely was the argument with the Americans concluded than the Icelandic Government turned on its other principal ally, Britain. In June 1958 it announced its intention to extend from three to twelve miles the limit within which foreign fishing vessels might not operate round the coasts of the island, from 1 September following. The Minister of Fisheries at the time was a Communist. Britain refused to recognize the new limits, and there followed a number of violent incidents between British and Icelandic naval vessels as British trawlers tried to maintain their rights. At the end of 1958 the Icelandic Government was reconstructed without Communist ministers. Although neither side formally gave way, and although Iceland would not accept the British proposal to submit the dispute to the International Court, the conflict tacitly became less severe, but the potential friction remained.

On the European continent in particular there were sources of friction left over from the war in which Britain had no direct interest, but which tended to compromise the harmony of her alliances. One such case was that of Trieste, which was disputed between Italy and Yugoslavia until the Free Territory was divided between them by agreement in October 1954. Another was the Saar, which was at first economically linked with France, then designated as a 'European' territory to be controlled by a statute under W.E.U., and finally reincorporated into Germany after a referendum in October 1955. In each of these cases the dispute was not at its origin one between two allies of Britain, but in both cases circumstances changed during the course of the dispute, so that the British Government came to regret in the later stages commitments which it had given to one side rather than the other at the beginning. In neither case were vital British interests engaged, though British troops were sharing with the Americans the occupation of Trieste until the dispute was settled. In both cases it was an obvious matter of relief to have the disputes eventually cleared out of the way of developing Britain's alliances.

Neutrals

With such cases as the Saar and Trieste, the field of this survey of British commitments and their complications passes over from consideration of allies who had always been close friends of Britain to that of countries with whom Britain's relations during and after the Second World War were very different. These presented moral problems of another kind to offset the material advantages of reconciliation. In the case of Yugoslavia the problem was not severe. The Yugoslavs had been greatly admired as allies during the Second World War and the British had generally regretted the hostility which ensued from 1945 until the breach between Tito and the U.S.S.R. in 1948. Although Yugoslavia did not become formally an ally of Britain, she did become an ally of Britain's allies, Greece and Turkey, by the Balkan Pact signed in August 1954.

Tito continued to be critical of N.A.T.O. even while he was receiving American arms and British and American economic aid. But this seemed a small price to pay for the gap which his defection opened up in the Soviet Bloc. As that gap was partly closed from 1955 onwards, and as the Balkan Pact of 1954 proved itself to be increasingly a nullity, without actually being allowed to lapse, Tito appeared to have succeeded in establishing himself as a genuine neutral, a position which other leaders of the new post-war powers, such as Nehru and Nasser, desired to share. These developments were not entirely unwelcome to British policy, though less acceptable to the U.S.A.

The case of Spain was very different. Memories of the Civil War were still lively in England, though livelier on the Left than on the Right, and therefore more potent under the Labour than the Conservative Government. Franco's conduct during the Second World War was not easily forgiven; and Spain's persistent claims to Gibraltar were resented. The British Government readily agreed, at the Potsdam Conference in July 1945, to the exclusion of Spain from the United Nations. Although it saw no advantage in the U.N. resolution calling for the withdrawal of ambassadors from Spain in December 1946, the British Government conformed to the decision. In May 1949, when the Latin American states presented a resolution to the United Nations in favour of the restoration of full freedom of action over diplomatic relations with Spain, Britain abstained from the vote. It was not until early in 1951 that a British Ambassador returned to Madrid. The opposition to Spain's admission to N.A.T.O., which the U.S.A. and Portugal both advocated, continued as before. It was declared to be 'unnecessary' by a British minister in February 1951, a few weeks after Ambassadors had been reappointed; and to all American arguments in favour of it there was the counter-argument that Spain's adherence to N.A.T.O. would almost certainly entail the loss of the Scandinavians, particularly Norway, whose Labour Government retained an implacable hostility to Franco. It would also have alienated Socialist opinion throughout the Western Alliance.

The case for Spain's admission to N.A.T.O. on strategic grounds was plain from the map. It was repeatedly pressed by American defence chiefs, and also by members of Congress. Although they were unable to change their allies' convictions, they were successful in securing military aid for Spain and establishing air bases, independently of N.A.T.O., on Spanish soil. In November 1955 Dulles visited Madrid and spoke publicly in favour of Franco. In July of the same year the House of Representatives voted in favour of admitting Spain to N.A.T.O., and military aid was increased. There appeared to be no weakening on the British side so far as political and military matters were concerned. But economic relations were regarded as another matter, in which no useful purpose would be served by boycotting a European state. Anglo-Spanish monetary and trade agreements were made as they were required; and in July 1959, after a devaluation to bring Spanish currency into line with the rest of Europe, Spain was admitted to O.E.E.C. and granted a credit by the International Monetary Fund. It was possible that this last step, which constituted a recognition of economic respectability, might also prove eventually to have opened a back door to Spain's rehabilitation with the Western Allies in other contexts.

Former Enemies

It proved less embarrassing in practice for Britain to become reconciled with her former enemies than with Spain, even though the latter had been nominally neutral. Italy caused the least difficulty of all, thanks to eighteen months of 'co-belligerence' in the closing stages of the war. Diplomatic relations were actually restored with Italy by all the major allies (the U.S.S.R., the U.S.A. and Britain) before the defeat of Germany, and a peace treaty was signed in February 1947. Thereafter the only difficulties that stood in the way of reconciliation were the future of the free territory of Trieste and the disposal of Italy's former colonies. In both cases Britain, like the U.S.A., was inclined sympathetically towards Italy by reason of the fact that rival claims were laid on Italian territory by Communist Powers: Yugoslavia claimed Trieste, and the U.S.S.R. claimed to be granted trusteeship over one or other of the ex-colonies.

Both disputes led to protracted wrangles before they were eventually settled in 1954. Italy acquired possession of the City of Trieste, while Yugoslavia acquired the southern part of the Free Territory. All overseas possessions passed out of Italian sovereignty, as had been a declared British aim during the war: some, like Libya, to become independent, some, like the Dodecanese, to pass under other sovereignty. But Italy had the satisfaction of being granted trusteeship in 1950 over one former colony, Italian Somaliland, with a view to complete independence in 1960. The moral rehabilitation of Italy was thus completed by her new allies, which led the Italian Government to ask for the 'moral extinction', or at least the revision, of the peace treaty in 1951; but this could not be done without Soviet consent.

Subsequent friction in Anglo-Italian relations was happily slight. One case was due to the attitude of the British National Union of Mineworkers towards the employment of Italian miners in England – a particular symptom of the difficulties in the way of British participation in European economic institutions. A more general danger for the future lay in Italy's growing interest in the Middle East, where some

Italian businessmen foresaw the possibility of inheriting something of the traditional British position as it declined, particularly during the Anglo-Iranian oil dispute of 1951–3. Oil and natural gas became a special interest of Italian industrialists when they were discovered in northern Italy itself; and the exploiters of it showed a marked reluctance to conform to international conventions and practices developed mainly by the Americans and the British. An Italian firm, for instance, was the first to depart from the fifty-fifty principle governing oil concessions in the Middle East, when it signed an entirely novel agreement with the Iranian Government in 1957. This was an example of the conflicts of interest which were bound to arise within the Western Alliance from the fact that all the allies also had interests lying outside the Alliance's scope, either geographically, economically or politically.

In the case of Germany far more serious questions stood in the way of reconciliation. It was impossible, and still remains so, to forget the crimes of Nazism; and more than once in the post-war years allegations were made that former Nazis were returning to positions of influence. The cases of Otto Remer in 1952 and Wernher Naumann in 1953 were only the most notorious of many. But few things could in fact be more unlikely than a repetition of that particular conjunction of circumstances, each of them unusual and each necessary to the result, which brought Nazism to power in 1933. It was encouraging to sober students of Western Germany that the initiative in suppressing signs of Nazi recrudescence was always taken by the Germans themselves, though not always in the first instance by the official authorities. It is also encouraging that most of the notorious names of a few years ago have become forgotten by today. But the mistrust and suspicion of the post-war years between Englishmen and Germans did not entirely disappear, as was shown when President Heuss made a state visit to England in 1958, and again when Chancellor Adenauer in a broadcast in 1959 sharply criticized what he called a systematic attempt in England to damage Anglo-German relations. On the other hand, German relations with the U.S.A. were much more easily restored: the war was hardly over before it was true to say that the average American's favourite Europeans were the Germans. Policy towards Germany was therefore a potential source of friction between the U.S.A. and Britain as well as between Britain and the German Federal Republic.

During the first post-war years, when Germany was not a free agent but a passive object of allied policy, the main problem was economic. In 1945 much of Western Europe's economy was in ruins, that of

Germany more so than most. Food supplies in particular were desperately insufficient. Bread rationing was introduced in England for the first time in 1946 to help save Europeans, including Germans, from starving. It was soon recognized in the West that the economic recovery of Germany was vital to Europe. But the allies were committed to reducing Germany's industrial potential to a level which would make new aggression impossible; and the Soviet authorities, by their methods of collecting reparations, were draining off at one end the economic aid which the U.S.A., in particular, was supplying at the other. In August 1947 the U.S., French and British Governments held a conference in London on their own to settle the level of German industry, but they could not agree even among themselves. For instance, the U.S.A. and Britain disagreed about public ownership of industry in the Ruhr, which the Labour Government desired and the Americans opposed.

As the three zones of occupation were progressively merged, these disagreements were gradually settled, usually in a sense closer to American ideas than to British or French. By November 1948 agreement had been reached on draft laws for the reorganization of West German industry. In the meantime the crucial step had been taken towards accelerating German recovery, by means of the monetary reform of June 1948, which was also the indirect cause of the Soviet blockade of Berlin. From 1948 onwards German economic recovery was assured. It proceeded on a scale far more spectacular than had ever been envisaged, and one which caused uneasiness in Britain from the first. In place of the economic problem, there was then a political problem to be faced.

The political problem was to establish an acceptable form of sovereign government in Germany in spite of the country's division by the Iron Curtain. Local government at the level of *Länder* was restored as quickly as possible in the West. The process of 'de-Nazification' was handed over to their responsibility as early as 1946 by the Americans, and in 1947 by the British. A *Länderrat*, or co-ordinating agency of the provincial governments, was created in February 1948. In the same month the Western Allies began separate discussions on the future constitution of Germany. A Western six-power conference was held at Frankfurt in April to discuss a German constitution. A German 'parliamentary council' was convened at Bonn in September 1948.

From then on the steps towards sovereignty, though not always swift nor free from criticism and anxiety in Britain, were virtually automatic:

the Occupation Statute in April 1949; the Basic Law in May; the first federal elections in August of the same year; admission to the Council of Europe in November; a revision of the Occupation Statute in March 1951; the formal ending of the state of war with Britain in July; participation in the new institutions of European unification from 1951 onwards; the agreements linked with the signature of the E.D.C. Treaty in May 1952; and finally, by a rapid series of steps in 1954, the full restoration of sovereignty and admission to N.A.T.O. Once again there was uneasiness both in Britain and France. There was still a basic antinomy of feeling towards Germany, which was seen both as an essential partner of the West and as a potential enemy. Even after the collapse of E.D.C. in 1954 the French Prime Minister, Mendès-France, seems still to have hoped to keep the German Federal Republic out of N.A.T.O., although the British and American Governments had long since and repeatedly assured the French that it was inevitable.

By 1954 the field of debate over Germany had shifted again, from the political to the strategic. There were two reasons why German participation in N.A.T.O. was considered essential: firstly, more manpower was needed to offset the Soviet Union's numerical advantage; secondly, more depth and room for manœuvre on the ground was needed for the allied forces in Europe. German rearmament was nevertheless an extremely contentious subject, not only in Britain and France but also in Western Germany itself, where the new generation had been so effectively purged of militarism that the popular reaction towards the prospect of rearmament was expressed in the slogan 'ohne mich' ('leave me out'). As early as March 1950, however, Churchill had called for a German contribution to Western defence, which was repudiated by Bevin as well as the Labour rank and file. Later Bevin accepted the need for German rearmament, but he had to carry the point against strong resistance within his party. In August 1950 Adenauer himself asked to be allowed to form an 'armed mobile police' to counter the East German *Bereitschaften*, or security police, who were already under arms. A few weeks later the three Western Foreign Ministers met to discuss the problem of German defence. At the end of the year the North Atlantic Council agreed that a German military contribution was indispensable.

The intention was that the contribution should be made through the medium of the European Defence Community, under overall European instead of national control; but a long debate ensued on the level of command at which units should begin to be purely national.

Although the technical details were finally settled, and the E.D.C. Treaty was duly signed by the six participating powers (Germany, France, Belgium, the Netherlands, Luxembourg, Italy), the failure of the French to ratify it finally left Germany with much greater freedom of action than had been intended. Admitted to N.A.T.O. on equal terms at the end of 1954, the German Federal Republic has sometimes exercised an influence on Western policy second only to that of the U.S.A. As the debate over the future of Germany shifted ground again, to become an argument across the Iron Curtain about reunification and the status of Berlin, it seemed more than once in 1958–9 that Adenauer was dictating Western policy to both the British and the American Governments.

In Eastern Europe the fear grew, or was purported to grow, that the Federal Republic would eventually try forcibly to recover the territories lost to Poland and Czechoslovakia in 1945, although Adenauer had expressly abjured the use of force to recover them. Similar fears were not unknown in Britain. In France, however, especially after de Gaulle returned to power in 1958 and formed a close friendship with Adenauer, fears of Germany seemed almost extinct. This meant, of course, primarily fears of German aggressiveness directed towards the West. But even to be certain, as it seemed possible to be in 1959, that there could never again be a war between the great nation-states of Western Europe, was a considerable advance on the past and worth a high price.

Western Germany as an ally was therefore judged to rate a qualified optimism in the West. The last of the major ex-enemies was a more uncertain case, at least from the British point of view. Japan, Britain's first ally in the twentieth century, did not become formally an ally again, as she did with the U.S.A.: but circumstances made a degree of *rapprochement* inevitable, if only because Japan was the ally of Britain's own most important ally. In this case too there were bitter memories to be lived down: not only of wartime aggression and atrocities but also of unscrupulous trading practices before the war. But Japan could not be permanently excluded from international society, if only because, being placed by nature in economic and physical circumstances similar to those of Britain, she had either to trade or starve; and rather than starve, she might even again go to war. From the British point of view it was awkward, though natural, that some of Japan's most important industries (ship-building and textiles, for instance) were in direct competition with Britain's, and were favoured in foreign markets by lower wage-rates. Nevertheless, the British Government recognized that these difficulties had to be accepted lest worse should ensue. But they led to a protracted battle before Japan was admitted to full membership of the General Agreement on Tariffs and Trade (G.A.T.T.), reluctantly so far as Britain was concerned, in September 1955.

Japan was looked on primarily as an American responsibility after the war, and the responsibility was exercised without much regard for the U.S.A.'s allies. But the British Government supported the U.S.A., with its eyes open, in the process of rehabilitating and restoring Japan. As early as 1947 the prospect of a peace treaty was discussed with the Commonwealth Governments, of which India, Australia and New Zealand were particularly concerned. The Peace Treaty was not signed until September 1951, and then only at the price of leaving out many interested powers, particularly the U.S.S.R., which would not accept the American terms. Moreover, even the Australian and New Zealand Governments felt uneasy about the future of the Pacific area with Japan again a potential great power. It was to meet this uneasiness that the A.N.Z.U.S. Pact (named after the initials of Australia, New Zealand and the United States) was signed in September 1951 – the first which those two Commonwealth countries ever signed with a foreign power to the exclusion of Britain. The Japanese Peace Treaty also had the awkward consequence of providing a precedent for the Soviet Union to sign a separate peace treaty with Eastern Germany, if it so chose, a few years later.

British relations with Japan continued to be marked by intermittent friction. In July 1952, when some British sailors were arrested in Japan after a brawl, it was found that they were not covered, as American forces were, by a 'status of forces' agreement. They were eventually released, and the lacuna was later remedied; but the incident left an unpleasant effect on both sides. So did the persistent opposition of the British Government to the admission of Japan to G.A.T.T.: and so did the British refusal in 1958 to be moved by Japanese protests against conducting nuclear test-explosions in the Pacific. Anglo-Japanese relations were marked by probably less cordiality than Anglo-German relations, but they were also more remote and not bound by a formal alliance. Britain's principal interest was economic: Japan was a market as well as a competitor. But it was impossible to ignore the possibility of both countries being drawn into a war in the Far East by their respective alliances with the U.S.A. Although, for instance, Japan lay north of the S.E.A.T.O. area as defined in the Manila Treaty of 1954, the same was true of Hong Kong, an obvious prize for an aggressor;

and a war involving S.E.A.T.O. might easily spread to become a general Far Eastern war, whether on Chinese or on American initiative. It was not to be forgotten that in April 1954 Vice-President Nixon had declared, at the height of the crisis over Dien Bien Phu, that the real stake in Indo-China, as in Korea, was Japan. Japan and Britain were inevitably bedfellows, however uneasy they might be.

Other Alliances

With the case of Japan, this survey of Britain's post-war need for allies and friends, and the complications created by it, has moved away from Europe to Asia. This serves as a reminder that both of Britain's multilateral alliances other than N.A.T.O. lie outside Europe, in S.E. Asia (S.E.A.T.O.) and in the Middle East (the Baghdad Pact, later known as the Central Treaty Organization). It should also be remembered that the most intimate of Britain's overseas associations, the Commonwealth, though not a formal alliance, is world-wide. But the implications of these relations are of a somewhat different kind from those with the powers that have so far been discussed. In the case of S.E.A.T.O. and the Baghdad Pact, they are essentially relations with small or new countries whose participation in an alliance with Britain could not help being on something less than completely equal terms. Such relations are dealt with in chapter 9 below. In the case of the Commonwealth the relation is so peculiar that it can only properly be given a chapter to itself, and this is done in chapter 8, supplemented in part by chapter 12. The relation with the U.S.A. is also, as has been explained, for similar reasons treated separately in chapter 7. Each of these cases will add further substance to the argument of this chapter, that Britain's relations with her friends and allies were an important and unavoidable factor in her post-war foreign policy, and one which was at the same time in many respects most welcome, in others inhibiting.

6

The National Economy

THE importance of economic factors in foreign policy is a commonplace of the post-war years. It is amply illustrated by the Defence White Papers, since defence is by far the most expensive element in foreign policy. 'Economic rehabilitation at home' was one of the two imperative needs defined in the 1946 White Paper; and since the other was 'to carry out our responsibilities abroad', the potential conflict of interest was laid bare from the start. The 1947 White Paper re-emphasized the dilemma of seeking 'healthy social and economic conditions' at home without 'ill-considered jettisoning of defence responsibilities'. The next White Paper, in 1948, mentioned balance of payments difficulties for the first time, and stressed the need for 'a strong and sound economy, with a flourishing industry'. All this emphasis on what was needed suggests that it was not being achieved. The impact of rearmament from 1950 onwards naturally worsened the situation, until by 1957 it came to be admitted that the burden was intolerable and must be cut down. It was then that the concept of 'interdependence' was invoked to rationalize the reduction of the country's expenditure on defence. Britain's post-war economy, even at its most prosperous – and it was in the period of the latest reductions that it reached its maximum prosperity – could not afford the defence bill of an entirely independent power.

During most of the post-war period, however, Britain was not at her most prosperous. She was constantly struggling with economic adversity. There have been many explanations by the experts of the reasons why this was so. It was due, they say, to the sacrifices of the war, or to a national loss of dynamism; it was due to spending too much at home, especially on services, and selling too little abroad; it was due to a slow rate of economic growth caused by too low a level of investment and too much conservatism (or alternatively, Communism) in the trade unions; it was due to the overwhelming impact of the American economy on all other national economies, coupled with the selfishness and ineptitude of American policy; it was due to the failure to fund the wartime sterling balances, or to the improvident policies of other members of the Sterling Area; it was due to one government's passion for redistributing the national income rather than increasing it, and to the other's worship of the fetish of a strong pound; it was due, of course, to spending too much on defence, and to investing, lending or giving away too much overseas.

All these arguments were used, but all agreed upon two things. One was, in words used by Eden when he was Prime Minister, that Britain needed to be economically sound at home in order to play 'our special part in world affairs'. The other was that we were finding it extremely difficult to do so. Some people would even have argued that the Prime Minister's logic was inverted: that the real purpose of 'our special part in world affairs' should be to make Britain economically sound, not vice versa. But no one, in any case, would have denied the connexion.

The economic history of the years 1945–59 shows that there were very few and brief periods when it was possible to look on the struggle for a soundly based prosperity with any confidence. The struggle was essentially one to achieve a favourable balance of payments; that is to say, to earn more by exports than was spent on imports, since it is on foreign trade that the entire national economy depends. The annual fluctuations of the balance of payments are directly related to the broad trends of foreign policy, and the relation is reciprocal. Thus, it was the boom consequent upon the outbreak of the Korean War that led to the first large favourable balance of payments (£300,000,000 in 1950). The same chain of events caused the disastrously unfavourable balance in the following year (a deficit of £403,000,000), when Britain had to sell abroad in a falling market the goods produced from raw materials bought at peak prices in 1950; and when additionally a large proportion of the raw materials were being converted into defence production instead of export goods.

The process happened again in reverse from 1956 to 1959, when the burden of defence began to be cut down, thus facilitating the re-expansion of exports; and when incidentally the terms of trade moved on balance strongly in Britain's favour, thanks to the declining cost of some of her principal raw materials. It was not entirely an accident (though luck certainly played a part) that the worst year in the post-war period for the balance of payments was 1951, when defence began gravely to overstrain the national economy; and the best one was 1958, when it was stated in the Defence White Paper for that year that 'the favourable effects of the new defence policy, announced a year ago, are already beginning to make themselves felt'. This was particularly true of the demands of defence on manpower, metal-using industries, and scientific and engineering skill, for which the export industries' needs were also great.

To look at the broad trend over a period of several years, however, is to over-simplify the picture and to ignore the almost daily problems harassing a Government that was seeking to meet the responsibilities of a great power without any margin of resources. Foreign policy is made from day to day, not simply from decade to decade. Ministers were not merely battling with trends or swimming with tides: they were also taking fences as they came to them. The chronicle needs to be read as it unfolded, not merely summed up in distant retrospect.

It began as soon as the first post-war Government came to power, when the U.S. Government in August 1945 terminated the wartime Lend-Lease arrangements. The gap was later filled in part by the U.S.-Canadian loan, which was agreed in December 1945, though the terms were not easy. In the meantime the economic prospect for Europe as well as for Britain was grim. In the first two post-war years the British adverse balance of trade reached the disheartening levels of £298,000,000 (1946) and £443,000,000 (1947). These were also the years in which food shortages led to the rationing of bread and potatoes in Britain for the first time. The same problems were general throughout Western Europe.

The winter of 1946–7 sharply aggravated the weakness of the British economy, and drew attention to it in a dramatic way, though it did no more than that. While the Foreign Secretary was arguing that with a few million tons of coal for export he could save Europe from political disaster, stocks in England dropped so low that electric power-stations had to close or reduce their generating hours, and factories producing goods for export had to stop work or work part-time. In February 1947 there were temporarily 1,800,000 unemployed in Britain. The effect on foreign policy was immediate. In every direction the Government looked for relief and economies.

The commitment in Greece was surrendered to the U.S.A. in March. The cost of occupying Germany was cut down by negotiating an agreement with the U.S.A. through which the latter bore three-quarters of the burden of the combined Anglo-American Zone and relieved Britain of all dollar expenditure in Germany. Trade negotiations were opened with the U.S.S.R., though with little success. Attempts were made to negotiate with countries holding large sterling balances as a result of the war, in order to scale them down, but again with little success. The

Defence White Paper led to demands in parliament for even more drastic reductions of Britain's commitments. Imports were severely cut in June. In July and August came the attempt at convertibility of sterling, prescribed by the American loan agreement but foredoomed to failure. Relief was already in sight, however, thanks to the offer of comprehensive aid to Europe made by the U.S. Secretary of State, General Marshall, on 5 June.

The Marshall Plan was intended not only to relieve Europe, which was suffering collectively, like Britain, from an adverse balance of payments, particularly with the dollar area, but also to transform its economic way of life. When the Foreign Assistance Act was finally passed in 1948, its preamble stressed the value of 'a large domestic market with no internal trade barriers', and this was what the U.S. Government hoped to see created in Europe. That it did not come about so fast as the Americans desired was due partly to the circumstances of Europe, which were far more different from those of the U.S.A. than most Americans would allow; and partly to the fact that the initiative in giving concrete form to the Marshall Plan was taken by the British Government, and in particular by Bevin, who had all the Englishman's congenital distrust of what were thought of as 'continental entanglements'. The most that the Marshall Plan was able to achieve in liberalizing European trade was the creation of the Organization for European Economic Co-operation (O.E.E.C.) in 1948, which in turn created the European Payments Union (E.P.U.) in 1950. From the European point of view, these were valuable and fruitful institutions. But the Americans' disappointment that more was not immediately achieved was reflected in their later encouragement of other more radical supranational developments in later years.

For Britain the Marshall Plan meant salvation, though not immediate salvation. While it was under discussion and until the first fruits were received in 1948, emergency measures continued. Further cuts of imports were announced in October 1947, and a supplementary budget was introduced in November. In December Churchill sombrely predicted that the population of the British Isles would have to be reduced by a quarter. Capital construction was cut back in January 1948. The Chancellor of the Exchequer inaugurated a policy of wage and dividend restraint, and imposed a capital levy for the first and only time in the 1948 Budget. Meanwhile the policy of nationalization was well under way. The coal industry had been taken over by the State in January 1947; electricity was taken over in April 1948, and rail and road transport in May. These developments of Socialism were looked upon with mixed feelings by the U.S. Government, which was about to provide so powerful an economic relief to Britain; but it was accepted as the primary object of American policy to ensure that the European democracies should not founder, whatever form their democracy might take.

As the dollars began to flow, things began to look up in other ways as well. Nineteen-forty-eight was the first post-war year to show a favourable balance of trade for Britain, even if only by a minute margin. The pre-war level of production was surpassed early in 1949, and the target for exports, which had been set at 175 per cent of the pre-war level in 1946, was achieved by 1950. The first wartime rationing scheme to be abolished was that of clothing and textiles in March 1949. But the shadow of the new crisis was already gathering. In July the Chancellor reported to the House of Commons on an adverse turn in the balance of payments, and the Government's purchasing departments were instructed to postpone dollar expenditure. The devaluation of sterling was rumoured, then denied, then carried into effect on 18 September. Crisis measures were announced in October, including new cuts in capital expenditure. The object of the whole operation was to stimulate exports still further, but the results were inadequate. The year 1949 showed a favourable balance of only £31,000,000. The following year showed a much more substantial surplus of £300,000,000, by far the biggest since the war, but this was largely the result of the boom which followed the outbreak of the Korean War, and it was not sustained into 1951.

Despite the stringency of the times, the Labour Government took during this period a number of costly but far-sighted and courageous decisions, which later events justified. One was to give a special priority to developing the aircraft industry, with the help of public funds. Another was to develop atomic energy independently of the U.S.A. – which indeed had made further co-operation impossible by the McMahon Act of 1946 – and to give it the same kind of stimulus as the aircraft industry. In both cases the initial motive was military, but the benefit was also economic. Both aircraft and nuclear reactors have since taken a place among the most valuable earners of foreign exchange by export.

A third case was the decision to build a major oil refinery in England in order to be less dependent on refineries in politically uncertain areas near the point of production of crude oil, such as the Persian Gulf, or on dollar imports. The inauguration of the refinery at Fawley in September

1951, as the Anglo-Iranian oil crisis reached its peak and Abadan was about to go out of production for three years, was a notably fortunate coincidence. Without it, petrol rationing (which had ended in May 1950) would certainly have had to be restored. The damage done to Britain by the Iranian nationalists was thus limited to the loss of investment in Iranian oil (partially recovered in 1954 after the fall of Mussadiq's Government); though that is not to say that it was not extremely severe, given that oil accounts for over half of the net income received from British overseas investment.

To make matters worse, the terms of trade turned against Britain in 1951. The burden of defence also grew by 50 per cent between 1950 and 1952, and it absorbed a large proportion of the country's productive capacity. Another adverse factor was the re-emergence of Germany and Japan as competitors. Both had been eliminated by the war, but both had once been great manufacturing powers and were bound to be so again. It was impossible to keep them permanently depressed and economically dependent on their conquerors. Even though their competition would be a particular danger to Britain – perhaps even unscrupulously so in the case of Japan – it was judged necessary to encourage them to redevelop their industrial capacity rather than to remain as a drain on the Western taxpayer and a prolific source of future trouble, perhaps even of renewed war. Their revival began to make itself felt in the early 1950s.

It was the more powerful because they had not yet any burden of defence to carry. British resentment also began to revive against Japanese commercial practices. Japan was, for instance, one of the few countries that undertook to buy Iranian oil after the Iranian Government had nationalized the industry and evicted the A.I.O.C. The British Government struggled long and hard, but eventually in vain, to exclude Japan from the General Agreement on Tariffs and Trade (G.A.T.T.), which had been created in 1947 to promote the reduction of tariffs and discriminatory practices. The expansion of world trade had drawbacks as well as advantages, and some of these were now beginning to be felt.

The last year of the Labour Government began with a black outlook, quite apart from the fateful involvement of China in the Korean War. In February 1951 there was again a shortage of fuel supplies. There was also a dock strike, and the beginning of the Anglo-Iranian oil crisis. The nationalization of steel took effect in the same month, which was likely to have some dislocating effect on the industry to begin with, whether or not it were ultimately to prove a success. In April the Government admitted that there was bound to be a general rise in prices, including food. Bevan and two other ministers resigned from the Government on the ground that the rearmament programme launched in 1950 was too costly, and was bound to prejudice the welfare services at home. Restrictions were increased on capital issues in April, and the building programme was cut in June. In July severe restrictions were imposed on dividends, bank advances, some prices and dollar imports. A major crisis was clearly impending, and a new approach to the U.S.A. was made for help in September. In the following month the Labour Government was defeated at the General Election. The extreme seriousness of the economic situation was the main preoccupation of its Conservative successor, which showed its intention to depart decisively from the recent course of economic policy by raising the Bank Rate in November for the first time since the war.

Other emergency measures followed at the beginning of 1952: more restrictions on imports and also on hire purchase, more cuts in capital investment. Again the major object was to restore the balance of payments, which had slumped to a deficit of £403,000,000 for 1951. Apart from restrictive measures, the Government sought relief in three positive directions. One was by strengthening the co-ordination of policy within the Sterling Area, some of whose members had been pursuing an erratic course to the detriment of the whole association. A conference of Commonwealth Prime Ministers, devoted to economic problems, was held in London in December 1952, which yielded many important decisions, especially in the emphasis it laid on the need for all members to curb internal inflation.

A second positive measure was to urge the U.S.A. to adopt a more liberal commercial policy. This was the principal object of a visit to Washington by the Foreign Secretary and Chancellor of the Exchequer in March 1953, when the slogan 'Trade not Aid' was first heard. Fortunately the slogan appealed to the new Republican President of the U.S.A., who had taken office in January committed to cut Government expenditure. The first fruits of his re-examination of American foreign economic policy were the report of the Douglas Committee in August, which proposed measures to increase the U.S.A.'s level of imports, and the appointment of the Randall Commission on foreign economic policy in the same month, under a chairman whose liberal views on international trade were well known. A slow but definite trend towards lowering U.S. tariffs and other barriers was set in motion.

The third positive measure adopted by the new British Government was one which was by no means new, but was now bitterly resented in the U.S.A. This was to promote increased trade with the countries of the Soviet Bloc. British trade with China in particular was regularly denounced in the U.S. Congress, where legislation was actually introduced for the express purpose of cutting off American aid to countries engaging in such trade, meaning specifically Britain. The charges were regularly and effectively rebutted so far as they alleged infringement of the embargo imposed by the United Nations in May 1951; but outside the limits of the embargo the British Government regarded itself as morally free.

A note was sent to the Chinese Communist Government in April 1952 proposing an increase of trade. The reply was not received until July, and then it was unaccommodating. The subject was discussed in Washington by the Foreign Secretary in March 1953, to try to overcome American objections, and new attempts were made. In April the Economic Commission for Europe, an organ of the United Nations, held a conference on East-West trade. In June an unofficial British trade mission visited Peking, but with no substantial results. For some time the matter of trade with China lay dormant, and the slightly less contentious problem of trade with the U.S.S.R. was pursued in isolation. But it was not until 1958 that the barriers in either case were broken through with any measure of success.

Nevertheless the years 1953–4 showed a real improvement in other directions. The terms of trade turned in Britain's favour, and the two years showed surpluses of £188,000,000 and £228,000,000 in the balance of payments. Nineteen-fifty-three was the first odd-numbered year since the war to break the cycle of financial crises every alternate summer or autumn. Earlier restrictions were relaxed. Nineteen-fifty-four was a singularly untroubled year, which led up to the comment[1] that '1954 looks like the last of the post-war years', with the complete abolition of rationing and controls, the great increase of prosperity, and the apparent containment of inflation. But there were latent seeds of trouble that had been overlooked. The agreement by which Western Germany was admitted into N.A.T.O. had been signed without any provision for the cost of stationing British troops there after the occupation ended; and this was later estimated at £50,000,000 a year above what they would cost at home. It was a significant burden on the balance of payments, but one which the German Federal Republic pertinaciously refused to

[1] *Financial Times*, 1 January 1955.

accept as its own responsibility, until at last a compromise was reached in May 1958.

Another unsatisfactory feature of the time, which was not sufficiently recognized for the dangers it entailed, was the easy-going inflation which was accompanying increased prosperity. In this respect the experts quoted above proved wrong. It was called, both then and later,[1] a 'wage inflation', though this is not so much to accuse organized labour of forcing the employers' hands as to convict the employers of being too ready to outbid each other for labour in the prosperity of a buoyant and easy home market. With the level of unemployment falling below 1 per cent of the labour force in the middle of the year, the temptation to both sides was strong.

The signs of danger began early in 1955, despite the complacent atmosphere in which it had opened. Bank Rate was put up in February and restrictions were imposed on hire purchase. A railway strike in May (the month of the fourth post-war General Election) increased the Government's handicap. More serious emergency measures were taken in July, and in August the new Prime Minister, Sir Anthony Eden, warned the country that the balance of payments was in danger. Rumours of another devaluation were vigorously (and this time correctly) denied by the Chancellor in September. Instead, a Supplementary Budget was announced for October, which was assumed to portend drastic measures. What actually emerged was surprisingly mild, though again capital investment was cut. The measures so far taken gave the appearance of being inadequate and indecisive, but in February 1956 Bank Rate was put up to 5 per cent, the highest level it had reached since 1932. By the end of the year crisis measures were again called for: this time from new causes, in the aftermath of the Suez Canal crisis.

Considering the magnitude of that crisis and the horrific predictions that were made of its consequences, the British economy recovered from it with remarkable ease and speed. This was in large measure due to the generosity and vigour with which the Western Allies reacted once the first shock was over. For instance, the International Monetary Fund lent Britain £201,000,000 to help counter the pressure on sterling in December 1956; O.E.E.C. created an emergency oil pool in January 1957 to help minimize the shortage caused by the closure of the Suez Canal; and the U.S. Government diverted its own oil supplies to help stock the pool. On Britain's side, the waiver of the interest and repay-

---

[1] e.g. in the first and second *Reports* of the Council on Prices, Productivity and Incomes (February and August 1958).

ment due on the 1945 American loan, and the imposition of fuel oil rationing for six months, were almost the sum total of the direct damage inflicted. Though the opportunity was taken at the same time to scale down drastically the cost of defence in the 1957 White Paper, this was to meet a need which had long existed already, and for which the drama of November-December 1956 provided only the occasion, not the cause.

Similarly, when a new financial crisis gathered in the autumn of 1957, it was in no way due to the aftermath of the Canal crisis of 1956. It was due rather to a new round of 'wage inflation' leading to a rise in prices and a loss of confidence in sterling abroad. To scotch rumours of devaluation and to remedy the weakness of sterling, if possible once for all, the Government introduced the most drastic emergency programme since the war, with Bank Rate raised to 7 per cent. On this occasion, if it is not premature to judge, the remedy seems to have worked a lasting cure, although the Chancellor responsible for it resigned with his two junior ministers in January 1958 on the ground that the Government was not pursuing its anti-inflationary course with sufficient rigour and determination.

The years 1958-9 were the first since the war in which Britain's economy appeared to be both prosperous and soundly based. This was so despite a fairly severe recession in world trade, particularly in the U.S.A. in 1957, and despite a temporarily high level of unemployment in the winter of 1958-9 and a disappointingly low level of production, both of which were attributed by the Government to the recession abroad and by the opposition to the Government's own anti-inflationary measures. By the latter part of 1959, whatever their origins, both the rise in unemployment and the lag in production appeared to have corrected themselves. In the meantime a series of bold steps had shown the Government's confidence that the improvement in the economy was lasting and not fortuitous.

Bank Rate was reduced by stages; hire purchase restrictions were successively relaxed and abolished; control over bank advances was ended; the ceiling on public investment was raised; control over capital issues was largely removed; non-resident sterling was made freely convertible; and restrictions on dollar imports were substantially reduced. From the long-term point of view, two events which took place in December 1958 were probably the most significant. One was the abolition of the European Payments Union, which followed upon the co-ordinated action of the West European Governments in unifying their currencies and adopting convertibility simultaneously. The other

was the breakdown of the attempt in O.E.E.C. to negotiate a Free
Trade Area associated with the Common Market, which had been
created by the Treaty of Rome in 1957. The E.P.U. and the F.T.A.
lapsed for precisely opposite reasons, the one because it had fulfilled
its functions, the other because it was never given a chance to do so.

The creation of the European Economic Community, or Common
Market, by the six powers which had already linked themselves in the
European Coal and Steel Community (France, Western Germany,
Italy, Belgium, the Netherlands, Luxembourg) presented Britain with
the hardest single problem in the economic field that remained unresolved at the end of the period under review. With the E.C.S.C.
Britain had signed a treaty in December 1954, which operated satis-
factorily; and it led to a further agreement in 1957, by which British
tariffs on steel were substantially reduced. But to negotiate a *modus
vivendi* with the Common Market, and with its companion body
Euratom, proved a more intractable problem, largely because of the
diametrical opposition of French and British views.

The negotiations began in 1957 under the auspices of O.E.E.C., and
proceeded through 1958 until the French took the initiative in terminat-
ing them on 14 November. In 1959 the British Government evolved a
substitute European Free Trade Association consisting of what were
called the 'outer seven' powers (Britain, Norway, Sweden, Denmark,
Portugal, Switzerland, Austria) which had not been able to join the
European Economic Community. The resultant division of Western
Europe into two separate economic leagues was a discouraging feature
of the years 1958–9, whose long-term consequences for Britain's
economic future could not be foreseen. Many well-qualified judges
considered that the association of the Outer Seven would tend to harden
the division rather than to act as a bridge between the Six and the rest
of Europe.

In the short term, however, the importance of these two years in
relation to Britain's foreign policy is that they were the first since
demobilization in which the country's overseas commitments were
brought within the limits of her economic capacity. This was done by
squeezing at both ends, as it were: by increasing the capacity and
decreasing the commitments. More satisfactory though the prospect
appeared, it would have been a mistake to suppose that either part of
the process could be abandoned: for instance, to have made the
stronger national economy of 1959 sustain the defence burden laid
upon it up to 1957. That burden absorbed, as the 1957 White Paper

pointed out, on average over the previous five years, 10 per cent of the gross national product, 7 per cent of the working population and one-eighth of the output of the metal-using industries. At the same level of commitments, the figures would not have been different in 1959, and they were in the long run intolerable. The burden had to be shared. The economic situation of the country was thus one of the major factors that made 'interdependence' necessary. Equally, interdependence was intended to be one of the factors that would enable Britain to achieve the sound economic basis needed for playing her 'special part in world affairs'.

7

The Relation with the U.S.A.

THE U.S.A. does not appear among the allies or commitments specifically mentioned in the Defence White Papers until 1950, between the signature of the North Atlantic Treaty and the outbreak of the Korean War. At the end of the Second World War the 'special relation' created by Churchill in his dealings with Roosevelt had virtually lapsed. This was not because of the change of Government in Britain in 1945: many Americans, including those in responsible positions, had a sympathy for Britain's great political experiment, and none, whatever their misgivings, denied Britain's democratic right to follow her own course in domestic affairs. The reason was rather that the U.S.A. was disenchanted with allies generally, and Britain was seen only as one ally among the rest. The reaction of American sentiment was given exaggerated expression by the fact that a new and inexperienced President had suddenly taken office just before the end of the war. President Truman later criticized himself for his first major post-war decision, which was to terminate Lend-Lease in August 1945.

The total value of Lend-Lease to Britain since its inauguration in 1941 had been $29,000,000,000, which was reduced to $23,000,000,000 by reverse Lend-Lease. The sudden cut-off of this subvention was, in Lord Keynes's words, 'what might be called without exaggeration a financial Dunkirk'. The effort to negotiate some kind of replacement for it was led by Lord Keynes himself, and resulted in the Anglo-American Financial Agreement of December 1945. The loan which Britain received under the agreement amounted to $3,750,000,000 from the U.S.A., plus another $1,250,000,000 from Canada. But the terms were hard, especially those that were aimed against discrimination of the kinds that Britain had built into the system of Imperial Preference. The Americans refused, for instance, to regard the Sterling Area as a single financial unit, a concession that was to come only when the European Payments Union was set up in 1950. The hardest condition of all was that sterling should be made freely convertible by the middle of July 1947. Lord Keynes revealed the extent to which the agreement was a disappointment when he told the House of Lords that he had hoped, in vain, for a free grant from the U.S.A. Post-war Anglo-American relations were on a new footing.

The economic weakness which was revealed in July and August 1947, by the inability of sterling to stand up to the strain of premature convertibility, led to a new approach. It was by then clear that Britain, as well as the rest of Europe, would be dependent on economic help from the U.S.A. for some years; and the Marshall Plan was already in gestation when the Anglo-American Financial Agreement broke down. Britain, however, was still just one among a dozen other friends of the U.S.A. in the same predicament. Help was to be given on a strictly practical basis, which again involved measures of a kind traditionally unwelcome to British opinion: in this case, a degree of merger with the economies of continental Europe. A new 'special relation' had still to be formed with the U.S.A. Churchill tried to apply his unique prestige to the purpose, when he spoke at Fulton, Missouri, in March 1946, of the 'fraternal association' of Britain and the U.S.A. But this intervention was not appreciated by the Labour Government's supporters, who were already critical of Bevin for taking sides with the U.S.A. against the U.S.S.R. in international questions. In a broadcast in December 1946 Bevin scouted the idea of a new Anglo-American alliance, with explicit reference to Churchill's speech at Fulton.

From the American point of view Britain was at this date not merely an ally not much better than the rest, but in some respects worse. The spectre of colonialism was still lively. The restoration of British sovereignty in all the enemy-occupied colonies, sometimes by force of American arms, was resented. The process which gave India and other Commonwealth countries their independence had not yet begun. There were signs, too, as it appeared to the Americans, that British imperial influence might even expand instead of contracting: for instance, the continued presence of British troops in Greece as a major case, and the Anglo-Siamese agreement of May 1947 as a minor one.

There was also the tragic case of Palestine, which remained a major stumbling-block in the way of Anglo-American accord throughout the period, in spite of the early hope of co-operation inspired by the appointment of an Anglo-American Committee of Inquiry in November 1945. The report of the Committee, and especially President Truman's comments on it in May 1946, in fact served to worsen relations. In this case again Churchill tried to exercise a mediating influence by stressing the impossibility of continuing the Mandate without American support. But at the date when Churchill spoke, in the summer of 1946, President

Truman was faced with the prospect of losing ground in the mid-term Congressional elections. The President therefore chose to cajole the Jewish vote by openly supporting the Anglo-American Committee's proposal that 100,000 Jewish refugees should be admitted at once to Palestine. From that date there was no prospect of Anglo-American agreement on Palestine until after the Mandate was surrendered; and recriminations on both sides continued for many years.

Only in Europe, and especially in dealing with Eastern Europe, was there some harmony between British and American policy, largely because the U.S.A.'s disenchantment with the U.S.S.R. was even more rapid than with her other allies. Towards the former enemies and former allies who were passing under Soviet control there was a common attitude of indignant sympathy, which the American Government was generally quicker to express than the British. Towards the major ex-enemies, Germany and Italy, a united front was adopted against the U.S.S.R.: for instance, in opposition to the Soviet reparations policy in Germany, and in maintaining the Anglo-American occupation of Trieste against Yugoslav claims. But in both cases there were also internal disagreements: in Germany over the question of public or private ownership in the Ruhr, in Italy over the speed of political rehabilitation and economic reconstruction. At the United Nations, the common front against Soviet intransigence – it was too soon yet to speak of Soviet aggressiveness – was qualified by tactical disagreements. The British Government was not consulted by the U.S. Government, for instance, before General Marshall put forward his plan for an Interim Committee of the General Assembly, or 'Little Assembly', in the autumn of 1947; and the British representative supported it only grudgingly.

The post-war period up to 1949–50 was one in which Britain and the U.S.A. were both independently adjusting themselves to their new status in the world. Readjustment involved an incidental adjustment of their mutual relations at the same time, which would have been easier if only one of the two had been undergoing the process of change instead of both. For both countries there was a basic dilemma in the relation with the other. Britain was gradually coming to stand out for the Americans as their sturdiest ally in Europe: for instance, it was Britain that was first able to dispense with financial aid under the European Recovery Programme in 1951. But Britain was also a colonial power, which was a bad thing in American eyes, and it was the fact of being a colonial power that constituted a large part of her strength. For Britain the U.S.A. was simultaneously a necessary ally and economic support on the one hand and a competitor, both politically and economically, on the other. One of the early post-war objects of British policy was to involve the U.S.A. in greater responsibility in some areas of the world, for instance S.E. Europe and S.E. Asia, but at the same time to preserve other areas as British spheres of influence, especially the Middle East. American participation in the Allied Mission for Observing the Greek Elections in 1946, and in the Anglo-American Commission to help Siam in stimulating the export of rice in the same year, was in each case welcome. But some of the activities of the American oil companies on the Persian Gulf were much less so.

The Americans, being a strong, energetic and competitive people, are not a people for half-measures. It was impossible for weakened British Governments to harness them for one purpose and not for another; and harnessing them at all was rather like harnessing an elephant with an ox to pull the same load. It thus turned out that the U.S. Government was a difficult body to co-operate with. Either it would not co-operate at all, or it would take over the whole responsibility. This happened in succession, with first the one thing and then the other, in Greece, with the turning-point in 1947, and in Palestine, with the turning-point in 1948; and eventually it happened also in Western Europe. The Far East was another matter, since there the responsibility was recognized as predominantly American from the first. It is noteworthy that it was in the Far East that almost every case occurred of the Americans taking action which affected their allies without consulting them: for instance, in permitting the first post-war Japanese whaling expedition in August 1946, and in many of General MacArthur's decisions during the Korean War.

The outbreak of the Korean War was perhaps the most crucial of all turning-points in the U.S.A.'s relations with the rest of the alliance, especially with Britain. The preponderant role played in the war by U.S. manpower, equipment and money gave to the U.S. Government an undisputed leadership, which became world-wide because the threat was seen as world-wide. Rearmament at once became general, not related simply to a local emergency. American military aid, through 'counter-part funds', figures in the British defence budget for the first time in 1952. The Anglo-American relation has therefore to be considered henceforth as a factor in British foreign policy everywhere. It will be convenient to consider it region by region, as the locus of crisis moved to different parts of the world from 1951 to 1959, taking in order the Far East, S.E. Asia, the Middle East, Europe, and other areas; followed by particular contexts affected by the status of Anglo-American relations, such as strategy, weapons, atomic energy and trade.

The Far East

In the Far East where Britain's only independent interest was Hong Kong, with a related commercial stake in China until 1950, British Governments were generally content to follow the American lead with little question. To this rule there were two qualifications and one major exception. The first qualification concerned Japan, with which Britain's relation was different from the U.S.A.'s for reasons which have been explained.[1] The Japanese Peace Treaty of 1951 was criticized in the House of Commons for subordinating British interests to American; but it could be shown that the final draft embodied a number of British amendments.

The other qualification concerned Korea. Although it was on a British motion that the United Nations command was created under an American general, the tactical conduct of the campaign was subject to constant criticism by British politicians. At the end of 1950 Attlee flew to Washington to dissuade the American government from extending the war to China; early in 1951 Churchill gave a warning against a serious Anglo-American rift over the campaign; and Labour members accused General MacArthur of conducting policy (for instance, the decision to cross the 38th parallel) without reference to his U.N. allies.

These recriminations did not end with the dismissal of MacArthur in April 1951. For instance, the American air-raid against installations on the Yalu River in June 1952 was planned while the British Minister of Defence, Field-Marshal Lord Alexander, was in Korea, but without his knowledge; and in April 1953 the American command publicly offered a large reward to anyone on the other side who would bring across specified Russian aircraft, again without consulting the allies. There was also some divergence on the lengths to which the two Governments were prepared to go in the event of a renewal of the fighting by the Chinese; and the British Government additionally made it plain that it would not be committed to further fighting if the armistice were to be broken by the South Korean President, Syngman Rhee.[2] Even the conclusion of the armistice negotiations in July 1953 was the occasion of an Anglo-American disagreement on the next steps to be taken towards the convening of a political conference on Korea.

[1] See pp. 107-8.
[2] Sir Anthony Eden, *Full Circle*, pp. 18, 27.

The major exception, as distinct from the above qualifications, to the British Government's rule of following the American lead in the Far East concerned China. After 1949, it concerned the two rival Chinese Governments. The main issues were firstly the recognition of the Communist Government in Peking; secondly, the possession of the 'offshore islands' lying between Formosa and the mainland; and thirdly, trade with the Chinese People's Republic. The first two were matters of disagreement on tactics, but did not lead to major disputes on principle. The British Government, having consulted the Commonwealth Governments, decided to recognize the Chinese Communist Government, at least in part because the Indian Government was determined to do so. British business interests also favoured recognition, in the hope, which proved illusory, of maintaining their commercial position; and American business interests followed the same course, but without success.

At one time American recognition seemed probable sooner or later: Acheson described it only as 'premature' in January 1950, and Bevin hinted that it would come before long. The Korean War frustrated this prospect for a long time, though Dulles realistically admitted in October 1958 that the U.S.A. of course recognized the existence of the Peking Government as a fact. In 1954 their representatives met face to face in Geneva, and thereafter the American and Chinese Ambassadors in Warsaw had a long series of meetings on specific problems. On the other hand, successive American Governments of both parties set themselves firmly against admitting Communist China to the U.N. For some time the British Government sought to obtain a majority in the Security Council in favour of this course, but American opposition made it impossible. That did not, however, cause any ill-feeling between the British and American Governments. Both recognized that so long as Chinese sovereignty was irreconcilably divided, there were perhaps mutual advantages in the recognition of different Chinese Governments by the two allies. Both Labour and Conservative Governments voted for postponement of the question of China's seat at the United Nations.

The second problem, that of the islands between Formosa and the mainland, was more delicate. The British position was that legally the sovereignty of Formosa was unsettled, but that of the offshore islands rested undoubtedly with the recognized Government in Peking, that is to say with the Communists. On the other hand, the Chinese Communists were not justified, as they repeatedly threatened, especially in 1955 and again in 1958, in using force to obtain possession of the offshore islands. But Britain was not committed to going to war either for Formosa or for the offshore islands. The U.S.A., on the other hand, was committed by the Mutual Defence Treaty of 1955 to fight for Formosa, provided that Chiang Kai-Shek did not provoke attack by infringing the terms of the treaty.

Whether the U.S.A. was also committed to defend the offshore islands was less certain. Dulles was cautious on this point in 1958, but it was strongly suggested that the Chiefs of Staff believed the principal islands to be essential to the defence of Formosa. Although the British and American attitudes differed, therefore, they did not formally conflict. But to many people in Britain the distinctions seemed to be merely theoretical, because if war came in the Far East it would be hard to localize; and once Hong Kong were involved, Britain would be also. On the allied side, therefore, all depended on the exercise of American responsibility, and on the control of Chiang Kai-Shek. Given these requirements, and given tact and clarity on both parts, there was no reason why Formosa and the offshore islands need seriously prejudice Anglo-American relations.

In the third case, that of trade with China, nothing could conceal the basic conflict of British and American interest. Britain's main interest in China had been commercial, and the *raison d'être* of Hong Kong was trade with China (though the economy of the island was transformed by other developments after the Second World War). British Governments and traders were exceedingly reluctant to give up their commerce with China: on the contrary, they wished to build it up. Although, therefore, Britain supported the embargo on strategic trade with China voted by the U.N. in May 1951, trade which was definable as non-strategic continued on a fairly considerable scale. Hong Kong became a licensed loophole for this purpose. But many Americans, including particularly General MacArthur, could not see the fine distinctions drawn between strategic and non-strategic trade, while Americans were being killed by Chinese troops in Korea. Bitter attacks were made in the U.S.A. on British trading with China, and some of them were echoed in the House of Commons, though the published figures seldom supported the charges made.

The attacks continued even after the end of the Korean War, becoming particularly virulent in the summer of 1953. This was one instance, however, in which Britain refused to bow to her ally's wishes. Most of the other European members of N.A.T.O. which had overseas trading interests shared Britain's resistance to American policy; and so did Canada. Finally, in May 1957, restrictions on trade with China were modified to coincide with those on trade with the U.S.S.R., having previously been much more severe; and in August 1958 both were further relaxed. The U.S.A. expressed disappointment, but no more. By 1959 it had become unlikely that anything short of a new major crisis would revive this once controversial issue as an irritant between the British and U.S. Governments.

South-East Asia

In S.E. Asia there were no serious questions affecting Anglo-American relations until the Indo-China crisis of 1954. Before the rise of Communist China American interest in the area was slight, though the U.S. Government was sufficiently discriminatory in its supply of arms to its allies to permit their shipment to Malaya, during the emergency beginning in 1948, while it would not permit the same to Indonesia or Indo-China. One of the few early embarrassments to Anglo-American relations was caused by the establishment of considerable Kuomintang Chinese forces in northern Burma after their defeat in China. Burma, in spite of having left the Commonwealth, looked upon Britain still as a kind of protecting power; and the Americans were suspected of clandestinely supplying the Chinese forces there. The British Government's suggestion in February 1952 that a fact-finding mission should be sent to northern Burma was resented in the U.S.A.

Prior to 1954, the only other serious rift in Anglo-American relations that deserves mention in the context of S.E. Asia was the formation in 1951 of the A.N.Z.U.S. Pact by Australia, New Zealand and the U.S.A., from which Britain was excluded. The formal reason for the exclusion was that if Britain were included, then Malaya must be covered by the treaty (as it later was by the A.N.Z.A.M. defence agreement); and then there would be no justification for excluding Indo-China and the French.

By 1954 the Americans' reluctance to be involved with French responsibilities for Indo-China had been completely reversed. Published accounts of the allied consultations in March and April 1954 show that by then the U.S. Government was contemplating the extension of the Indo-China war by a major intervention, possibly including the use of nuclear weapons. The British Government resisted this policy, and the French viewed it without enthusiasm. A serious disagreement took place between Dulles and Eden during hurried consultations in London and Paris in April, as a result of which contradictory accounts were given out of what had been agreed and recriminations followed. The U.S. Government continued to plan a possible intervention even while the Geneva Conference on the Far East was in progress.[1]

The essence of the disagreement, however, was not whether Britain should become involved in the fighting then in progress in Indo-China, against which the British Government's mind was firmly set. It was rather whether steps to form a collective defence organization should be begun at once, as Dulles wanted, or only after the Geneva Conference on the Far East, which was about to begin, as Eden wanted. The latter policy prevailed, and S.E.A.T.O. was the result. But even after S.E.A.T.O. had been created by the Manila Treaty in September, uneasiness was felt in Britain about the reservation which the U.S. Government unilaterally attached to the treaty, limiting its application only to the case of Communist aggression. After 1954 British and American policies moved more harmoniously in S.E. Asia, particularly in supporting the unexpectedly successful Government of Southern Vietnam under Diem.

The Middle East

In the Middle East Anglo-American relations followed a more chequered course, partly no doubt because both powers, instead of only one of the two, have important interests. Since the Second World War the principal episodes in which their respective policies became mutually involved were the emergence of Israel, the Iranian oil crisis of 1951–3, the various Anglo-Egyptian discords from 1951 to 1956, the Baghdad Pact, the conflicts between Saudi Arabia and the British-protected sheikhdoms on the Persian Gulf, the Cyprus dispute from 1954 to 1959, and the crises in Iraq, Jordan and the Lebanon in 1957–8. These episodes span practically the whole period under review, and show American sympathies fairly equally divided. They were mainly against British policy over the emergence of Israel (but not later), in the early stages of the Anglo-Iranian oil dispute (but not at the end of it), and above all in the final stages of the protracted Anglo-Egyptian dispute (but not throughout it). They were mainly in agreement with British policy in the formation of the Baghdad Pact and in reacting to the crises of 1958. In the conflicts between Saudi Arabia and some of the minor rulers under British protection on the Persian Gulf, there appeared to be some ambivalence between the policy of the U.S. Government, which supported the British Government, and the conduct of the

[1] Sir Anthony Eden, *Full Circle*, chapters V and VI.

principal American oil company in Saudi Arabia, ARAMCO. There was even talk of the oil companies having their own foreign policy during the Anglo-Iranian oil dispute. But such gossip was exaggerated.

By the later 1950s there was in fact no fundamental difference of purpose between Britain and the U.S.A. in the Middle East. It was always customary to announce complete agreement whenever the area was discussed: in September 1949, for instance, between Acheson and Bevin in Washington; in May 1950, when the U.S.A., Britain and France made their Tripartite Declaration guaranteeing the *status quo* in the Middle East; in January 1952, when Churchill and Eden visited Washington soon after returning to power; and in February 1956, again in Washington, when Eden visited the U.S.A. as Prime Minister. Actions seemed sometimes to bely the words, however. When the Iranian and Egyptian crises began in 1951, there was a strong impression in Britain that the U.S. Ambassadors in both countries were markedly hostile to British interests; and it was no secret that in 1954 American pressure preceded, if it did not cause, the British decision to sign a new Anglo-Egyptian Treaty. It is fair to say, however, that the differences were matters of tactics, interpretation and emphasis, not of fundamental aims. They arose from the fact that the two countries had interests which, though similar, were not identical. In each case these interests fell under the same three heads: political, economic and strategic.

The political interest of both countries lay in the stability, prosperity, peace and independence of the states of the Middle East. But each had different commitments. After the war the British had a commitment to the Jews under the Balfour Declaration of 1917, and conflicting commitments to various Arab states: some as a result of undertakings also made in the First World War; some as a result of inter-war Mandates (Iraq and Transjordan); some as a result of treaties of more or less recent date (the sheikhdoms on the Persian Gulf, the Aden Protectorates, Egypt and Iraq); and many as a result of occupation and undertakings in the Second World War (Egypt, Iraq, Libya, the Levant states). American commitments were different. To the Jews they had a moral commitment arising from Jewish suffering under Hitler coupled with the strength of Zionism in the U.S.A. and the influence of the Jewish vote in American politics. To the Arabs they had no formal engagements at the level of governments, but an important stake in the oil of Saudi Arabia. As events developed it proved in fact more difficult to harmonize the British and American interests internally than with each other, for almost any promise to the Jews and almost any promise to the Arabs were likely sooner or later to come into conflict.

The high-water mark of Anglo-American co-operation in the Middle East was reached in the Tripartite Declaration made jointly with the French in May 1950, guaranteeing the peace and stability of the area and the maintenance of the existing frontiers and armistice lines against violation by force. The lowest ebb was reached twice. The first occasion was in the Palestine War of 1948–9, when American and British nationals were in fact engaged, though only as individuals, on opposite sides, and the Jews and Arabs were using American and British weapons against each other. The second low ebb was reached in the Suez Canal crisis of 1956, when the lines of co-operation were paradoxically reversed. The latter was the one major occasion of mutual interest when a British Government acted without consulting the U.S. Government, though not without knowing what its advice would have been.

The conflict between Jews and Arabs was not the only political source of disagreement between the U.S.A. and Britain in the Middle East. There was also the social and political revolution within the states of the area, which had been precipitated by the impact of the West since the nineteenth century. The whole process of modernization had been set in motion by the Western impact: industry, medicine, civil administration, education, the armed forces and so on were all, in their modern forms, created by the West. So was the ferment of political ideas, including nationalism and military Socialism. The revolutionary tide of which President Nasser became the symbol was therefore the product of British, French and American influences. But the degree of sympathy shown towards these new developments was not the same. The French had resisted them, except in so far as they conformed with French cultural and political predominance, and had lost. The Americans and the British broadly sympathized with them, except in so far as they conflicted with existing engagements to the older political systems.

In the American case, the exception consisted at first only of Saudi Arabia, to whose ruling family the U.S.A. owed the tenure of the ARAMCO oil concession and its air base at Dhahran. In the British case, the exception covered the monarchical régimes originally established in most of the area: Egypt, Libya, Jordan (formerly Transjordan), Iraq, the Persian Gulf sheikhdoms (especially Kuweit), as well as Iran (which is not an Arab state). Both the Americans and the British were uneasy about their associations with political systems which were so easily represented as archaic and undemocratic. Each was also readier to see the mote in the other's eye than the beam in his own. Neither could find a ready-made way out of the dilemma. Indeed, by 1957 the U.S. Government actually enlarged its commitment to the seemingly outdated type of political system by declaring the integrity of Jordan (which meant the maintenance of the Hashemite dynasty on the throne) to be of vital importance. By that date British and American policies were very close together; but they were united in a dilemma and not a solution.

The economic differences between British and American policy were matters of degree. To Britain the Middle East is vital as a source of oil: between 40 and 50 per cent of the oil consumed in Britain comes from Kuweit, more than 10 per cent from Iraq, and Iran and the other Persian Gulf states are also important suppliers. Middle East oil also makes a large contribution to the balance of payments. And the Suez Canal is valuable, if not vital, as an artery of trade. None of these considerations applies in anything like the same degree to the U.S.A., which is not yet dependent on Middle East oil (though some is imported to the American continent) and which has little trade through the Suez Canal. These facts account for the relatively detached view that the U.S. Government was able to take of the Anglo-Iranian oil dispute in 1951 and of the long-drawn-out dispute with Egypt from 1951 to 1956. When American intervention eventually came in these disputes, it was not because American economic interests were involved: there has probably never yet been an American economic interest outside the American hemisphere so crucial as to make the risk of war acceptable to the U.S.A. In each case the danger which involved American interests was strategic. In Iran there was the possibility that Mussadiq would be succeeded by Communism and hence by Soviet control in 1953. In Egypt there was the possibility that the Western defence position would be fatally weakened, if not destroyed. The flow of Iranian oil and traffic through the Suez Canal, which were Britain's main preoccupations, were relatively matters of indifference to the U.S.A.

Strategically, the Middle East is from the American point of view a large and important link in a global chain of defence round the Soviet periphery. It is also the land-mass between the Soviet Union and Africa. For Britain the strategic view is different. The Middle East had once been important as the land-mass lying across the route from

Europe to India, but with the liquidation of the Indian Empire this had become less important. After the Second World War, with the emergence of many new and discontented states, the military danger to peace and stability in the Middle East arose no longer primarily from external attack but from internal conflicts, within or between the new states. The external danger still existed, and the Baghdad Pact was formed to contain it; but the main source of potential conflict lay within the area, particularly in the creation of Israel. What was therefore chiefly needed, in the British view, was no longer a major base in the Middle East to support a major theatre of war against external invasion, but an advanced protective post from which minor operations could be quickly launched against eruptions within the area. This was the military argument which justified the signature of the Anglo-Egyptian Treaty of 1954 and the transfer of the British Middle East G.H.Q. from the Canal Zone to Cyprus. The argument was reinforced by Churchill's belief that the invention of the hydrogen-bomb had enormously reduced the danger of a Third World War, and had also rendered the Canal Zone base obsolete.

British strategic thinking was thus guided by new considerations. The danger of global war and the threat of the Soviet Union to the Middle East were both regarded as secondary to the danger of local war and the explosive potentialities of local nationalism. From the American point of view the balance of danger was the opposite. Neither party discounted the other's calculations and fears, but each made its own rather different assessment. To the Americans, the threat of war in the Middle East was seen rather in terms of war involving the U.S.S.R. and the U.S.A. and therefore a global and not a local war; and the dangers of nationalism were secondary to those of Communism. What provoked strong American reactions was the fear that Iran would go Communist in 1953, or Syria in 1957, or Iraq in 1959. What concerned Britain, at the same time, was primarily the danger to British interests from nationalist dictators, not the loss of allied bases to Soviet control. The consequence was that the British and U.S. Governments often took different views of the same nationalist movement or leader in the Middle East; and when they took the same view, it was often for different reasons. In the British calculation, economic interests would tend to be uppermost, and in the American, strategic.

The contrast was well illustrated by the two concurrent interventions in the Lebanon and Jordan in 1958. The Americans intervened in the Lebanon to prevent the security of the Middle East being undermined by what they saw as Communist-inspired subversion. The British intervened in Jordan to safeguard the oil supplies of the area against the risk of an extension of the Iraqi revolution. Defence played a part in British calculations, too. In the intervention against Egypt in 1956 strategic and economic considerations had equal weight. In the struggle to retain Cyprus, strategic considerations were uppermost; though over Cyprus too Eden pointed out in June 1956 that the crucial consideration was oil. But in any case defence always meant, to the British, primarily the defence of trade. To the Americans it did not: it meant world-wide defence against the global threat of Communist aggression.

The primacy of strategy in the Americans' thinking was shown by their support, though not unwavering, of the British policy in Cyprus and in the Baghdad Pact. When American support wavered, it was because of the traditional instinct to encourage nationalist movements for independence among small and formerly dependent nations. When, for instance, the participation of American negotiators alongside the British in the Anglo-Iranian oil dispute in 1951, or in the Anglo-Egyptian treaty negotiations in 1953, led to objections by the nationalist leaders that the West was combining against them, the Americans soon dropped out, instinctively avoiding the implied reproach of 'colonialism'. That instinct was more fully developed in the State Department than in the Pentagon. The dilemma between them was apparent in American policy everywhere, and Dulles was the embodiment of the dilemma.

Africa

In other parts of the world overlapping British and American interests were not generally a source of disagreement, either because there was no overlap, or because the interests were identical. Africa outside the Middle East presented the Anglo-American relation with few problems up to the late 1950s. In North Africa the difficulties lay almost entirely between the Americans and the French rather than the British. South of the Sahara the strictly international aspect of Africa's problems was only just beginning to emerge. It was noticeable, however, that the Americans were showing increased interest in Africa in the late 1950s. They were much less insistent there than they had been in Asia on the evils of 'colonialism' and the desirability of an early end to colonial rule, though its early end was already certain.

There were, no doubt, two reasons for this new attitude, which were both aspects of the desire that Africa should not be exposed to Soviet and Communist influences. One was that Africa is so located strategic-ally that it could be an important bastion against further extensions of the Soviet empire, whereas its loss to Soviet control would constitute a serious threat to the security of the U.S.A., on the assumption that Soviet intentions were aggressive. The second reason was that Africa is an important and largely untapped source of minerals, in which the American continent is becoming progressively less self-sufficient. This fact had been recognized by the Materials Policy Commission as early as 1952. The upshot was that Britain appeared to be able to count on a more sympathetic attitude towards colonial developments in Africa than elsewhere.

Latin America

In the American hemisphere British interests are slight compared to those of the U.S.A. That would seem to point to a natural sense of solidarity, but it has not always been the case. The British and American governments had a common interest in the oil resources of Venezuela, where few differences arose between them. They agreed in disliking the Peronista régime in the Argentine, though for different reasons. They also generally agreed in disliking the other dictatorships of Latin America, but as the overthrow of one dictator so often led only to the establishment of another, there was a danger that the two Governments might unwittingly get out of step. The American Government resented the British Government's refusal to support its condemnation of the quasi-Communist Government of Arbenz in Guatemala in 1954, to which in fact arms were being supplied in British ships at the time when the Americans were helping to contrive its overthrow. Similarly in 1958 British arms were supplied to the Government of Cuba under Batista at the height of the rebellion against it led by Fidel Castro; but American sympathies for Castro later turned sour. On the other hand, the U.S. Government showed rather more sympathy for British commitments in Latin America. At meetings of the Organization of American States, for instance, both at Bogotà in 1948 and at Caracas in 1954, the U.S. representatives opposed resolutions, which were otherwise over-whelmingly supported, against European powers possessing territory on the American continent.

Europe

In Europe, once out of the aftermath of war (when there had been serious Anglo-American rifts over liberated Greece and Italy), there was an interlude of passivity until after the establishment of N.A.T.O. The Americans regretted, though perhaps they understood, the British reluctance to join European institutions such as the European Coal and Steel Community, the European Defence Community and the European Economic Community or 'Common Market'. Though both countries agreed upon the essentials of defence against the Soviet Bloc, the Americans showed a greater sense of urgency in extending the North Atlantic Alliance: first, paradoxically, to the Eastern Mediterranean, to include Greece and Turkey, in which Britain more hesitantly acquiesced; and then, more logically, to include Spain, from which Britain recoiled. Over the admission of Germany to N.A.T.O. they were agreed, though perhaps for different reasons. Over the appointment of an American Admiral in 1952 to command the allied naval forces in the Atlantic, British pride (and in particular Churchill's) suffered a painful humiliation. The appointment of an American Admiral to command the allied naval forces in the Mediterranean was also suggested, but not put into effect. In all these matters, the Americans again showed their primary concern for the most efficient organization of the allied defence and strategy rather than for inter-allied politics. The same consideration remained paramount whenever negotiation with the Soviet Government was in view.

For the Americans friendship and hostility were absolutes. There were no gradations between them: that is why Indian policy was so much disliked in the U.S.A. Dulles argued that neutrality was an obsolete conception, though Eisenhower appeared to hold a more elastic view. By the same argument, it was difficult for the Americans to accept partial settlements, such as 'disengagement'. The fundamental questions were: should American troops remain in Europe or not? – should Germany be democratically reunited or not? – should the allies make an overall settlement with the U.S.S.R. or not? These questions demanded categorical answers, not diplomatic ambiguities. If the allies wished the answers to the first two questions to be affirmative, as they apparently did, then the answer to the last must be negative. The British Government sought a more flexible approach, as was shown both by the popularity of the debate on 'disengagement' in 1958–9 and by the general feeling that the Prime Minister did well to visit Moscow in the spring of 1959. The Americans, with the encouragement of the West German Government, still favoured a more uncompromising position, and largely had their own way so far as the approach to the Summit was concerned. But a changing pattern of relationships was already emerging, as was shown by the eventual exchange of visits at the highest level between the U.S. and Soviet Governments. Eisenhower with Herter as his Secretary of State appeared to be a different man from Eisenhower with Dulles.

So far as Anglo-American relations were concerned, two elements of the changing pattern can be distinguished. In the first place, although far from total independence, Britain was growing steadily stronger on her own. Possession of nuclear weapons up to the megaton range was not the only symbol. There was also a great and steady improvement in the balance of payments, not least in the American market. This showed itself in the approach to convertibility at the end of 1958, and the relaxation of controls on dollar imports. British competition in the U.S. market in particular became strikingly successful, in part because of a more liberal attitude towards protection on the part of Eisenhower's Government. There were setbacks, such as the rejection of the lowest tender by a British firm for the Chief Joseph Dam in 1953 and the delay in granting B.O.A.C. the right to operate a service across the Pacific in 1959; but these were exceptions that caught the public eye, and they generally ended in satisfactory compromises. The diminution of British dependence on American aid is shown by the following comparison: from 1945–51 Britain received in grants and loans from the U.S.A. about £1,800,000,000 and repaid nothing; from 1952–9 Britain received about £673,000,000 and repaid £230,000,000. The country was thus well on the way to fulfilling Eden's condition for playing its special part in the world.

In the second place, the U.S.A. was finding that 'interdependence' was a relationship just as necessary to the biggest ally as to the smaller ones. The illusion of self-sufficiency was over. The U.S.A. was becoming a net importer instead of a net exporter; and among the imports were certain goods, particularly strategic minerals, which could not be replaced from within the U.S.A. The capacity of the U.S. Government to play Santa Claus to the world was seriously reduced by 1959. There were even serious balance of payments difficulties owing to the scale of foreign aid. Moreover, considerations of defence in the age of missiles made alliances an absolute necessity, at least so long as the U.S.S.R. had a lead in long-range missiles such as the *sputniks* appeared to imply. It was necessary for the U.S.A. to establish missile bases in Europe to offset the Soviet advantage, at least temporarily, and Britain was among the most dependable and best-located allies for the purpose. In return, the U.S. Government became more forthcoming about pooling resources in atomic research and weapons supply. The McMahon Act of 1946, which forbade the sharing of U.S. atomic secrets, was partially superseded by fresh legislation in 1958, of which Britain was the immediate beneficiary. A series of agreements in 1957 and 1958 gave Britain a privileged position in co-operating with the U.S.A. in the nuclear field, and also the promise of American ballistic missiles under British control. These agreements went some way to restoring the Anglo-American partnership of the Second World War in the atomic field.

Thus the U.S. Government was becoming more conscious of its dependence on allies, particularly Britain, at the same time as Britain was becoming more conscious of her ability to stand on her own legs. But simultaneously there was also a paradoxically contrary trend in the American view of the great-power relation. It seemed as if there were a growing awareness both in Washington and in Moscow that the two greatest of the great powers stood out so conspicuously from the rest that the ultimate issues, as has been said, lay in their power alone; and that they could and therefore must be resolved by those two powers alone. This thinking, disguised though it was by an elaborate parade of preliminary inter-allied consultation, appeared to lie behind the dramatic decision of Eisenhower and Khrushchev in 1959 to exchange visits to each other's countries, even though only half of the decision was eventually carried out.

Their personal conversations *tête à tête* were perhaps more important in the eyes of both leaders than the four-power Summit Conference to which they were supposed to be a preliminary. Second in importance, and again probably surpassing the Summit, were the preliminary soundings which each took in the capitals of Europe and Asia, each among his own friends. So far as Eisenhower was concerned, London was at best *primus inter pares* in this context. The one forum in which the British Government (and incidentally the French Government also) would sit exclusively on equal terms with the U.S. and Soviet Governments was perhaps the least decisive in the long run, though the most prominent in the short. In the traditional four-power form, it was perhaps also obsolete. It was still uncertain whether the U.S. and Soviet heads of Government would eventually prefer a bilateral or a multilateral settlement of the world's problems, but they were increasingly less likely to persist with a quadrilateral settlement. This was a probability of which any British Government must take note.

8

The Devolution of Empire

THE Commonwealth is not an alliance, but it appears in the great majority of the post-war Defence White Papers as an important factor in one form or another, beginning with 'the Empire' and 'the Dominions and India' in 1946. The present chapter is not concerned with the structure, function or significance of the Commonwealth, which will be later discussed in chapter 12, but with the particular influence of the Commonwealth countries, singly and collectively, on British policy from 1945 to 1959. There are two parts to this question: the role of the independent countries, and the evolution of the colonies towards self-government or independence.

In the first category come Canada, Australia, New Zealand and the Union of South Africa throughout; India and Pakistan from 1947; Ceylon from 1948; the Central African Federation, with qualifications, from 1953; Ghana and Malaya from 1957. Nigeria is to be added to the list from 1960, Sierra Leone from 1961, and the West Indies eventually. Singapore and Cyprus entered into an intermediate position in 1959. The rest of the former British Empire consisted still of dependent territories in various categories, which will be described collectively by the loose but convenient term of 'colonies'. The term 'Commonwealth' is normally used only to cover the independent states: those, that is, which are represented at the periodical conferences of Prime Ministers, and with which relations are conducted through the C.R.O. (Commonwealth Relations Office) instead of the Foreign Office; though there are exceptions to both rules.

Since the importance of developments in the Commonwealth and Colonies is habitually underestimated in Britain as a factor in international affairs, and since it is impossible to attempt a complete historical survey of such developments in the post-war period, it may be convenient to take a sample period for scrutiny, to serve two purposes. One purpose is to show that Commonwealth and Colonial affairs necessarily bulked very large indeed among the influences on British foreign policy, especially towards the end of the period under review. The other is to give a brief synoptic view of the comparative progress of developments in different parts of the world, showing success in some areas, failure in others, and the general international context for all. The most useful period for this purpose, because one of the most crowded and most recent, is the first few months of 1959. The initial survey which follows is merely chronological: it is simply a diary of Commonwealth and Colonial events from January to May 1959 inclusive.

On 5 January the Malta Constitution of 1947 was revoked after the final breakdown of discussions between the British and Maltese Governments in London. On 8 January Nkrumah, the Prime Minister of Ghana, left India after an official visit. On his return to Ghana, he reconstructed his Government as a consequence of an alleged conspiracy to destroy it by force. On 19 January the so-called 'Treason Trial' of persons accused of conspiracy against the Government opened in South Africa. On 21 January proposals were announced for a new constitution of Basutoland, a British protectorate geographically within the Union of South Africa. On 25 January an open-air meeting of followers of the African National Congress took place in Nyasaland, which later gave rise to official belief in a conspiracy against the Government of the Central African Federation. At the end of the month a meeting of the ministerial council of the Baghdad Pact (including Britain and Pakistan) took place in Karachi. During the month progress was made towards a settlement of the dispute over Cyprus, at a meeting in Zürich between the Greek and Turkish Prime Ministers.

In February a settlement was reached for the future of Cyprus, first by an agreement between the Greek and Turkish Governments on the 11th, followed by a tripartite agreement between them and the British Government on the 19th. It was left uncertain at that stage whether Cyprus would remain within the Commonwealth when it became independent in 1960. During the month there were debates on both Cyprus and Malta in the House of Commons. A new political party was formed in the Central African Federation, led by Garfield Todd, who as Prime Minister of Southern Rhodesia had proved too advanced a liberal for most of his previous followers in 1958. In the middle of the month the Indonesian Foreign Minister visited Australia and New Zealand. There was criticism in Australia of the communiqué issued after the visit, so far as it touched on the disputed territory of West Irian (Western New Guinea), on the ground that its tone was hostile to the Dutch. At the end of the month the South African Government introduced bills for the enforcement of *apartheid* in the universities. The British Prime Minister and Foreign Secretary visited the Soviet Union from 21 February to 3 March, and it was emphasized later in the House of Commons that the Commonwealth Governments had been kept informed of what passed.

At the beginning of March grave disorders broke out in Nyasaland, which were attributed by a subsequent inquiry[1] to African distrust of the Central African Federation. The leader of the African National Congress, Dr. Hastings Banda, was arrested, and so were many of his followers, under emergency regulations. Almost simultaneously incidents at a camp for Mau Mau detainees at Hola in Kenya led to the deaths of eleven Africans. These ugly events distracted public attention from the fact that on 2 March the House of Commons gave an unopposed extension to the Colonial Development and Welfare Act until 1964. On 6 March a Ghana Regiment of Infantry was formed with the Queen as Colonel-in-Chief. On the same day a new Defence Agreement was signed by Pakistan with the U.S.A. and bitterly attacked by Nehru. On 13 March the Ceylon Government terminated the state of emergency which had been proclaimed in May 1958. On the same day the General Assembly of the United Nations approved resolutions on the future of the British and French Cameroons: the latter being due for independence in 1960, and the former to be the subject of a plebiscite. On 15 March the Northern Region of Nigeria acquired internal self-government. Two days later the Tanganyika Legislative Council met after the first elections to be held for thirty elected seats, which were mainly won by supporters of Julius Nyerere. On 23 March the appointment of an Indian general as Deputy G.O.C. of the Malayan Federation Army was announced. On 27 March the first General Election was held in British Somaliland, and on the same day the first provisional Cypriot Government was formed under Archbishop Makarios.

At the beginning of April Michael Blundell, a Minister in the Kenya Government, resigned in order to form a new party of moderates of all races. On 5 April the Dalai Lama of Tibet arrived in India after a dramatic escape from Chinese Communist forces. On 6 April a new African Affairs Board of the Central African Federation was appointed. On the same day the Ghana Government secured the passage of a bill unseating two opposition M.P.s. On 9 April the commission of inquiry into the riots in Nyasaland, under Mr. Justice Devlin, arrived

[1] *Report of the Nyasaland Commission of Enquiry* (Cmmd. 814, July 1959), usually known as the 'Devlin Report'.

in the Central African Federation. On the following day a prominent South African Nationalist, Du Plessis, was expelled from the party for criticizing its racial policy. On 15 April the former Mau Mau leader, Jomo Kenyatta, was released from imprisonment, but his movements were restricted. On 17 April the Governments of India and Pakistan signed a provisional agreement ending their dispute over the Indus waters. By the end of the month the St. Lawrence Seaway, connecting the American and Canadian lakes with the Atlantic, was open to navigation. In May self-government was conferred on Jamaica within the Federation of the West Indies. In the same month the first elections under the new constitution were held in Singapore, and won by the left-wing Chinese, the People's Action Party.

The foregoing paragraphs contain an indiscriminate, kaleidoscopic picture of events taking place under the ultimate aegis of the British Crown, or at least within the Commonwealth of which the Queen is titular Head, during a brief, arbitrarily chosen period. Incomplete as they are, they serve nevertheless to illustrate the fact that for Britain, Commonwealth affairs are an integral part of international affairs: for instance, the catalogue of events involves, apart from the Commonwealth, seven other sovereign states as well – the U.S.S.R., the U.S.A., China, France, Indonesia, Greece and Turkey. The catalogue also serves to illustrate all the types of question raised in Britain's foreign policy by her Commonwealth connexions. There is, first, the growing independence of action of the members of the Commonwealth; secondly, the desire for consultation between them; thirdly, the progress of former colonies towards either complete independence or responsible self-government; fourthly, the setbacks experienced in many cases during that progress; fifthly, the impact of disputes within the Commonwealth; and sixthly, the importance of economic considerations to both the independent members of the Commonwealth and the Colonies.

Independent Countries

The trend of the Commonwealth countries towards independent policies became most marked after 1947, when India and Pakistan became independent. Before 1947 independent action by the Dominions in the field of foreign affairs had been relatively rare. Canada had entered into separate defence commitments with the U.S.A. in 1940, for obvious reasons connected with the progress of the war, but the first treaty signed by Australia and New Zealand to which Britain was not a party, the A.N.Z.U.S. Pact, came only in 1951. A new era began in 1947, marked by the change of title of the Secretary of State for the Dominions to the Secretary of State for Commonwealth Relations. The leading roles in enlarging the sphere of independent action were then taken jointly by one of the oldest and one of the newest member-states, Australia and India; for although Canada also developed a strong individuality, it was chiefly in association with the U.S.A. and Britain, and as a bridge between the two, that she did so.

Events in S.E. Asia provided the context for the joint début of Australia and India as independent agents at the United Nations. They combined to bring the Indonesian situation to the attention of the U.N. in July 1947, when Britain was more concerned with the question whether this was a matter of 'domestic jurisdiction' for the Dutch. The Dutch 'police action' of December 1948 was bitterly criticized by Australia at the U.N., although Britain continued to argue that the U.N. was not competent in the dispute. The Indians took the initiative in convening a conference at Delhi on Indonesia in January 1949. Thereafter the paths of the two Dominions divided. Although Nehru criticized the Indonesian Government, he could never support it against the 'colonial' Dutch. Australia, on the other hand, supported the Dutch Government in its retention of Western New Guinea (West Irian), the eastern half of which was under Australian administration. In May 1950, when President Sukarno claimed West Irian, Australia withdrew her Ambassador from Indonesia. But being acutely conscious of the size and potential importance of her northern neighbour, Australia sedulously avoided a decisive conflict, and tried to play so far as possible a neutral role between the Dutch and the Indonesians. Britain was of course interested in Australian policy in this matter, and was fully informed of it; but it was an Australian and not an Anglo-Australian policy.

S.E. Asia and the Far East were naturally the areas where Australian policy was most distinctive. Defence planning in the Pacific was expressly devolved on to Australia as a result of the conference of Common-wealth Prime Ministers in 1946. The Australian Government took a strong line against easy terms for Japan in the Peace Treaty, and her anxiety led to the formation of the A.N.Z.U.S. Pact in 1951. A series of attempts by the British Government to secure at least observer status in the Pact were unsuccessful: President Eisenhower said pointedly in May 1954 that the Commonwealth countries most concerned in S.E. Asia were Australia and New Zealand. Neither country had any

intention of weakening its connexion with Britain, as they both showed
later by joining in the A.N.Z.A.M. defence system, under which they
contributed forces to the defence of Malaya in 1954. But in Australia,
if less so in New Zealand, there was a determination to have a separate
foreign policy, in which countries outside the Commonwealth would
also play a part. The same rule applied in matters of trade. Australia
did not regard the system of Imperial Preference as sacrosanct when it
was found necessary to impose import restrictions in 1955; and in 1957
a new trade agreement was negotiated with Britain, superseding the
Ottawa rules. But still in matters of national interest lying outside
Australia's direct experience, such as the Middle East, she was content
to follow Britain's lead. The Australian Government agreed to take
part in the abortive plan for a Middle East Defence Organization in
1951, and loyally supported the British Government throughout the
Suez Canal crisis in 1956.

India showed less deference to Britain's policies and judgement.
Nehru pursued a distinctive line towards the Korean War, the Japanese
Peace Treaty, and the recognition of Communist China; towards the
formation of defence pacts such as S.E.A.T.O. and the Baghdad Pact,
which he abhorred; towards the Soviet Union, from which he received
economic aid; and particularly towards the Suez Canal crisis and the
concurrent crisis in Hungary. He established himself as a figure, not
merely of regional, but of world-wide importance, especially by his
visits to the U.S.A. and to Europe in 1956, and also in the conferences
of Commonwealth Prime Ministers. He found himself constantly at
loggerheads with his Commonwealth neighbour, Pakistan, and also
with the U.S.A., which distrusted the policy which it called 'neutralism'
and he called 'non-alignment'. Nehru was personally responsible for
India's decision not to leave the Commonwealth, either on attaining
independence in 1947 or after Britain's action against Egypt in 1956.

He came to be regarded as a major asset to the Commonwealth,
particularly as a bridge of communication with Communist China and
with the new states both inside and outside the Commonwealth. There
was almost no subject in the field of international affairs on which his
opinion was not valued, and in some cases it might usefully have been
followed when it was not: for instance, the Indian plan for the Suez
Canal at the London conference in August 1956 would have been
difficult to oppose if Britain had adopted it, and would have salvaged
more for British interests than did the use of force. On the other hand,
many people in Britain as well as the U.S.A. disliked the closeness of

Nehru's association with the Communist Powers; and his principal representative abroad, Krishna Menon, was widely disliked.

Of the other independent members of the Commonwealth, each asserted some degree of separateness of foreign policy in its own way. Pakistan entered into defence treaties separately with the U.S.A. as well as into S.E.A.T.O. and the Baghdad Pact. Alone of the countries in the Sterling Area, Pakistan decided against following Britain's lead in devaluation automatically in 1949. Ceylon openly evaded the embargo on strategic trade with Communist China from 1951. Ceylon and South Africa both insisted on the closure of British bases on their territory in 1957. Canada played a leading part in bringing to a halt the Anglo-French expedition against Egypt in 1956. Perhaps to the surprise of the British Government, the Commonwealth Governments in general rather encouraged than discouraged Britain's participation in European institutions, particularly those of an economic character. All of them, however, were agreed upon one cardinal point, which was the importance of consultation within the Commonwealth on matters of international importance. In the nature of things this meant primarily consultation by the British Government of the Commonwealth Governments, for the Commonwealth was still a community with much closer and readier links between the centre and the periphery than around the periphery. But at the United Nations consultation was genuinely multilateral. The desire for it had an important limiting effect on British policy, as was shown by the one major exception to the practice.

It was not a new policy. For instance, consultation of the Commonwealth played a crucial role in the abdication crisis of 1936 and in the Munich crisis of 1938. It was constantly practised during the war, though not always so much as some Governments wished. After the war, it became more perfunctory for a time, apart from the series of Prime Ministers' conferences, which became at least biennial and sometimes annual events. But consultation could never be treated lightly. As an example, when in May 1946 Attlee incorrectly told the House of Commons that the Dominion Governments had been consulted about negotiations then in progress with Egypt, he later had to withdraw the statement. The growing practice of consultation was exemplified by the discussions between Dominion representatives in London in March 1947 before the conference at Geneva on an International Trade Organization; by the conference in Canberra in August 1947 on the possible terms of a Japanese Peace Treaty; by discussions in 1948 on the desirability of Britain's participation in European institutions; by the negotiation of a joint Commonwealth loan to Burma in 1949; by discussions on the recognition of Communist China in 1950, which led to separate decisions in favour of recognition by Britain, India and Pakistan, and against recognition by Canada, Australia, New Zealand and South Africa; and by constant discussions between delegations at the United Nations, especially on critical matters such as the Korean War.

The outstanding exception was the Anglo-French action against Egypt in 1956, about which the Commonwealth Governments were neither consulted nor informed in advance. Since it was known in advance what advice they would give if consulted, it is arguable that the British Government, having no doubt what action it ought to take, did better to act without their advice rather than against it. Eden has also argued that there was too little time for effective consultation.[1] But not to have informed them in advance was less easily forgiven; and the shock caused by this case was so severe that in subsequent actions of importance, such as the intervention in Jordan in 1958 and Macmillan's visit to Moscow in 1959, special stress was laid in the public announcements on the fact that Commonwealth Governments had been either consulted or informed.

Between 1945 and 1959 the circle of consultation was enlarged by the addition of India and Pakistan (1947), Ceylon (1948), and Ghana and Malaya (1957). The Central African Federation, though still not fully independent, was represented at Prime Ministers' conferences by Lord Malvern as a mark of his personal eminence from 1953, and his successor, Sir Roy Welensky, inherited the same right. The Federation of the West Indies came into being in 1958 and Nigeria was due for full independence in 1960. During the same period three states either left the Commonwealth or rejected the opportunity to join it: Burma (1948), the Republic of Ireland (1949) and the Sudan (1953). One other diminution of numbers was due to the merger of Newfoundland, a former Dominion and the oldest associated with the British Crown, with Canada in 1949. Of all these developments, the most difficult and painful were those of India and Malaya. India's destiny occupied a great deal of the British Government's time and energy from 1945 to 1947, and Malaya's from 1948. The two were also overlapped by the problem of Palestine, a British commitment if not a British colony.

The policy for India which the Labour Government inherited from

[1] *Full Circle*, p. 526.

the wartime coalition was intended to achieve independence within the Commonwealth without partition. In the closing months of the war a White Paper was issued proposing reform of the Executive Council to make it more representative, and a conference was held at Simla by the Viceroy to plan the course ahead. It was on that occasion, in June 1945, that Jinnah, the leader of the Muslim League, insisted irrevocably on the formation of two separate states as the first essential. After the British General Election of 1945, it took the new Government some time to address itself to the problem of India, but in January 1946 the Viceroy announced the intention to establish a new Executive Council and to summon a Constituent Assembly. In the following month a Cabinet Mission was sent to India to discuss the future, which it was still hoped need not involve partition. The Cabinet Mission's proposals were published in May. They did not automatically entail partition, but Jinnah nevertheless accepted them, while still insisting on the creation of 'Pakistan'. The Congress, under Nehru's leadership, accepted them on conditions, but declined to enter an interim government. The Viceroy, unable to reconcile the two responses, formed a 'caretaker government' of civil servants, which Jinnah declared to be a breach of faith.

In July the Viceroy proceeded with the attempt to form an interim government in accordance with the Cabinet Mission's plan. He offered six seats to the Congress, five to the Muslim League, and three to the other minorities. The positions of Nehru and Jinnah were now reversed. The Muslim League refused, and the Government was formed without them in August. In October Jinnah changed his mind, and allowed the Muslim League to join the Government; but Pakistan was still his objective. Because there were still sharp differences of interpretation of the Cabinet Mission's proposals, the Indian leaders were invited to London for a conference in December. There the differences ended in deadlock, and led to acrimonious debate in the House of Commons. In January 1947 the Indian Constituent Assembly, without Muslim participation, voted to establish an independent republic. A month later the Labour Government announced its intention to transfer power to the Indians by June 1948, and appointed Lord Mountbatten Viceroy in place of Lord Wavell.

Mountbatten quickly convinced himself, and the British Government, that June 1948 was too long to wait. There was, he argued, no practical alternative to a rapid withdrawal, leaving power in the hands of the two main communities. Jinnah had in fact won his claim to Pakistan, as was publicly conceded by Nehru in April. In June the plans for the transfer of power were presented to the two communities. On 4 July (another Independence Day) the necessary legislation was introduced in the House of Commons. It received the Royal Assent with extraordinary rapidity two weeks later. On 15 August India and Pakistan became two independent states. A bloody aftermath followed between the two religious communities, in which it is said that the casualties numbered millions, and so did those who had to find new homes. Yet little blame was cast on the British Government or the last Viceroy, until later when the unresolved problems emerged: for instance, the fate of the princely states, particularly Hyderabad and Kashmir, and the division of the life-giving waters of the Indus River. At least, however, one of the problems which had most vexed the British Government for years was no longer their problem.

Another still was. Palestine, though not a colony, was administered under the Colonial Office, and therefore falls into this chapter, along with the neighbouring mandate of Transjordan. The background of the Palestine problem is too complicated to trace in detail, but three points antecedent to the Labour Government's accession to power must be mentioned. The first was that in the First World War the British Government had made what seemed to be conflicting promises about Palestine to the Jews and the Arabs; and even if those promises could be reconciled in pure logic, neither party was inclined to be purely logical. The second was that in a White Paper published in 1939, the National Government had limited Jewish immigration to 75,000 a year for the next five years – a policy which was nullified by the outbreak of war, but which remained an enduring source of bitterness for the Jews. The third point was that in preparation for the Labour Party Conference in December 1944, the National Executive had put out a policy statement which in effect proposed to admit Jews to Palestine without limit and to encourage Arabs to emigrate. This policy was approved by the Party Conference. Many supporters of the Labour Party, and all Zionists, considered that the Labour Government was in effect committed to rescind the White Paper and to allow an immediate and substantial increase of Jewish immigration, especially of the survivors of Hitler's massacres. But the Arabs thought otherwise, and so did Bevin.

The Jewish Agency made strong and repeated representations in that sense. The Government met its representatives with compromises which were not accepted as satisfactory. Bevin, meeting Weizmann in October 1945, is said to have talked of 'a fight'. By November, when the announcement was made of an Anglo-American Committee of Inquiry into Palestine, violence and sabotage by the Jews had already begun. Early in 1946, while defence regulations were being tightened in Palestine, Bevin announced the Government's intention to make Transjordan independent. To the Jews, Transjordan was a part of Palestine, but the original mandate of 1922, which covered both countries, permitted the British Government to administer them separately, as had always been done. Nevertheless, the decision was resented by the Jews, as were many other steps taken by the British Government during 1946. Violence grew throughout the year, reaching a climax in the destruction by high explosives of a wing of the King David Hotel in Jerusalem in July. Stern measures were taken against the illegal immigration of Jews, and leaders of the Jewish Agency among others were arrested. No way could be found to reconcile Jewish and Arab claims in the future development of Palestine, nor even to bring their leaders together for discussion. The periodical interventions of the U.S. Government were found unhelpful by the British Government, and tartly criticized by Bevin. After a last attempt at compromise had been refused by both communities early in 1947, the Government referred the problem to the United Nations in April.

The United Nations was little more successful. It appointed a Special Committee on Palestine, which eventually recommended partition into a Jewish and an Arab state. Partition was finally accepted by the General Assembly in November 1947, though only after bitter debate and under the shadow of an explicit threat by the Arab Powers that they did not regard the decision as binding and 'reserved full liberty of action'. The British Government, having given repeated warnings that British troops would not be available to enforce a settlement, finally announced that it would give up the mandate and accept no further responsibility after 15 May 1948. As the final date approached, violence grew in intensity between Jews and Arabs. The prospect of an orderly partition on the basis of the U.N. plan was plainly hopeless. On 15 May, when the State of Israel was proclaimed, instant war broke out between it and its Arab neighbours. The rest of its story lies outside the context of British colonial history.

These events in India and Palestine have been narrated in some detail, though very incompletely, only to emphasize the preoccupation and anxiety which they imposed on the British Government. They illustrate, in the case of Palestine, a resounding failure of British colonial policy, perhaps foredoomed from 1917; and in the case of India, on balance, a success. The story of India, so far as this chapter is concerned, culminates in the renewed acceptance of India as a member of the Commonwealth, although a republic, from 1950. The precedent of India was probably decisive in some subsequent cases of development within the Commonwealth. Pakistan followed automatically; and so did Ceylon, virtually without a struggle. With these three the new Commonwealth was born. It was now multi-racial and multi-constitutional, and could accommodate an unexpected range of varieties. Thus it was made easier for future members to reach full independence within the Commonwealth after much less painful processes than in the case of India. Ghana, Nigeria, Sierra Leone and the West Indies have all had an easier course; and the difficulties they have experienced have generally arisen from conflicts within their own component parts rather than between their national leaders and the retiring colonial power.

The case of Malaya was very different from any of the above. A first attempt to devise a new constitutional structure for the Malay States had begun in 1945, but had broken down over the suspicions of the Malay rulers and the general fear of the Malays that they would be dominated by the Chinese population. This would have been especially probable if, as was intended, Singapore with its very large Chinese majority were eventually united with Malaya. The British proposals for a Malay Union, which had already received the Royal Assent in 1946, were revised and replaced by a looser Federation, which was inaugurated in February 1948, only a few weeks before the emergency began. The emergency was essentially a Chinese Communist rebellion designed to destroy the Federation. It was never popular: the maximum strength of the rebels never exceeded 5,000. Nor did it succeed in disrupting Malaya's economy: the production of tin and rubber, the two staple commodities, was virtually unaffected by the rising. But politically it was exceedingly damaging, and militarily it represented a major drain on Britain's resources for more than five years. More than once it was feared that Britain intended to abandon the country. Attlee denied this in April 1949, but the suspicion revived when the Conservative Government took office in 1951, until the decisive appointment of General Templer as High Commissioner and director of military and police operations in February 1952.

Even while the situation was at its gravest, constitutional development was never set aside. In January 1949 a Communities Liaison Committee was formed on the initiative of the Commissioner-General for S.E. Asia, Malcolm Macdonald. The aim of self-government was declared in September; and the first step towards it was taken a year later, when quasi-ministerial responsibility was transferred to nine heads of departments. In April 1951 a Malayan Executive of fourteen members was created, though it was not until October, a year later, that General Templer could say that the 'shooting war' was being got under control. In 1953 began a relaxation of emergency measures and gradual reduction of troops. Constitutional questions were already under discussion again: a conference on the future Government of the Federation reported early in 1956. By August 1957, although the last of the Chinese rebels were still at large, independence was finally achieved.

During the ten years of uncertainty over Malaya, it had come to be accepted by British public opinion that complete independence, preferably though not necessarily within the Commonwealth, must be the goal for all colonies in which it was practicable in terms of size, geography, economic viability and other relevant factors. The bitter struggles which had preceded Indian independence were not repeated with anything like the same intensity in the cases of Ghana, Nigeria and the British West Indies. Although the movement towards independence was inevitably accompanied by friction between the colonial administrators and the Nationalist leaders in the colonies, the conflict was no longer due to a reluctance of the former to give up their power but only to differences about the terms on which it should be given up, and to whom. Once this fact was recognized, the problem of reconciling rival forces within each colonial territory displaced the more traditional conflict between Nationalist leaders and colonial governors.

The last period of office of the Labour Party, 1950–1, was perhaps the decisive period in this process, so far as the most recent accessions to independence are concerned. In December 1950 a new constitution for the Gold Coast (later Ghana) was proclaimed, on the basis of the report of a Committee on Constitutional Reform in 1949, which had itself made history by being the first to consist wholly of African members. It is noteworthy that these steps had not been impeded by the outbreak of grave riots at Accra in February 1948, nor by the arrest and imprisonment of Dr. Nkrumah in 1950 on charges of fomenting civil disobedience. When the first elections were held in February 1951, and overwhelmingly won by Nkrumah's party, he was released within a week by the Governor to become Leader for Government Business in the Executive Council. Once this critical turning-point was passed, the colony's progress towards independence within the Commonwealth was unchecked. It was achieved in March 1957. Even so, there were undercurrents of opposition to the process within Ghana, particularly in Ashanti. These persisted after independence and led to reactions by Nkrumah's Government which were not encouraging to the prospects of democracy in Africa.

Internal stresses, rather than conflicts with the colonial power, also lay at the heart of the difficulties of those other colonial territories, or former colonies, which stood at the threshold of full independence by the end of 1959. The Central African Federation is a case apart, which will be discussed below.[1] Nigeria and the British West Indies both took their decisive steps on the road in the years 1950–1. The new Nigerian constitution, providing for a majority of African ministers, came into force in June 1951, and was succeeded in October 1954 by a fully federal constitution. Again there were internal conflicts over the relations of the three regional governments to the Central Government and the protection of minority rights. But these were considered to have been resolved by a constitutional conference in London in September 1958, after which independence in 1960 came to be regarded as a foregone conclusion. The cohesion of the Federation still remained to be tested.

The progress of the Federation of the West Indies in the same direction earned less publicity, although it was in some ways more remarkable because of the number and diversity of the races merged in the Caribbean as well as the vast geographical extent and separation of the colonial territories. In March 1950 the Standing Closer Association Committee recommended federation with a view to Dominion status, as it was then called, and the recommendation was accepted and elaborated at a conference in London in April 1953. After prolonged discussion and modification to meet the anxieties of some of the colonial territories concerned, it was agreed to establish the Federation by the end of 1956. The first Governor-General was appointed in 1957; the first federal elections were held in March 1958; and the site of a federal capital was chosen. Nevertheless doubts about the principle of the Federation remained, particularly in Jamaica. By the end of the period under review, it was still not yet possible to foresee a precise date for full independence within the Commonwealth, though the intention to bring it about was not in dispute.

With the last two examples, the discussion has already strayed across the borderline between fully independent states and colonial territories

[1] See pp. 157-9.

still under British rule; and the same trespass will be committed in reverse in discussing the Central African Federation in the next section. Such untidiness is unavoidable, because the borderline is constantly shifting, and there is a kind of moving staircase between the two categories of territories. It is satisfactory that so far the movement has been virtually without exception in a single direction, though in some cases it has been spasmodic and irregular. Experience has also begun to suggest that in some cases it may have gone too far and too fast. Many unsolved problems were handed over along with political responsibility to the new states, and many new problems have emerged since independence. A number of them will have become apparent in the foregoing survey.

Ghana and Nigeria, though they amply pass the test of economic viability, both lack natural homogeneity in their populations, and in each case there was a danger that minority problems might lead to serious attempts at secession or disruption of the State. The Government of Ghana in particular took drastic steps against such possibilities in 1958 and 1959, in a manner which led to sharp criticism and heart-searching in Britain. Pakistan and the West Indian Federation both suffer from another factor militating against unity: the wide geographical separation of their component territories, with more or less serious economic consequences. Pakistan abandoned the attempt to preserve a parliamentary democracy in October 1958 in favour of an authoritarian régime under a military leader. Ceylon equally failed to make the system inherited from Britain work, and came near to anarchy in 1958. India also had serious domestic problems to contend with, both economic and political, of which the most notorious was the election of a Communist Government in the province of Kerala in 1957 and its deposition by the Central Government in July 1959. Such internal problems of the new Commonwealth countries concerned British policy not only in the way that the problems of her allies concerned her, but even more so in affecting her judgement of the future course to be adopted in other dependent territories.

Apart from internal strains, there were also damaging tensions between some of the member states of the Commonwealth. The general rule in the past had been that Commonwealth countries were all more interested in their connexions with Britain than with each other. Post-war developments modified this rule in some cases. Canada, for instance, became by force of circumstances a power with interests all over the world, including Canadian troops in Europe, Korea and the Middle

East and an observer mission in S.E. Asia. She developed a particularly intimate connexion with India. South Africa, on the other hand, kept herself rather aloof from the Commonwealth after the defeat of Smuts's Government in 1948, and did not, for instance, even have a diplomatic representative in New Zealand. Unfortunately, when relations did develop more strongly within the new Commonwealth, they were sometimes relations of hostility rather than friendship.

India and Pakistan had numerous quarrels over matters left unsettled by partition in 1947, particularly the distribution of the Indus waters, which was provisionally settled in 1959, and the sovereignty of Kashmir, which India formally annexed in January 1957. All the Asian members of the Commonwealth also had a grievance against South Africa over the policy of *apartheid*, with special reference to Asians living in the Union. When India took the case to the United Nations in 1946, and more than once subsequently, Britain supported the South African contention that the matter was one of domestic jurisdiction. But the quarrel remained irreconcilable, and in 1954 India severed diplomatic relations with South Africa.

Even with Australia the Asian countries had something of a grievance against the so-called 'White Australia' policy. The Australian Government denied that there was any such policy. It argued that the restriction of immigration rested rather on economic grounds, to maintain the Australian worker's standard of living; and it was not a result of Australian discrimination that the class of would-be-immigrants who would depress the standard of living by providing cheap labour happened to be Asians rather than other races. The explanation may have been well-grounded, but it did not satisfy the Asians of the Commonwealth. It was widely felt that if the Commonwealth, with its overwhelming predominance of non-European peoples, could not solve its own problem of race relations, then it might not survive at all. The outbreak of racial riots in Britain in 1958, though on a minor scale, was a disquieting portent.

Dependent Territories

The area where the racial problem was most severe, and could most easily damage the Commonwealth as a whole, was Africa. So far as Britain's direct responsibilities were concerned, the crucial parts of the continent were East and Central Africa. In the Union of South Africa, the problem was also acute and embarrassing, but outside Britain's jurisdiction; though the responsibility still held by the British Government for three territories geographically within the Union (Bechuana-land, Basutoland and Swaziland), and the repercussions of policy throughout the continent, made it impossible to take a detached view of what was happening in the Union as well. Elsewhere in Africa the problems were less acute. Ghana and Nigeria were almost wholly African in population, and could therefore become independent without raising serious problems of the relations between an African majority and a European minority. Other territories were small and still largely in the colonial stage. In each of them, nevertheless, substantial advances were made in the post-war period, even if not always without setbacks. A brief *tour d'horizon* of the minor territories will serve both to show the complexity of the colonial problem in Africa and to emphasize the contrast with East and Central Africa.

British post-war policy was governed everywhere by the principle that 'colonial rule could be justified only by its success in preparing the way for its early supersession by political self-government'.[1] The first steps took different forms in different circumstances, but they usually included provisions for an expansion of the Legislature to include representative Africans, an enlargement of the franchise, and the introduction of ministerial responsibility. Sierra Leone took the first steps in 1956 and finally become due for independence in 1961. Zanzibar had its first election in 1957, Somaliland in 1959. In the latter case independence was then barely a year away. Tanganyika and Uganda, both relatively untouched by the troubles in neigh-bouring Kenya, held their first direct elections of Africans to the Legislative Council in 1958. A new constitution for Basutoland was planned in 1959, and the British Government steadily resisted the claims of the South African Government to incorporate this and the other two High Commission Territories, Bechuanaland and Swaziland. Beyond the borders of Africa, but within its orbit, Mauritius had ministerial government from 1957; in Aden elections to the Legislative Council began in 1955; and in 1959 a federation was achieved between six Arab Amirates of the West Aden Protectorate, to which others might adhere.

The tale of development was not without its setbacks. The dispute in Uganda between the colonial Government and the Kabaka of Buganda in 1953 was notorious. It resulted in his exile for two years, and gave rise to suspicions which handicapped constitutional progress later. A different case which had only superficial similarities was the exile of Seretse Khama, the hereditary Bechuana chief, on account of

[1] Lord Hailey, *An African Survey*, revised 1956 (O.U.P. for R.I.I.A., 1957). p. 203.

his marriage with an English girl. He was debarred from his homeland from 1950 to 1956, and returned only after abdicating his chieftainship. In some cases there were problems created by the interest of other countries or the United Nations. For instance, in 1954 a mission from the Trusteeship Council of the United Nations visited the trust territory of Tanganyika and its Belgian-administered neighbour, Ruanda Urundi, and proposed that both should be guaranteed self-government within twenty years. Although the British Government's intentions proved by 1959 to be even more far-reaching, such advice seemed irresponsible at the time. Even more embarrassing, because it touched a sensitive point of conscience, was the sequel to the British Government's decision in 1955 to cede a small strip of Somaliland to Ethiopia. The complaint of the Somali inhabitants was taken to the United Nations by Egypt, and the British Government agreed to reconsider and reopen the negotiations. Such were the constantly, almost weekly, recurring difficulties of colonial administration.

All this was small beer, however, compared to the tragedies played out in Kenya and Central Africa. The problems of those territories were both racial and economic. If they were to be developed towards independence within the Commonwealth, with the requirement of economic viability fulfilled, it seemed necessary to group them in larger units. Geography pointed to the possibility of an East African unit consisting of Kenya, Uganda, Tanganyika and Zanzibar, and a Central African unit consisting of Northern and Southern Rhodesia and Nyasaland. An East African High Commission, consisting of the three governors concerned, was formed in 1948, together with a Central Assembly equipped with defined powers in inter-territorial matters; but subsequent progress in the direction of unification was slow. A Central African Federation was created in 1953, with a possible prospect of full independence not earlier than 1960. But in both areas formidable difficulties arose in the intervening years.

East and Central Africa did not have the advantage of the West African states, Ghana and Nigeria, which were wholly African in population and lacked a dominant European minority; nor did they enjoy the special circumstances of South Africa, where the European minority had achieved independence before the idea of self-government by native Africans had been seriously contemplated. In East and Central Africa (with the exception of Southern Rhodesia, which had been self-governing since 1923), the Europeans were at the same time too numerous to allow a development similar to that of Ghana and Nigeria and too few to follow the course set by South Africa, even if that course had been thought acceptable. The problem was not unlike that of the French in Algeria, and the attempt to find a compromise was likewise nearly disastrous.

In Kenya, the Mau Mau rebellion broke out in 1952, just as the emergency in Malaya was beginning to come under control. A state of emergency was proclaimed in October. In the following year Jomo Kenyatta, the leader of the Kenya African Union, was convicted of being a principal organizer of the Mau Mau and imprisoned. Even two years later, however, the Colonial Secretary said that the eradication of the Mau Mau might take a very long time. Emergency regulations continued after the end of the fighting in 1956, and were lifted only towards the end of 1959. Even then a hard core of terrorists remained to be rehabilitated or retained in indefinite confinement. Constitutional developments were delayed but not entirely frustrated as a result of the emergency.

The British Government refused the European settlers' demand for full self-government at the outbreak of the emergency, but presented a plan for ministerial government in 1954. The intention was that the Government should be multi-racial, representing Europeans, Africans and Asians alike, and that eventually the system of election should be based on common and not communal electorates. But after the first Africans had been elected to the Legislative Council in 1957, they refused to co-operate in the multi-racial Government and demanded a large increase of their representation. A new plan was announced in November 1957, which went some way towards meeting the African demands, but the Colonial Secretary announced that in any future expansion there would be no additional seats based on election by purely communal electorates. The ultimate success of multi-racialism in Kenya remained still in the balance; and its prospects were handicapped by fears of a possible recrudescence of Mau Mau. The tragic events in 1959, leading to the death of eleven former terrorists at the Hola camp, intensified the unhappy atmosphere in which Kenya was seeking to develop its own future. On the other hand, there was some progress in the direction of forming multi-racial political parties; and in 1959 a far-reaching decision was taken to open the so-called 'White Highlands' to Africans as well as Europeans. The next steps were to depend upon the constitutional conference in 1960, but the underlying tensions remained unresolved.

The second major tragedy of British Africa came to a head at the same time as the disaster of the Hola camp. It was the climax of six uneasy years in the history of the Central African Federation. The Federation had been opposed from the first by the African National Congress in Nyasaland, and particularly by Dr. Hastings Banda, who eventually became its leader, on the ground that it would be dominated by the Europeans of Southern Rhodesia. The Labour Opposition in the House of Commons asked in May 1953 that the Federation should be postponed, although it had itself taken the first steps when it had been in power. The arguments in favour of the Federation were mainly economic, since Nyasaland, which supplied a considerable labour force to Northern and Southern Rhodesia, was not a viable unit on its own. The Conservative Government refused to delay and established the Federation in August 1953, with a provision for review after not less than seven years. Some constitutional changes were introduced in Nyasaland in 1955 to give stronger African representation, and the African National Congress was successful at the following elections. But suspicion and racial hostility were deeply ingrained. Early in 1959 the fears of the pessimists were justified by an outbreak of violence, followed by the declaration of a state of emergency.

The subsequent inquiry by the Devlin Commission strongly suggested that the fact of federation was itself the main cause of the trouble, but that implication could only be accepted by the Government if it were prepared to dissolve the Federation. There would then remain the problem of the disposal of the constituent parts, for which there was no obvious solution. It had been suggested by some that Southern Rhodesia might eventually join the Union of South Africa; and an alternative federation of Northern Rhodesia, Nyasaland and Tanganyika was favoured by some of the Nyasaland Nationalists. But decisions of such immense consequence could not be taken in a hurry. The long-term future of Central Africa remained one of the gravest unsolved problems of British policy at the end of 1959. It was to be the subject of examination by an advisory commission under Lord Monckton early in 1960, followed by a full-scale constitutional inquiry into the working of the Federation. But the prospects were darkened by the fact that the Labour Opposition, and consequently the principal African Nationalists, had little confidence in the Government's intentions.

The problem was aggravated by the much-abused policy of *apartheid*, or racial segregation, in practice in the Union of South Africa immediately to the south. It could be argued by doctrinaire Nationalists on a strict interpretation that *apartheid*, in the sense of politically separate development, was in fact the state of affairs already realized in Ghana and Nigeria, and now demanded by the Nyasaland African Congress in seeking to break up the Federation. But these were sophisticated afterthoughts. By the same logic, the gravamen of the case against the Nationalist Government of the Union of South Africa was not that it preached *apartheid* but that it did not conscientiously and consistently practise what it preached: it enforced the externals and withheld the substance. But even though some educated Africans might prefer a genuine opportunity of independence to insincere 'partnership' (which Lord Malvern once called the partnership of a rider and his horse), the fact remained that the problem of race relations within the Commonwealth was crucial and was not getting easier to solve.

Apart from the vast problems presented by Asia and Africa, the British Government had also to deal with a large number of smaller territories all over the world. These were mostly either small islands, like Malta or Mauritius, or small enclaves in mainland territories, like Sierra Leone or the Gambia on the west coast of Africa. Often they were claimed by neighbouring powers, as Gibraltar was by Spain, British Honduras by Guatemala, Aden and the protectorates by the Yemen, and Hong Kong by the Kuomintang Chinese Government (though much less vocally by the Chinese Communists). Each of these claims was made and resisted at least once during the post-war years. There were also the Argentine claims to the Falkland Island Dependencies, the Iranian claim to Bahrein, and the Greek claim to Cyprus to be withstood. Other islands whose status presented problems were Mauritius, Singapore and Malta. Of all these, the last two and Cyprus were the ones that caused the acutest problems in the period under review, but none was ever so completely dormant as to be negligible.

The case of Cyprus was not a colonial problem in the normal sense at all. Independence was not originally at issue. Until the Greek-Cypriot leader, Archbishop Makarios, offered to accept it *faute de mieux* in September 1958, no one in Cyprus had ever asked for independence. Nor was it disputed that the Cypriot people was capable of self-government. What was disputed was whether there was such a thing as the Cypriot people, as distinct from a four-fifths majority of Greeks and a one-fifth minority of Turks. What the Greek Cypriots wanted, almost to a man, was union with Greece (*énosis*). What the Turkish Cypriots wanted was either to remain under British rule, or to pass back under Turkish rule, either by retrocession or by partition of the island. The problem was aggravated, though not created, by the

British Government's need for a military base on the island, especially after the withdrawal from the Suez Canal Zone in 1954. It was also increased by the fact that Cyprus was not viable on its own, at least at the standard of living to which people had become accustomed under British occupation.

The dispute broke into open violence early in 1955. In the late summer the British Government acknowledged the Greek and Turkish interest in Cyprus to the extent of convening a tripartite conference in London; but when the conference had broken down, accompanied by violence against the Greeks in Turkish cities and by Greek threats to withdraw from N.A.T.O., it was decided that the time was one for a firm stand. In October the retiring C.I.G.S., Sir John Harding, was appointed governor; in November a state of emergency was declared; in March 1956, after further fruitless negotiations, the Greek-Cypriot leader, Archbishop Makarios, was deported to the Seychelles. Negotiation and bloodshed still proceeded side by side for nearly three years, the worst period of strife being that in which the Anglo-French expedition against Egypt was mounted from the island. Archbishop Makarios was released in 1957, but not allowed to return to Cyprus; until at last in February 1959 the quarrel was patched up by an agreement to establish Cyprus as an independent republic early in 1960. Independence eventually came into effect in August 1960, under Archbishop Makarios as President.

It was an open question whether the unique and experimental solution of the Cyprus problem could be applied elsewhere. Possibly Singapore was moving in the direction of a similar status. The problem of racial disunity in Singapore was not dissimilar, with the predominance of Chinese over Malays in about the same proportion. It was this predominance which made union with Malaya unattractive to the Malays, but many experts considered that some form of union was the only possible solution. For the present – or for good, as the British Government hoped – it was decided as the result of a constitutional conference in 1957 to create a self-governing State of Singapore, which came into being in August 1958. The first independent elections in May 1959 were overwhelmingly won by the left-wing Chinese People's Action Party, which began its tenure of office with a number of pointedly anti-British measures. On the other hand, it persisted in its desire to achieve some kind of union with Malaya, which entailed a more conciliatory policy towards the Malays.

The story of Malta was different again. Like Cyprus, it was not a viable unit on its own, but amalgamation with any other Mediterranean territory was neither desired nor seemingly possible. Like Cyprus, too, its importance had been as a base, but the Royal Navy's requirements of it were diminishing. Unlike Cyprus, it had self-government from 1947. An imaginative proposal emanated from the Maltese Government for union with the United Kingdom itself, on which discussions began in 1955. An all-party parliamentary committee from Britain reported (with two dissentients) for the integration of Malta in December 1955, and discussions on the execution of the plan proceeded throughout the next two years. It became clear, however, that the Maltese were expecting a great deal more than Britain could give in the way of material benefits; and the run-down of employment in the dockyards led to bitter recriminations. The argument turned to violence in April 1958, when a state of emergency was proclaimed, and in January 1959 the constitution of 1947 was revoked. The solution of the problem of a small strategic island was not easily to be found, Malta probably not being the last example. There still seemed even to be some truth in the generalization uttered by a former Minister of State for the Colonies, that 'there are certain territories in the Commonwealth which, owing to their particular circumstances, can never expect to be fully independent'.

The foregoing incomplete and superficial review of some of Britain's colonial problems since the war shows that they were a grave enough preoccupation even without external interference. But there was also constant external interference to aggravate them, partly from well-meaning and less well-meaning antagonists of 'colonialism' at the United Nations, and partly from the Communists. In July 1949 the then Colonial Secretary told the House of Commons that the British Communist Party was deliberately stirring up trouble in the colonies. The 'front organizations' of the international Communist movement entered upon a large-scale campaign against colonial rule from 1950 onwards. The rebellion in Malaya in 1948 was of Communist inspiration, as also was the abortive rising in British Guiana which led to the dispatch of British forces and the suspension of the constitution in October 1953. Only anti-Soviet crusaders could see Communist inspiration behind the emergencies in Kenya (1952), Cyprus (1955) or Nyasaland (1959); or in the lesser disorders in the Maldives or Fiji (1959). But it remained a fact that such disorders signified trends which could be exploited by Communism. The increased interest of the Soviet Union in Africa in particular was an important new phenomenon of the later 1950s.

Mutual Benefits

Churchill said in 1942 that he had 'not become the King's First Minister in order to preside over the liquidation of the British Empire'. In view of the distractions caused to British foreign policy by imperial commitments after the war, it might well be asked 'Why not?' What was the point of trying to preserve and develop the Commonwealth at such cost? A sense of political responsibility cannot be the whole answer, though it is a major one, applicable in particular to the smaller and poorer territories. Strategic necessity is also an important part of the answer. Quite apart from the world-wide system of alliances to which Canada, Australia, New Zealand and Pakistan all belong, there are the strategically located bases which are still far from obsolete: particularly Gibraltar, Malta, Cyprus, Aden, Singapore and Hong Kong. The gap created in that chain by the withdrawal of the bases on Ceylon had to be replaced as recently as 1957 by the establishment of a new base on the Maldive Islands, which in its turn led to political troubles there in the following years. Such troubles were not courted from an instinct for imperialism, but because of imperative strategic need.

There were also strong economic motives holding the Commonwealth system together. Indeed, it might be argued that, from the economic point of view, the system was virtually impossible to liquidate. All members of the Commonwealth except Canada belong to the Sterling Area, of which Britain acts as the central banker; and since the central 'bank' is one whose liabilities exceed its assets some six times over, to liquidate it would be a declaration of bankruptcy. It is a system of closely interlocked advantages from which any member could withdraw, but perhaps none is likely to do so. Britain has had advantages from the great majority of its members since the war: loans from Canada and South Africa, grants from Australia and New Zealand, and crucial contributions to her dollar earnings from Malaya, Ghana and Nigeria. The colonies as a whole have been the main savers and the main dollar-earners of the Sterling Area, but that is not to say that they would gain by leaving it.

Every member of the system has some advantage from it, though perhaps each has a different set of advantages. Some rely on the London capital market for loans, some base their currencies on their sterling reserves, almost all do a high proportion of their trade in sterling, and for most of them Britain is the most important single customer. For the less developed territories, economic and technical aid organized by

Britain are important benefits: in particular, under the Colonial Development and Welfare Acts of 1940 and subsequently, through the Colonial Development Corporation established in 1947, and through the Colombo Plan for South and S.E. Asia in 1950. Such contributions towards development in backward countries are motivated by self-interest as well as humanitarianism, for a higher standard of living in Asia and Africa means larger markets eventually for British goods. But it is worth recording that the one resounding failure of the post-war years was the one venture that was almost wholly selfish. This was the scheme for growing groundnuts in East Africa, which was finally liquidated in 1952 after producing 9,162 tons of shelled nuts (against an estimate of 609,000 tons) at a total cost of £35,000,000.

Although reciprocal advantages are the binding factor of the Commonwealth and Colonies on the economic plane, the system has never been regarded as a closed or exclusive one. The Commonwealth Prime Ministers' conference at the end of 1952 emphasized in its communiqué that the Commonwealth was an outward-looking, not an inward-looking, economic association. The same thought was repeated at the Commonwealth Finance Ministers' conference in Montreal in August 1958, with the slogan 'an expanding Commonwealth in an expanding world'. Britain continued to be the largest single investor in the Commonwealth, though some of the newer countries (notably India) observed that private investment from London was much more easily attracted to the older European-descended countries than to the newer non-European ones. India in particular began to look elsewhere (particularly to the U.S.A., but not ignoring the U.S.S.R.) for her loans. At the same time the value of the Imperial Preference system was steadily waning, as the older members of the Commonwealth developed their own industries and their own commercial relations outside it.

None of this was a matter for regret or recrimination. The Commonwealth was still there; Britain was still unavoidably the centre of it; and it was a major factor in the evolution of Britain's foreign policy. Although the responsibilities of maintaining this association some-times limited Britain's freedom of action, they were also the foundation of her status as a global power. They gave her a means of influencing events everywhere not less potent than the dollar in the hands of the U.S.A. or international Communism in the hands of the U.S.S.R. And they continued to be a source of honourable pride. The implications of these facts will be further examined in chapter 12.

9

Small States and New Nations

ANY consideration of foreign policy since the Second World War must take account of the greatly increased importance of the small states and the new nations: those, that is to say, which either carried no weight in international affairs before the war, or which did not even exist as independent political units. The point can be illustrated by a simple comparison of the United Nations with the League of Nations. The U.N. had eighty-two members in 1959.[1] The maximum number of nations that belonged to the League at one time or another was sixty-three; and of these only half a dozen (five of them European) carried any real weight. The difference in numbers is mainly accounted for by the small states and new nations, no less than twenty of which were dependencies of other powers (eight of them British, six French) at the outbreak of the Second World War. At that date, too, if people other than specialists discussed 'the colonial question' at all, they often meant by it only the question whether Germany's former colonies should be restored to her. Today the only question is how quickly the colonial problem can be liquidated altogether by abolishing colonial status. Some people argue that the process has gone too far too fast; and they are disquieted by the numerical preponderance of the new nations at the U.N., on the ground that both in size and level of development most of them ought not to have equal votes with the major powers. But whether for good or ill, the change is a fact and the trend irreversible.

To show in detail the effect of this change on British foreign policy would require a large book in itself, and to try to compress the detail into a bare chronology would serve no useful purpose. The most that can be attempted is to sketch the impact of these new phenomena on British policy in broad outline, and to analyse the reasons why successive British Governments were obliged to give them so much attention. The first part of the assessment can be done by breaking down the post-

---

[1] By the end of 1960 the total was near the hundred-mark, the increase being mainly accounted for by the addition of new African states.

war years into three roughly equal periods, which happen to coincide more or less with the natural joints of the historical continuum, in order to see what were the major preoccupations of the British Government in each of them. The periods are 1945–9 inclusive; 1950–4 inclusive; and 1955–9 inclusive. They are, roughly speaking, the quinquennium of the cold war in Europe; the quinquennium of the fighting in the Far East and S.E. Asia; and the quinquennium of crises in the Middle East and *détente* in Europe.

In the first period, 1945–9, the most important development was the creation of the Atlantic Alliance. But apart from that achievement, almost all the other main preoccupations of the British Government were with the small states and new nations. There was firstly the sometimes painful process of creating independent states: India, Pakistan, Ceylon, Burma out of the former British Empire; Israel, Jordan, Iraq out of former British mandates; Syria and Lebanon out of former French mandates; Indonesia out of the Dutch East Indies; and the Philippines out of an American dependency. All except the last case were matters of direct British concern. There were other miscellaneous problems of the same kind, and involving states in the same categories, left over from the war: the security and restoration of Greece, the negotiation of a new treaty with Egypt, the disposal of the former Italian colonies, the safeguarding of the British interest in the oil resources of Iran and the Persian Gulf, the future of divided Korea, and the French entanglement with Communism and Nationalism in Indo-China. These too were all directly or indirectly British commitments. And there were the problems of development in the non-self-governing colonies, particularly the emergency in Malaya. In Latin America there were Guatemala's claims to British Honduras and Argentina's and Chile's claims to the Falkland Islands.

In the second period, 1950–4, the major preoccupations were virtually all concerned with the small states and new nations. The period was dominated by the war in Korea, which involved indirectly the fate of other small states in the Far East and S.E. Asia. In S.E. Asia it was also the period of the French disaster in Indo-China, the continued emergency in Malaya, the multilateral civil war in Burma, and the protracted dispute between the Netherlands and Indonesia. In the Middle East, it was the period of the Anglo-Iranian oil dispute, the continuing conflict between Egypt and Israel, and the long-drawn-out negotiations for a new Anglo-Egyptian treaty, which were interrupted by an Egyptian revolution. Those negotiations created new problems even as they more or less solved old ones: for instance, the transfer of the British base from the Canal Zone to Cyprus led to the violent stage of the campaign for *énosis*, and the agreement on the former Anglo-Egyptian Sudan created yet another new state bringing fresh complications in its train. On the periphery of the Middle East, there were also the problems of achieving the independence of Libya, Tunisia and Morocco, followed by the outbreak of a nationalist revolt in Algeria. Among Britain's own colonies, it was the period of the Mau Mau rebellion in Kenya, and a major crisis in British Guiana.

The third period, 1955–9, was dominated by a seemingly endless succession of crises in the Middle East, the gravest of them being that over the Suez Canal in 1956. There was virtual war between Egypt and Israel; a threat of war between Syria and Turkey; and armed clashes involving British troops in the Aden Protectorates, the Buraimi Oasis, and the Sultanate of Muscat and Oman. There were emergencies in Cyprus and Malta, revolutions in Iraq, Pakistan and the Sudan, and armed interventions by American and British troops in Lebanon and Jordan respectively. There was the formation of the United Arab Republic and frequent tergiversations in Egypt's relations with her Middle Eastern neighbours, particularly Iraq, Jordan, Saudi Arabia, the Sudan and Tunisia. In North Africa there was the continuing revolt in Algeria and the completion of independence for Tunisia and Morocco. Later there were even more far-reaching developments in French colonial policy, including the emergence of a new state, Guinea, and other new associations in West Africa. British policy was inevitably involved in these developments, both indirectly, because nothing in Africa now happened in isolation, and directly, because British West Africa consisted essentially of a number of enclaves in the French Empire: witness the decision of Ghana, which gained independence within the Commonwealth during the same period, to form a union with Guinea in 1958.

Britain also had special problems in Africa, particularly East Africa and the Central African Federation. Asia was relatively quiet, but that did not mean without problems. Malaya achieved independence and peace; Burma, Siam and Pakistan underwent bloodless revolutions; a Communist incursion threatened Laos, and China suppressed a revolt in Tibet; Indonesia brought its quarrel with the Dutch to a head and approached near to internal chaos; India annexed Kashmir and tried to annex Goa. The new nations of Africa and Asia organized a conference at Bandung, in Indonesia, which gave a new name to them as a group; and further conferences of similar composition were held in Egypt and Ghana. Latin America too was more prominently in the news; in one country after another, beginning with Argentina and ending with Cuba, dictatorships were overthrown, though they were not always succeeded by democracies. As the catalogue by itself shows, the third quinquennium was even more agitated by the activities of the small states and new nations than the first two. In terms of telegrams and dispatches, the Middle East and Africa between them may perhaps have exceeded even Europe as a principal preoccupation of the British Government. At the same time, however, Britain's relations with her principal European allies became more uneasy than at any time since the war.

The simple questions which require an answer are why the affairs of the small states and new nations should concern the British Government so much, and why they should be allowed to have so great an impact on British foreign policy? Some of the answers are immediately obvious. One is that the small states and new nations are directly or indirectly represented at the United Nations, where their votes collectively amount to more than half the total. Another is that the Soviet Union has developed a great interest in what it calls 'colonial and dependent territories', which include most of the countries in question, even if we do not accept the nomenclature. But these reasons are not by themselves sufficient. They are in a sense secondary: they operate only because the new countries are thought to be important, and do not explain their importance. More fundamental reasons must be sought in Britain's national outlook upon the world; and the reasons can be distinguished as partly moral obligation and partly self-interest. As will be seen, without any implication of cynicism, the one kind of reason merges in practice into the other.

To speak of moral obligation in this context is not merely to be self-righteous. Britain has, in the first place, obligations towards people in many parts of the world arising simply from past history, even if the historical origin of those obligations may well have been self-interested. Some go back far into history: examples are the old dominions, India, Egypt and many of the colonies. Their historical origins are generally to be found in the necessity of trade or the defence of trade; though sometimes (as in the case of Sierra Leone) a purely humanitarian motive was at work. Others are of more recent origin: for instance, the mandates between the wars. Others represented commitments arising from the circumstances of the Second World War: examples are the liberation of Libya and Greece or the accident that British troops received the Japanese surrender in Indo-China and Indonesia. All these historical circumstances created obligations and responsibilities which British policy could not simply shuffle off and ignore. It may be argued in some cases, particularly India and Palestine, that the responsibility was very imperfectly discharged; but every British Government recognized that it had a moral responsibility, which it had to do its best to handle. In most cases a residual responsibility still remains, however much attenuated it may be by the conferment of independence and subsequent developments.

There is also another aspect to the sense of moral obligation, which might better be called humanitarian. The countries and peoples with which this chapter is concerned constitute the bulk of the world's population, but they have a standard of living far below what would be considered tolerable, or even in many cases conceivable, in Western Europe and North America. The statistics illustrating these facts are often put on record, but seldom taken in, perhaps because they are so shocking. It would be beyond the scope of this book to reproduce them here, and they are on record with better authority.[1] But the essential point which has had to be grasped by all civilized governments is that the gap between rich countries and poor countries is growing wider, not narrower.

Although constant efforts to remedy the situation are made, they have so far been at best pitiful in the scale of their effect, and at worst self-defeating. A pitiful example is that with all the immeasurable generosity of the U.S.A., the population of India has so far benefited to the extent of less than one U.S. dollar *per caput* over the last decade, which is the price of a haircut in the U.S.A. A self-defeating example is that of the introduction of modern methods of hygiene and preventive medicine in overpopulated countries, such as India and Egypt, which has actually depressed the standard of living by providing more mouths to feed.

The question can be asked, why should the more advanced nations do anything about the troubles of people incapable of taking care of themselves? Most people in Britain have no doubt that the answer is a matter of common humanity, and all recent British governments have acted on this principle. A more sophisticated argument is that if the Western Powers do not help them, the Soviet Union will do so, and then they

[1] e.g. the sources quoted in J. P. Cole, *Geography of World Affairs* (Penguin Books, 1959), pp. 315–25.

will go Communist. There are fallacies in this argument. For instance, increased prosperity does not always act as an immunization against Communism; and the social revolution which is sometimes necessary to achieve any real material advance may well be a prelude to Communism. There may on the other hand very well be advantages in a joint contribution from both the Western and the Communist Powers towards the development of a new country, as in the case of India, since it may be preferable to both sides, on a sober calculation, that such a country should occupy a detached position rather than adhere to one bloc or the other. It would not be denied, in any case, by any political party in Britain that whatever the risks inherent in helping under-developed countries may be, the risks in not helping them are greater.

Leaving aside humanitarian considerations, there are two principal ways in which the new countries could damage Western interests, particularly British interests, if their policies were set on the wrong course by dissatisfied leaders. One way is by pursuing militantly anti-Western policies; the other is by pursuing local rivalries among their neighbours, to the point of involving other powers in war. Both dangers have been experienced since the Second World War, and at times there have been reasons to fear that Soviet policy has aggravated the dangers. The outstanding examples of anti-Western policy have been those of Iran under Mussadiq, Egypt under Nasser, and Argentina under Perón; and the first two cases certainly seem to have been aggravated by the U.S.S.R. On the whole, however, the virulence of anti-Westernism among the new countries appears to be on the wane. It was much less marked after the Iraqi revolution of 1958 than in Iran under Mussadiq six years earlier; and the widespread and rapid concession of indepen-dence in Africa has at least reduced the force of such sentiment in large areas of the continent. It is even possible that the Afro-Asian Conference at Bandung in April 1955 marked a turning-point in this respect.

On the other hand, the danger from mutual antagonisms between the new countries, especially among next-door neighbours, is greater than ever. Western imperialism at least had the advantage of blotting out the rivalries of local nationalism in Africa, the Middle East and Asia. In each area local nationalisms have now sprung to vigorous life, new or renewed: between Vietnam, Siam, Laos and Cambodia; within the Union of Burma; between Korea and Japan; between India and Paki-stan; between Israel and her Arab neighbours; between Syria and Lebanon; between Jordan, Iraq and Saudi Arabia; between Egypt and most of the other Arabic-speaking states; between Ethiopians and

Somalis; and both between and within several of the newly emerging West African states.

Several cases on the above list have caused a threat of war within the last few years, and such a war might easily spread into a major war involving other powers. Even if it were checked before it had gone so far, it might still damage their economic interests, as the Israeli attack on Egypt did in 1956 by leading to the severance of Western Europe's oil supplies. Britain is particularly vulnerable to such a danger, because her interests – economic, strategic and political – are world-wide. Any serious upheaval in the Middle East, Africa, S.E. Asia, the Far East or Latin America – in approximately that order of importance – could harm Britain's interests to a degree inferior only to the outbreak of war in Europe.

The Middle East

The Middle East was the most vital area of all in the post-war period. The object of British policy in the Middle East has not changed since the area came within Britain's sphere of interest a century and a half ago: it has been to ensure that the area should not pass under the domination of any potentially hostile power, so as to exclude Britain from it. But the reasons why that object is pursued have changed, and so have the conditions in which it has to be pursued and the means for pursuing it. Whereas up to a generation ago the importance of the Middle East was that it lay across the route to India, today its main importance lies in its oil resources. Its geographical position, at the crossroads of the east-west route between Europe and India and the north-south route between Russia and Africa, is still a matter of great importance, but not for the time being of primary importance. What is vital for the present is not where the Middle East is so much as what it has in it. The significance of the Middle East to Britain has thus undergone a revolution in the last half-century, since first oil was struck in prodigious quantities in Iran. There have in fact, however, been not one revolution but three: economic, strategic and political.

The three revolutions were interconnected. For instance, it was the discovery of oil at Masjid-i-Suleiman in 1908 which led the British Government to acquire a majority shareholding in the Anglo-Persian Oil Company[1] and to convert the Royal Navy from burning coal to burning oil. And it was the dissolution of the Ottoman Empire after the First World War which gave all the different nationalities of the Middle

[1] Later the Anglo-Iranian Oil Company (A.I.O.C.), now British Petroleum (B.P.).

East their chance to create separate nation-states, with unhappy results so far as their economic future was concerned. Some of them had oil some had not; some of the 'have-nots' lay across the routes that oil must travel to reach Europe, and some did not. Some had a problem of over-population and some of under-population; some were not economically viable; all had independent systems of communication, most of which did not communicate with each other; and so far as they had exportable products other than oil, their economies were not complementary but competitive. Even in the countries rich in oil, the resultant prosperity was very unevenly distributed by an archaic social system, though in Iraq and Kuweit at least something was done under British guidance to modernize it. The economic revolution was largely the product of the Western impact on the Middle East, and Britain in particular had a vital stake in it; but it has not so far had uniformly satisfactory results, and it is still full of possible dangers.

The best single example in British experience of the economic revolution and its consequences was the Anglo-Iranian oil dispute in 1951. Iranian oil was vital to Britain; the Anglo-Iranian Oil Company's investment in Abadan and the oil-fields was among Britain's largest overseas; and the royalties from the oil concession were Iran's main source of revenue. These facts pointed to a strong reciprocal interest, but Iranian nationalists thought otherwise. They considered their country's share inadequate, and they blamed the British Government for the fact that their own Government misused even the share they had. The A.I.O.C. negotiated a more favourable agreement with the Iranian Government under General Razmara in 1950; but his acceptance was withdrawn under Nationalist pressure, and in March 1951 he was murdered. After an uneasy interlude, the Government was entrusted to the Nationalist leader Mussadiq, who had introduced a law making oil concessions to foreign powers illegal as long ago as 1944. He announced the nationalization of the A.I.O.C. in April 1951, but both the British Government and the oil company refused to recognize it.

For six months the company and the Government, aided by American representatives, tried to negotiate with Mussadiq. By October, when negotiation was seen to be hopeless, the company's British employees were all withdrawn from Abadan and the refinery ceased work. It remained idle until 1954. In the meantime a further year was passed in a vain attempt to compromise with Mussadiq. Although the economic situation of the country grew worse daily, it made little difference to the mass of the people, who had never benefited significantly from the oil revenues even when they existed. Mussadiq still enjoyed enthusiastic popular support, including that of the illegal Communist-led Tudeh Party, which carried him back to power when the Shah dismissed him in August 1952. From that moment he seemed to carry all before him. He won a formal victory, which seemed more substantial than it was, over Britain in the International Court; and he severed diplomatic relations with Britain in October 1952. But in 1953 he carried his ambitions too far. He obtained extraordinary powers and tried to usurp prerogatives of the Shah; he allowed the Tudeh Party increasingly to dominate his policies; he sought to abolish parliament (the *Majlis*) by a referendum. In August 1953 a well-contrived *coup d'état* overthrew him for good.

Politically the consequences of the overthrow of Mussadiq were two: at home, a reversion to the situation as it had been before his heyday; internationally, a closer relation between Iran and the West, culminating in the Baghdad Pact. The further future was by no means secure. But economically things were much changed, both in Iran and in her international relations. The oil industry was brought back into operation by an international consortium in 1954, and Iran enjoyed more favourable terms than it had had with the A.I.O.C. But the demand for Iranian oil was not what it had been: the gap caused by its interruption had been filled with unexpected ease, particularly from Kuwait, which was the main beneficiary of the oil dispute. (This lesson was well learned by the Iraqi revolutionaries in 1958, who took care that their revolution should not interrupt Iraq's oil production.) On the other hand, Britain also suffered. In the new oil consortium the British stake was only 40 per cent, whereas American companies, which had previously held no stake in Iranian oil, now collectively held 40 per cent also. This was the most striking, though not the only, symptom of the growing presence of the U.S.A. in the Middle East. Others will be found, particularly in the strategic context.

The strategic revolution, which took place only after the Second World War, was partly a matter of changes in the nature of weapons and partly of developments within the area. Even up to the early 1950s the defence of the Middle East meant, from the British point of view, occupying a strategic point near the centre of the area to guard the perimeter against external attack, as it had been guarded in two world wars. That was the purpose of the Canal Zone base. But the invention of the hydrogen-bomb convinced Churchill's Government, firstly, that another major war of the kind envisaged was exceedingly unlikely, and secondly, that if it came the Canal Zone would be unusable. At the same time it became increasingly apparent that the chief threat to Middle Eastern security came from within the area and not from without.

Few states of the Middle East had any real sense of a threat from the Soviet Union. The few that did were the Soviet Union's neighbours, and these joined the Baghdad Pact in 1955. The rest saw the threat to their security principally from their neighbours, and this was especially true of the relations between Israel and the Arab states. Such local rivalries were the likeliest causes of war. It was to meet these dangers that the Tripartite Declaration of 1950 was signed. In addition, Britain had commitments to particular Arab states – treaties with Libya, Jordan, Iraq, and the Persian Gulf sheikhdoms – and an obligation of self-interest to safeguard the extraction and transport of oil. Such local commitments did not require a base on the scale of the Canal Zone. The headquarters was accordingly moved to Cyprus in 1954, with the intention of using it as a sort of advanced guard-post rather than a major base. Since a British foothold on Cyprus was still required even after the settlement of February 1959, it can be assumed that the strategic revolution had not yet gone a stage further, but not that it would never do so.

Both the economic and the strategic revolutions were accompanied, and indeed accelerated, by a political and social revolution, which was the most intricate of the three. It was again the product of the Western impact on the Middle East, like all the other major changes in the way of life of the area. In the political field the two ideas which the West introduced were those of nationalism and social reform; and the West also called into existence the new classes which were to carry them into effect – the bourgeois intelligentsia, the urban proletariat, the managers and administrators, and in particular the army officers. Both ideas were bound to produce revolutionary effects. Nationalism in its Middle Eastern form contributed to the destruction of the Ottoman Empire, only to create successor-states whose nationalist aspirations were mutually incompatible. Peoples who had coexisted without difficulty under the Ottoman *millet*-system became rivals as soon as national boundaries were drawn on the map behind which they had to separate themselves: not only as between Jews and Arabs, nor even between Arabs and Turks and Iranians, but within the Arab world itself between Iraqis and Egyptians, or between the Saudi and Hashemite dynasties. The determination to achieve modern social conditions let loose no less disruptive forces within each of the new states, precipitating the over-

throw in one after another of the traditional monarchies and aristo-
cracies. Both movements found in President Nasser their popular hero
and symbol.

All the revolutionary changes in the Middle East, but particularly
those in the military and political context, were illustrated by the
prolonged dispute between Britain and Egypt over the revision of the
1936 Treaty. The argument began in 1946 and ended only in 1954, so
that both Labour and Conservative Governments were deeply preoccu-
pied with it. The climax came, indeed, almost at the moment of transition between the two Governments, when in October 1951 Egypt
refused to join the Middle East Defence Organization, by which
Britain had hoped to replace the Treaty, and denounced the Treaty
itself. The two issues on which the argument turned were, firstly, the
future of the British base in the Suez Canal Zone and, secondly, the
status of the Sudan, which all Egyptian Governments wished to treat
as an integral part of Egypt. On 27 October 1951, as the new British
Government took office, the Egyptian Government brought both
matters peremptorily to a head by presenting a note calling on Britain
to evacuate both the Canal Zone and the Sudan.

Since the British Government refused to comply, the Egyptians
began to apply pressure. For the next three years negotiations were
accompanied by threats and violence. Egyptian labour was withdrawn
from the base. Bitter fighting took place within the Canal Zone, and in
reprisal for an attack by British troops on the police station in Ismailia –
itself, of course, also a reprisal – a violent and planned attack on
European property and lives took place in Cairo in January 1952. A
series of changes of government in Egypt led to no improvement. But
the Egyptian régime, and in particular the monarchy, had succeeded
in antagonizing not only the British but also its own people and, in
particular, the army. A military *coup d'état* on the night of 22–23 July
1952 brought to power a new government, led at first by General
Neguib and later by Colonel Nasser. For a time it seemed that negotiation with the new régime might be more fruitful; but the same obstacles
as before made it painfully slow. First the future of the Sudan and then
the Canal Zone base still obstructed progress.

The British Government had published a statute for self-government
in the Sudan in April 1952. In October it authorized the statute to be
put into effect, and in February 1953 an agreement with Egypt was
announced for self-determination of the Sudan within three years. The
Sudanese were to have the right either to unite with Egypt, or to be

fully independent, or to be independent within the Commonwealth. The Egyptians were no doubt confident that the Sudanese would make the first choice, and the British Government perhaps expected the third, but the result of the elections held in November was in fact the choice of a government pledged to complete independence. There were ugly disturbances before the first independent Sudanese parliament met in March 1954, and there were further difficulties and disturbances ahead for the new state, which eventually abandoned parliamentary democracy after a *coup d'état* in 1958. Egypt, too, did not hesitate to continue pressing her claims upon the Sudan, sometimes by violence. But from 1952 onwards the Sudan ceased to be an issue obstructing the Anglo-Egyptian negotiations.

Disagreement over the Canal Zone persisted for another two years after the advent of the new régime in 1952. There were vigorous forces opposing compromise behind both the Egyptian and the British Governments. But gradually the two Governments narrowed the issues between them, and finally the British Government gave way on the last points concerning the future management of the base. The base was to be kept in being by British civilian contractors and available to British use in certain defined cases of war; but it is doubtful whether either side regarded these arrangements as likely to last, nor did they in fact survive the Suez Canal crisis of 1956. The British Government entered into the new treaty, which was signed on 19 October 1954, because it regarded the base as obsolete in the new strategic situation and because it thought that the existing Egyptian Government was the best that it could expect to see in power. The Egyptian Government signed the treaty, having gained almost all it claimed, in order to free its hands for the work of consolidating the revolution at home and perhaps extending it elsewhere.

The revolutionary changes which have been illustrated in the Middle East – economic, strategic and political – all have two things in common. They all owe a good deal to Western influence, and they have all tended towards the extinction of Western power in the area. The former predominance of the Western Powers, particularly Britain, has become a thing of the past. But so long as their economies are based on oil, their dependence on the Middle East, which has three-quarters of the world's proved oil reserves, is greater than ever; and for Britain there is an additional dependence for the strength of sterling. The minute state of Kuwait illustrates the whole problem: it is about the size of Wales; it produces nearly half the oil consumed in Britain every day; it has larger proved oil reserves than the entire North American continent; and the Kuweit Investment Board is the largest single investor on the London Stock Exchange. One of the decisive shocks in the Middle East crisis of 1958, abortive though it proved, was perhaps the news that the Sheikh of Kuweit had gone to meet President Nasser in Damascus. For the traditional British policy that the Middle East must never be dominated by a potentially hostile power applied as much to a power within the area as to an external power. In the later 1950s President Nasser seemed, on his own nomination, to be a likelier candidate for that role than any other.

But Britain was no longer able to prevent such a prospect with her own unaided resources. As much as anywhere else, if not more so, she needed allies in the Middle East; and the irruption of the Soviet Union increased that need after 1955. The British Government sought American help over Palestine in 1946–7, and obtained American and French support in the Tripartite Declaration of 1950; it proposed that a token allied force should join in the defence of the Canal Zone in 1952; it invited American representatives to join in the negotiations with the Iranian Government in 1951 and with the Egyptian Government in 1953; it sought American and finally French help against Nasser in 1955–6; it invited the mediation of N.A.T.O. in the Cyprus dispute in 1957–8.

Not all of these steps were taken eagerly, or perhaps as soon as they might have been, for there was still reluctance to admit that Britain was no longer able to act alone in the Middle East. But after the Canal crisis the fact was inescapable; and the crisis of 1958 showed that, given the support of her allies, Britain was still a considerable Middle Eastern power. Moreover, it was not only impossible to act alone: it was also unnecessary, since Britain no longer had any exclusive interest that was not shared with other countries. The economic interest, which was oil, was shared with all Western Europe. The defence interest was shared with the other powers of the Baghdad Pact and with the U.S.A. The political interest, which was stability, independence and prosperity, was shared with everyone concerned, particularly the peoples of the Middle East themselves.

Africa

The interest in the Middle East was a familiar actuality to almost everyone in the British Isles in their everyday lives: witness the introduction of petrol rationing for six months after the Suez Canal crisis. The interest in Africa, on the other hand, was only gradually beginning to dawn in the 1950s. In 1945 the Scarbrough Commission reported that facilities for studying Africa in Britain were 'unworthy of our country and our people'. It was still the Dark Continent, and even the White Man's Burden. Today it is the Continent of the Future, though no one can say what the future will be. Its late development in international relations was no doubt due, apart from the climatic and psychological reasons, to the fact that it was poor in the first modern source of power, coal; and the second, which is oil, was only discovered in the Sahara late in the 1950s.

But in the future sources of power it is immensely rich. Its potential hydro-electric capacity is three times that of Europe: a quarter of the world's potential capacity lies in the Congo basin alone. The ex-Belgian Congo is also one of the world's major suppliers of uranium. For other industrial and strategic metals – manganese, chrome, copper, zinc, for instance – one or other of the African states stands first or second among the world's exporters. For Britain in particular the economic importance of Africa has greatly increased since the war. The cocoa of West Africa (Ghana and Nigeria being first and third among the world's suppliers) makes a major contribution to the strength of the Sterling Area. So does the facility of buying gold from South Africa for sterling instead of dollars.

The strategic importance of Africa has been still more slowly recognized, and that partly under American impulsion. During and after the Second World War, Africa was looked on only as the hinterland of Europe and the Middle East. Algeria was included in N.A.T.O. not only because it was constitutionally a part of France but also because North Africa provided a foothold for defending Europe. The long-debated plan to establish a British base in Kenya was realized only when the hostility of certain Middle East states (particularly Egypt and Syria, forming the United Arab Republic) set up a potential barrier by air, land and sea between the Mediterranean and the Indian Ocean. The phenomena which drew attention to Africa's strategic importance in its own right were partly economic and partly political. The former have already been described. The latter may be summed up in the explosive outburst of African nationalism, heightened by several outside influences: for instance, the encouragement of the newly independent Asian states, first expressed at Bandung in 1955; the declared ambition of President Nasser to be a leader of Africa as well as the Middle East and the Islamic world; and the growing interest of the Soviet Union, which lies at the other end of the north-south route that passes through the Middle East. It may be that the future importance of the Middle East will lie again in its position at the crossroads, as it did before the discovery of oil, and that the importance of Africa will become primary to it, as that of India once was.

In the 1950s the European Powers barely began to scratch the surface of the problems of Africa, which they had taken upon themselves and their successors in the scramble for African colonies during the nineteenth century and earlier. In some ways they made the problems worse by pursuing fundamentally different policies in their relations with the indigenous African peoples. Between the two poles of identity and differentiation of the white and coloured races, the French, the Portuguese, the Belgians, the British and the Afrikaners each adopted a different position, with greater or lesser gaps between them, and sometimes with no less great gaps between their theory and their practice. Nor were they operating in watertight compartments, insulated from each other's influence; for the boundaries of the African states are generally no more than the accidents of history, within which different peoples are brought together by chance and across which their sympathies freely move.

The problem of working out a new and permanent relation between Europeans and non-Europeans was complicated by the fact, and the varying extent, of European settlement in certain parts of the continent, ranging from 30 per cent of the population in South Africa and 14 per cent in Algeria to insignificant minorities in West Africa; not to mention the thinly but widely spread Asian immigration. It was becoming increasingly impossible effectively to pursue policies in fundamental contradiction with each other in the different territories: *apartheid* in South Africa, 'partnership' in the Central Federation, 'assimilation' in the French and Portuguese territories, and 'modified differentiation' in the Belgian. The cracks in the old pattern were already obvious in 1959, when the British and French dependencies were already well on the way to independence and even the Belgian Congo was within sight of it; but the shape of the future pattern was still obscure.

Asia

By comparison with Africa, Asia was lucky in the post-war period. Partly it was the luck of possessing an antecedent culture and civilization, which survived the imposition of European imperialism and took over what was valuable in it. Partly it was the luck of war, which proved in 1941–2 and again in 1950–1 that an Asian people could stand up to Europeans and Americans on equal terms (a lesson originally taught in 1905, but temporarily forgotten). After being driven out of Malaya, Singapore, Indonesia, Burma, the Philippines, Hong Kong, and being compelled to surrender Indo-China and barely saving the Indian sub-continent, it was inconceivable that Europeans and Americans should re-establish themselves as sovereign powers in Asia again. The French and the Dutch, who were slower than the British and the Americans to recognize this fact, learned it bitterly the hard way a few years later. But once the new situation was accepted, it seemed to make relatively little difference to the vital interests of the Western Powers, which were economic. Trade continued to flow in the channels to which it was accustomed, despite independence; though where independence was accompanied by Communism, political barriers were sometimes deliberately put in the way.

The removal of British sovereignty from all but a few Asian territories – Hong Kong and North Borneo being the most important still remaining – left the British economic interest unconcealed and needing no apology. S.E. Asia produces most of the world's rubber, one of the few raw materials that both the U.S.A. and the U.S.S.R. have to import. It also accounts for more than half the world's production of tin. In both cases one of the two leading producers is Malaya, to the great benefit of the Sterling Area. S.E. Asia is also the world's main producer of rice, of which Britain's Commonwealth partners, India, Pakistan and Ceylon, are the main importers. Other economic interests are on a smaller scale but not negligible: for instance, oil from North Borneo, and the *entrepôt* trade of Hong Kong, which has grown extensively since the war although China no longer accounts for so much as half of it. The strategic interest of Britain in the area, and therefore the purpose of Britain's participation in S.E.A.T.O., is to defend the economic interest: access to the raw materials, and trade routes to and from their sources, and beyond them to and from Australia and New Zealand.

Disorder and war are the chief dangers to the British interest in Asia, but both can spring from many different causes. Nationalism is a familiar one, which has largely been satisfied in so far as it was directed against Western imperialism, though not in so far as it is directed against rival Asian nationalisms. The dependence of so many national economies on one or two commodities, whose prices in the world market may vary abruptly, is another troublesome factor. International action has done something to mitigate it, though neither the U.S. nor the Soviet Government has gone out of its way to help the process. The third source of danger is the most serious: this is the explosive growth of population, particularly in the three most important Asian countries, India, China and Japan. It was the population problem of Japan, coupled with the island's shortage of raw materials and its need for foreign markets, that provided the economic impulse behind Japanese aggression in the 1930s. The war and its aftermath cured all the symptoms but left some of the roots of the problem untouched. Japan has learned that it is neither necessary nor desirable to impose political control abroad in order to secure markets and trade; and land-reform has mitigated the economic problem at home. But the basic problem remains: Japan's population will exceed 100,000,000 by 1970, and the greatest and most natural market for her trade, which is China, is still largely closed to her by political barriers.

China is also afflicted by the problem of a population growing too fast for her resources, and so is India. The fact that the two countries have similar problems in this and other respects, and that they have chosen diametrically opposite ways of trying to solve them, is crucial to the contemporary history of Asia. It is of extraordinary importance to the future of Britain and the Commonwealth that the democratic experiment in India should succeed, for if it does not succeed there democracy may well be abandoned altogether throughout Asia and Africa as well. Much, if not everything, depends on the ability of a democratic government to achieve an expansion of production, and therefore of national income, at a slightly higher rate than the expansion of population, which is itself about 2 per cent *per annum*.

India's national income is at present estimated at less than £30 *per caput*, which is well below one-tenth of Britain's. In the 1950s there were serious signs that the standard of living might be falling instead of rising. It was questioned even under the unchallenged leadership of Nehru whether democratic methods were capable of the drastic simultaneous operation which was needed to increase production and hold down the expanding population. Britain's interest in this crucial problem was represented in particular by the Colombo Plan, from which India was a major beneficiary. But as the sterling balances accumulated by India during the war were run down, it became increasingly plain that the main source of capital for the future would have to be the U.S.A.

Latin America

The contention that political independence is an essential prerequisite of modern economic development, which has been argued forcibly in Asia since the war and more recently in Africa, seems to be borne out by the experience of the remaining great continent of past colonialism, Latin America, even if only recently. Latin America is still best known in Europe for political disorder, but its economic development and potentiality were fast becoming recognized in the late 1950s. After more than a century of independence (though less in the case of Brazil and Mexico, two of the largest and now the most industrialized Latin American countries), the continent was beginning to achieve an economic status in the world commensurate with its potential resources. Although no Latin American country would figure among the richest 15 per cent of the world's population, no less than nine of them – Argentina, Brazil, Chile, Colombia, Cuba, Mexico, Peru, Uruguay and Venezuela – would figure among the next 30 per cent: that is to say, among the most prosperous half of mankind, although in an absolute sense still much underdeveloped. The sources of their prosperity were of particular interest to Britain: oil from Venezuela, bauxite from the Guianas and Jamaica, copper from Chile, tin from Bolivia, and other metals from half a dozen others. The evolution of a new member of the Commonwealth in the Caribbean, and the survival of two British colonies on the continent, constituted a moral as well as a material commitment for Britain.

The sources of anxiety for the future of Latin America were similar to those elsewhere. There was, firstly, nationalism, played upon by Communism: British Guiana was the first territory under the British flag to have elected a quasi-Communist Government. There was next the economic vulnerability of countries dependent upon a single major export commodity, to a degree even more accentuated than in S.E. Asia and scarcely less than among the oil-producers of the Middle East: in Cuba sugar, in Venezuela oil, in Colombia and Brazil coffee, in Bolivia tin, in Chile copper, all account for 50 per cent or more by value of the country's exports.

There was finally the dependence of most of the more important among them on trade with the U.S.A. More than half the imports of Mexico, Cuba, Venezuela, Colombia, Ecuador, Peru and Chile came from the U.S.A., with a consequent vulnerability to the effects of any American recession. For obvious reasons, since the Second World War

Britain played only a marginal part in the evolution of the American hemisphere, except in the Caribbean. Latin America was the very heart of the dollar area and the U.S. sphere of influence. When it came into the news in Britain, more often than not the occasion was an attack on British imperialism: by Guatemala on British Honduras, by Argentina or Chile on the Antarctic territories, or by revolutionary nationalists on the colonial Government of British Guiana. But the feeling was growing in thoughtful circles in Britain that the continent was becoming increasingly important to Britain for more material reasons.

The reasons can be generalized for all the underdeveloped areas of the world. They contain about two-thirds of the world's population and a very large proportion of the world's raw materials. For a country like Britain (and there are other such countries, for instance Japan) which has a population too large to feed from its own resources and practically no raw materials, the underdeveloped areas present two complementary assets: a source of supply and a market. It is obviously to Britain's advantage to safeguard the one and to develop the other. The security and stability of such areas can only be guaranteed by international co-operation, but to develop them as markets is a matter of national enterprise and competition.

The markets themselves change as the new countries develop their own secondary industries, and their demand switches from consumer goods to capital goods, as is already happening in Latin America since the war and will eventually happen in the Middle East, Asia and Africa as well. Such development, its orderly and stable progress and a mutually profitable participation in it, are the fundamental British interests in the new countries and the reason why British foreign policy is so much concerned with them. It has been said on high authority that 'scarcely any question relating to foreign affairs is exclusively political', and 'fully one-third of the work of the Foreign Service as a whole is preponderantly economic'.[1] This is nowhere more true than among the new countries, in which Britain's economic future lies as her sovereign responsibilities diminish.

There were thus reasons of self-interest, both economic and political, for the close attention paid by Britain after the Second World War to the needs and susceptibilities of the new countries, especially those which had once been British colonies. In a healthy state of international relations, self-interest and mutual interest are not far apart; and this

[1] Lord Strang, *The Foreign Office* (Allen & Unwin, 1955), pp. 21, 39.

fact was increasingly realized among the new countries towards the end of the period under review, in contrast with the immediate post-war years. But quite apart from the mutual interest of paying attention to them, it was in fact politically impossible not to do so. No great power could conceivably ignore the problems presented by the small states and new nations emerging after the Second World War. It was from them that the possibility of future wars arose; it was among them that the field of competition lay between Communism and Western democracy; theirs were the problems of poverty, over-population, race relations, nationalist rivalry and sovereign status, which had to be solved to secure the stability of the world; and theirs, collectively, were the decisive votes in the United Nations. As Europe settled down into a deadlock which might well mean permanent peace, Asia, Africa and Latin America became the world's stage.

10

The United Nations

A DIPLOMATIC historian wrote in 1923:[1]

'British statesmen have discovered that the highest interests and the abiding prosperity of their country are bound up with the vitality and authority of the one operative organization for the preservation of Peace – the League of Nations.'

The same soberly optimistic belief, applied to the United Nations, again inspired the first post-war Defence White Papers, in 1946, 1947 and 1948; but in 1949 a sense of 'grievous disappointment' was expressed instead. From 1950 onwards the United Nations is only perfunctorily mentioned in the White Papers, its Charter providing a 'framework' within which Britain's regional alliances would operate. Even its satisfactory reaction to aggression in Korea did not rehabilitate the United Nations in the eyes of the authors of the White Papers. N.A.T.O. rather than the United Nations became the hub of Britain's foreign policy. The United Nations was seen more as a diplomatic meeting-ground than as the embryonic World Government which had been envisaged, even by British representatives, in 1945. The general British attitude towards the organization became one of 'tepid acceptance'.[2]

The seeds of disappointment were sown even before the founding conference at San Francisco in April 1945. Churchill had argued in 1943 that the successor to the League of Nations should take the form of three Regional Councils (for Europe, the American hemisphere and the Pacific), under a World Council. His contention was that 'only the countries whose interests were directly affected by a dispute . . . could be expected to apply themselves with sufficient vigour to secure a settlement'. This conception was in part realized by the creation of the Organization of American States; but as a general principle it was

[1] *Cambridge History of British Foreign Policy*, vol. III, p. 538.
[2] Geoffrey Goodwin, *Britain and the United Nations* (O.U.P. for R.I.I.A., 1958), p. 421.

opposed by the U.S.S.R. and incidentally also by some of the Common-wealth countries. It was superseded by the conception of a universal organization in the Moscow four-power declaration of October 1943. By 1947 Bevin himself had been converted to Churchill's preference for regional arrangements, but it was then too late to undertake any serious reconstruction of the United Nations, although the Charter theoretically allowed for it.

Bevin's personal disillusionment began when the First General Assembly and the Security Council were meeting in London early in 1946. Apart from the criticisms of British actions in Greece, the Levant states and Indonesia, these were also the occasions of the first Soviet 'veto' and the first Soviet 'walk-out'. Although none of the criticisms of Britain was sustained, the experience had a permanently souring effect on Bevin's attitude towards the United Nations. The memoirs of the first Secretary-General indicate an unco-operative attitude on his part from the beginning:[1] for instance, over the election of the first Secretary-General himself, and the appointment of Assistant Under-Secretaries (one of whom was to be British) on his staff. Many of the complaints against the 'negative attitude', the 'self-righteousness' or the 'inaction' of the British bear particularly on the Palestine dispute,[2] which was referred to the United Nations by Britain in February 1947.

At the meeting of the General Assembly in April 1947 which first discussed Palestine, the British representative made it clear that Britain could not accept the sole responsibility for enforcing any decision that might be taken. The warning was more than once repeated in the following year. It was necessary because in the circumstances it was impossible that any decision should be reached which would not need force to impose it. In fact between the spring of 1947 and May 1948, when the British mandate terminated, the United Nations produced a series of complicated and unrealistic plans which showed without any need of commentary the futility of attempting such an operation through the medium of a large committee. When the General Assembly finally agreed that Palestine should be partitioned from July 1948, after the end of the mandate, the British Government declined to make any British troops available for carrying through the operation. The Secretary-General later strongly criticized the British Government's refusal, arguing that it should at least have co-operated with other powers in the task. In reality, however, there was no intermediate

---

[1] Trygve Lie, *In the Cause of Peace*, pp. 20, 47–8, 211, 285, 314.
[2] Ibid., pp. 160, 163–5, 183–6.

possibility between carrying all the responsibility and carrying none: for Britain alone had forces in Palestine, and no other power could or would have sent more than token forces to help in an operation that was bound to involve bloodshed, probably on a considerable scale.

When fighting broke out in May 1948 between the Jews of Palestine and their Arab neighbours, the United Nations was three times successful, in June, July and October, in persuading the combatants to cease fire, and eventually in bringing about a series of bilateral truces between Israel (which had been proclaimed as an independent state in May) and most of the Arab states concerned. The cost to the United Nations was the murder of Count Bernadotte, whom it had appointed as Mediator, and others of its officials. The conclusion was plain that such operations could not be effectively carried out unless the United Nations had some kind of armed force at its disposal. It was not until eight years later, and in connexion with the same problem, that a United Nations Emergency Force was formed, to occupy a buffer position between Egypt and Israel at the end of 1956. In the meantime the United Nations had to be content with nothing more forceful than Observer Missions.

It was not for want of trying that the organization failed to create its own permanent force. One of the earliest acts of the United Nations was to create a Military Staff Committee of the major powers, in accordance with Article 47 of the Charter, to plan the creation of a permanent U.N. force for the protection of peace. It first met in London in 1946, and presented a report to the United Nations in April 1947; but being unable to agree even on the size and arms structure of the international force, it achieved no result and never met again from 1948 onwards. The Secretary-General tried once more to create what he called a 'Field Force' in 1948, and actually secured a favourable vote from the General Assembly in November 1949; but again nothing came of it. When the first international force fought under the U.N. flag in Korea in 1950, it was in reality nothing but an American army with a large South Korean contingent and token contributions from elsewhere, as witness the proportions of casualties: South Korean 64 per cent, United States 32 per cent, remainder 4 per cent. Only in the most nominal sense can the forces in Korea be said to have been under U.N. command, though this is not to deny that the Korean War was fought, in Attlee's words, 'to vindicate the authority of the United Nations'.

Before 1950, the inability of the United Nations to place any physical sanction behind its decisions was a more severe test of Britain's loyalty to the conception of international organization than it was for almost any other power. For Britain was, more than any other, a power that desired certain definite things to be done by international agreement. The British Government's view was later expressed in Eden's argument that the Security Council ought to be the 'cabinet' of the United Nations,[1] which seems not to have been supported by other powers. The Soviet Government knew from the beginning that the United Nations would never decide anything in its favour against the wishes of the U.S.A. so long as the balance of power in the original membership was maintained; for of the first fifty-one members, twenty were Latin American states from which a substantial pro-American vote could generally be elicited. The Soviet Union therefore protected itself against adverse decisions in the Security Council by the 'veto', and used the General Assembly as a forum for exposing the misdeeds of other powers without expecting practical results.

The U.S. Government, on the other hand, seldom needed practical results from international agreement before 1950; and within its particular sphere of interest, the creation of the Organization of American States in 1948 provided the essentials of regional co-operation without the risk of interference by other great powers. Like the Soviet Government, it used the United Nations as a forum for public criticism of its antagonists; for instance, at the Economic and Social Council (ECOSOC) in February 1949, it demanded the inspection of Soviet labour camps, but without expecting that any result would be achieved. The same was true when the Berlin dispute was referred to the United Nations in September 1948, and the question of German elections in November 1951. These things were done for the record. But when the U.S.A. required action, it took the required action first by itself and obtained the sanction of the United Nations afterwards, as in the case of the intervention in Korea in 1950; or it never sought U.N. sanction at all, as in the case of the Truman Doctrine in 1947.

In the early years of the United Nations, the British position was different. Britain wished the organization to work, and to work collectively, in a way that the League of Nations had failed to do. The intended difference was implicit in the Charter, which lays responsibility on the organization as a corporate entity, whereas the Covenant of the League never referred to the organization, only to the responsibilities of its members. In the case of the League, 'the emphasis falls

[1] *Full Circle*, p. 495.

on the components, not on the construct';[1] or, put in another way, 'the emphasis was on the obligations of Members rather than on the authority of its organs'.[2] The U.S. Government, having had no direct experience of the League, was content to operate within the United Nations in accordance with the discarded principle. The British Government was determined to avoid a repetition of the League's failure, which had been precisely the failure of its individual members, by making the new principle work. It was unfortunate that all the early attempts by the British Government to secure some kind of collectively agreed action ended in failure.

In addition to the case of Palestine in 1947–8, the major disputes in which Britain was involved prior to 1956 were the dispute with Albania in 1946–7, the civil war in Greece from 1946–9, the Egyptian blockade of Israel since 1948, and the Anglo-Iranian oil dispute in 1951–2. In none of these did the British Government derive any satisfaction from the United Nations or its organs.

The case against Albania, arising from the mining of British ships in the Corfu Channel, resulted in the condemnation of Albania in the Security Council (against a Soviet abstention) and an award of damages, which were never paid, in the International Court. The Greek civil war led to frequent condemnations of Greece's northern neighbours in the United Nations, and to the appointment of a United Nations Special Commission on the Balkans (U.N.S.C.O.B.) in November 1947 to watch the frontiers; but what brought the civil war to an end was massive American military aid to Greece and the defection of Yugoslavia from the Soviet Bloc, rather than any action of the United Nations. The Egyptian blockade of Israel, especially the closure of the Suez Canal to Israeli ships or ships carrying goods to Israel, was expressly condemned by the United Nations on a British motion in July 1951; but it continued as before. Finally, the reference of the Anglo-Iranian oil dispute to the Security Council in October 1951 led only to an adjournment of the debate, pending a ruling of the International Court, to avert a moral defeat of the British case; and when the International Court reached its decision in July 1952, it was only to declare itself incompetent to judge the dispute. The British representative at the United Nations gave expression to a feeling of 'restlessness, not to say indignation', which was widely shared in Britain.

[1] H. G. Nicholas, *The United Nations as a Political Institution* (O.U.P., 1959), 38.

[2] Geoffrey Goodwin, *Britain and the United Nations*, p. 42.

There was naturally some pressure for a revision of the Charter, or at least of the rules of procedure at the United Nations. As early as November 1945 Eden spoke in the House of Commons of the desirability of reviewing the Charter, and a year later Bevin tried to get a 'code of conduct' accepted. But more drastic measures were needed if any real change was to be made. It was the Americans who initiated them, in the first place with General Marshall's plan for an Interim Committee of the General Assembly (the 'Little Assembly'), which would remain in session between sessions of the General Assembly itself and deal with matters which might have been blocked by the 'veto' in the Security Council. The plan was proposed in September 1947, and approved by the General Assembly in November, though the British Government was not enthusiastic for it. It functioned intermittently, and was prolonged indefinitely by a vote of the General Assembly in November 1949; but in 1955 it adjourned *sine die*.

A second initiative of the U.S. Government followed upon the outbreak of the Korean War in 1950. When the war began on 25 June, the Security Council was immediately summoned; but it was boycotted by the Soviet representative, who had absented himself since the Council had refused to give China's seat to the Communist Government in Peking earlier in the same year. His absence made it possible for the Security Council to condemn the North Koreans and to vote for collective military action against them. The absence of the Soviet representative was deemed not to constitute a 'veto', in accordance with precedents going back to 1947. But clearly such a lucky chance was unlikely to occur again. The U.S. Secretary of State accordingly took the initiative in proposing a resolution, under the title 'Uniting for Peace', to enable the General Assembly to take cognizance of a dispute when consideration of it in the Security Council had been frustrated by a veto. The resolution was supported by Britain and France and was passed in November 1950. Ironically, the first occasion when the General Assembly met under the terms of the resolution was to frustrate the Anglo-French action against Egypt in 1956, after Britain and France had vetoed two resolutions in the Security Council.

The intervention in Korea thus remained, from the British point of view, an exceptional example of effective action by the United Nations in the sense desired by British interests. Both before and after 1950, much more of the United Nations' interest appeared to be devoted to the grievances of the smaller and newer nations or the non-independent peoples, generally directed against the larger and older nations; and these were popular causes in which Britain was often, though not invariably, on the unpopular side. Sometimes the complaints were presented by the aggrieved states themselves: for instance, in 1946 by Syria and Lebanon against the presence of French and British troops, and by Iran against Soviet troops in Azerbaijan; in 1947 by Egypt against the presence of British troops under the 1936 Treaty; in 1953 by Burma against the incursion of Kuomintang Chinese troops into the north of the country; and in 1954 by Guatemala against incursions from Nicaragua with U.S. support. Complaints of the newer and smaller states against each other were less frequent, but they did occur: for instance, by Israel against Egypt and vice versa over incidents on their common frontiers; by Pakistan against India over Kashmir; by Siam against the threat to her frontiers from the Vietminh in May 1954; and by Jordan against the United Arab Republic in 1958. In none of these cases did any decisive action come from the United Nations.

The more difficult cases were those in which complaints were presented by a member of the U.N. on behalf of people not directly represented in the organization, because not independent. Such cases raised the issue of 'domestic jurisdiction', over which Britain, as a colonial power, usually felt obliged to support the view that the U.N. was not competent. Among the principal examples were the case against Dutch actions in Indonesia, raised by Australia and India in 1947–8; the attempts of the Arab states to compel discussion of French relations with Morocco in 1951, Tunisia in 1952, and, finally, Algeria in 1955; the Indian complaints against South Africa's policy of *apartheid* from 1946 onwards; the Egyptian espousal of the cause of the Somalis whose territory Britain had agreed to cede to Ethiopia in 1955; and the Cyprus dispute, repeatedly referred to the U.N. by Greece from 1954–8. The contention that such cases lay outside the U.N.'s competence may have been juridically valid, but it was not readily accepted; for the organization's right to interest itself in the political progress of dependent peoples is written into the Charter, in contrast to the Covenant of the League of Nations, which only laid upon the colonial powers the obligation to ensure 'the just treatment of the native inhabitants of territories under their control'. It was also questioned by some lawyers whether discussion at the U.N. amounted to 'intervention' under Article 2 (7) of the Charter.

The United Nations' political interest in non-independent peoples is expressed through two organs, apart from the General Assembly. The first is the Trusteeship Council, concerned with the eleven trust territories for which responsibility was divided between Australia, Belgium, Britain, France, Italy, New Zealand and the U.S.A. (South Africa is excluded from the list because its Government refused to place the former mandated territory of South-West Africa under U.N. trusteeship on the grounds that there was no legal obligation to do so – a view condemned by a majority of the General Assembly in 1947, but supported by the British Government and later upheld by the International Court.) The second organ, for which there is no clearly expressed or implied provision in the Charter, is the Committee on Information from Non-Self-Governing Territories, which was not intended to be permanent when it was created *ad hoc* in 1946, but took on a continuing lease of life in 1949.

The latter body concerns itself with colonies and other territories that might fall under the principle of 'domestic jurisdiction'. It has therefore been something of an embarrassment to the colonial powers. Although the British Government opposed the creation of the Committee, it has not refused to work with it. Nevertheless, Britain adheres to the principle of 'domestic jurisdiction' with some tenacity. It was this doctrine which prevented the Malayan emergency and the Vietminh rebellion in Indo-China from coming before the United Nations. The inability of the U.N. to solve the disputes between the Dutch and the Indonesians suggests that in S.E. Asia at any rate no substantial advantage was lost by the exclusion of the U.N. from intervention.

The most disagreeable case involving Britain to which the doctrine of 'domestic jurisdiction' could be, and was, applied was that of Cyprus.[1] The Greek Government tried to bring the case to the U.N. on five occasions from 1954 to 1958. On the first two occasions the subject did not even succeed in being inscribed on the agenda of the General Assembly. But it became increasingly difficult for Britain to argue that Cyprus did not concern Greece or Turkey, when it plainly concerned the whole Western Alliance and many other countries as well. At the third attempt the Greeks obtained a favourable vote on their resolution, but not by a majority sufficient to require action. At the fourth and fifth attempts, in 1957 and 1958, compromise resolutions were passed, the second much more innocuous than the first. By the end of 1958 the Greeks decided to give way, and a settlement was worked out between the Greek, Turkish and British Governments without further reference to the United Nations. It is difficult to say

[1] For full details, see *Cyprus: the Dispute and the Settlement* (O.U.P. for R.I.I.A., 1959).

exactly what effective role the U.N. played in this dispute. Certainly it did not find the solution. But it served to bring moral pressure to bear on Britain against her resolve to maintain the *status quo*; it probably served to convince the Greeks that world opinion was not sufficiently solid on their side to justify further intransigence; and for the rest, it only served to harden people in the opinions they already held, for or against British sovereignty over such a territory.

The tendency of the General Assembly to function as a forum for the grievances of small powers was increased after December 1955, when sixteen new states were admitted simultaneously after many years of wrangling between the great powers about each other's protégés. This was much the largest single accretion in the progressive expansion of the U.N. from fifty-one states in 1945 to eighty-two in 1959. So far as it is valid to speak of blocs, the distribution of the membership in 1959 was as follows: Western Europe seventeen, Soviet Bloc nine, Commonwealth ten, the Americas twenty-one, the Afro-Asians twenty-five. None of these groups in fact voted uniformly, but the American Bloc, which had shown some consistency, now amounted to only a quarter of the total, instead of two-fifths, as in 1951. What the U.S.A. had lost in preponderance passed to the so-called 'Afro-Asian Bloc', which was no more coherent and homogeneous than the rest. But the upshot was that even more attention had to be paid to the susceptibilities of small states and new nations than before. The same numerical trend went still further in 1960.

The expansion of the United Nations also had the effect – which is another aspect of the same thing – of increasing the disproportion between the General Assembly and the Security Council. The two bodies, neither subordinate to the other, had been to some extent rivals from the beginning. With the smaller body fixed at a membership of eleven and the larger increased from fifty-one to eighty-two, the number of members of the General Assembly who felt at any given moment that they could do the Security Council's work better than those at present on it was increased from forty to over seventy. This naturally aggravated the trend, which was already marked, towards the relative eclipse of the Security Council by the General Assembly. Whereas from 1946 to 1948 inclusive, the Security Council met on average 132 times a year, from 1949 onwards the average was between 40 and 50 times a year, with a maximum of 72 times in 1950.

The trend was unwelcome to the British Government, which had hoped for a small, strong, coherent nucleus of leadership within the

United Nations (its 'cabinet' in Eden's phrase) as the main guarantee
of international order, and regretted the open antagonism of the
U.S.A. and the U.S.S.R., which had turned the Security Council
virtually into an instrument of the cold war. It was doubly unfortunate,
from the British point of view, that 1956, the first year of the greatly
expanded General Assembly, was also the year of greatest crisis in the
United Nations since 1950. The double crisis of Hungary and the Suez
Canal proved to be an almost fatally severe test of the Security Council;
but it was perhaps the General Assembly's finest hour.

Of the two crises, the Suez Canal was the first to come before the
United Nations, though the later stages of both coincided. Britain and
France formally reported their dispute with Egypt to the Security
Council on 12 September 1956, the day on which they also announced
the formation of the Suez Canal Users' Association. On 24 September,
Egypt in her turn referred the dispute to the Security Council, not
merely by way of report but with a request for consideration of it;
and the Security Council met on the subject for the first time on
5 October. The British and French Governments presented a resolution, including six points fundamental to a settlement of the dispute,
which was adopted by the Security Council but vetoed in part by the
Soviet representative on 13 October. Two days later Jordan complained
to the Security Council about the allegedly aggressive intentions of
Israel. Before the Israeli threat and the Canal dispute came to a head
together at the end of the month, the Hungarian crisis had also burst
out.

The most serious outbreaks of violence in Budapest, which led to the
Soviet intervention, began on 23 October. Nagy became Prime Minister
the following day, but made no immediate appeal to the United Nations
against the action of Soviet troops, which indeed he was even believed to
have invited. On 26 October the U.S., French and British Governments
were reported for the first time to be considering a reference to the
U.N. of the Hungarian situation, and this was in fact made on 28
October. A motion in the Security Council condemning the U.S.S.R.
for repressing the rights of the Hungarian people was passed, but
vetoed by the Soviet representative. On the same day the Hungarian
Government addressed a note to the Secretary-General protesting that
the events on and after 22 October were 'exclusively within the domestic
jurisdiction of the Hungarian People's Republic'. No further communication to the U.N. came from Nagy's Government until 1 November,
when it sent a telegram asking that the Hungarian situation should be

put on the Agenda of the General Assembly – not, be it noted, the Security Council.

The General Assembly had been called into emergency session under the 'Uniting for Peace' procedure as a result of the ineffectiveness of the Security Council in dealing with the Middle East. On 29 October Israel's forces invaded the Sinai peninsula, and the U.S. Government announced its intention to put the matter to the Security Council on the next day. At the meeting of the Security Council on 30 October two resolutions, put respectively by the U.S. and Soviet Governments, urging all members of the U.N. to refrain from the use or threat of force in the Middle East, were both passed but vetoed by Britain and France. On the same day, and almost at the same moment, the British and French Governments presented an ultimatum to the Israeli and Egyptian Governments, which the former accepted and the latter rejected. With the British and French Governments thus committed to the use of force, and the Security Council unprepared for effective action, it was decided on a Yugoslav motion in the Security Council to summon an emergency meeting of the General Assembly. This was an application of the 'Uniting for Peace' procedure, and the General Assembly duly met on 1 November.

The General Assembly adopted a U.S. resolution on 2 November for a cease-fire and certain consequential measures. In the debate, the Canadian Foreign Minister, Lester Pearson, made the first suggestion of a U.N. force to occupy the frontier zone between Israel and Egypt. On 3 November the British and French Governments agreed to accept the resolution of the previous day provided that an effective U.N. force were formed and that Egypt and Israel both agreed to admit it. On 4 November the General Assembly passed a Canadian resolution asking the Secretary-General to produce a plan for such a force within forty-eight hours, which he did. On 5 November the British and French Governments formally welcomed the proposal for an international force, and on 6 November the Secretary-General's plan was circulated. It was welcomed generally, though not by the Soviet Government, which had sent notes to the British and French Governments on 5 November threatening to use force to halt their aggression, and had summoned the Security Council to endorse the joint use of Soviet and U.S. forces in the Middle East unless the Anglo-French operation against Egypt halted within twelve hours. The Security Council voted, by a narrow margin, against debating the Soviet proposal on 6 November. The cease-fire agreed upon in the General Assembly took effect at midnight that night. The U.N. Emergency Force (U.N.E.F.) began to arrive in the Middle East on 15 November.

During the same few days the Security Council had been proved equally ineffective in the Hungarian crisis. After the Soviet veto on 28 October and the appeal from Nagy's Government on 1 November, two further attempts were made by the U.S., French and British Governments to bring about a discussion of the Hungarian situation in the Security Council. These were both vetoed by the Soviet Government, on 2 November and 4 November. The Soviet delegate denied reports that Soviet armoured forces were moving back upon Budapest, after having been withdrawn on 31 October. It was not until 8 November, when Soviet forces had in fact almost completely regained control of Budapest, that the General Assembly discussed the Hungarian situation, on a motion submitted by Pakistan. On the following day the General Assembly passed a resolution calling on the Soviet Union to withdraw its forces from Hungary, and on 21 November it passed a motion condemning the Soviet Union for failing to obey. Further motions to similar effect in December had no better result. In January the General Assembly voted to establish a fact-finding committee on Hungary and on the basis of its report a further motion of condemnation of the Soviet Union was passed in September 1957. The committee's last public act was to ask the Soviet Government for information on the execution of Nagy in June 1958. But all was in vain.

Meanwhile the initiative of the General Assembly had been more effective in the Middle East. The withdrawal of British and French troops began in November, phased in relation to the build-up of U.N.E.F., and the salvage operation of restoring the Canal to use began under U.N. control in December. The withdrawal of the Israelis from the areas which they had conquered was slower and more reluctant: it began only in January 1957, and was not completed until March, under strong international pressure. The Emergency Force established itself so effectively that within a few months its very existence came to be generally forgotten, which argued that it was doing its job well. In April the General Assembly agreed to leave the operation of the Canal to the Egyptians on their own terms, which were criticized but not repudiated by the Suez Canal Users' Association. On 20 May 1957 the General Assembly adjourned discussion of the Suez Canal *sine die*. It had at least made the best of a bad job; and although it cannot be pretended that its intervention was the decisive factor in halting the action taken by Britain, France and Israel, the General Assembly came out of the crises of 1956 with much more success to its credit than the Security Council.

The French and British use of the veto on this occasion caused much heartburning throughout the world, not least in Britain, but hardly at all in France. The French took the realistic view, which was indeed the view of the founders of the U.N., that great powers must be allowed to retain the right, hitherto belonging to all powers, not to be overruled in matters affecting their vital interests. The veto had therefore been used strictly as it was intended to be used; and if that was wrong, it should never have been invented. The British took a more moralistic view of their own Government's action, and the debate for and against it is never likely to be settled. But it could fairly be pointed out that at the stage when the veto was used the Security Council was not thereby prevented from taking action because it had not been proposed that it should take any.

The Security Council was, in fact, seeking to frustrate action itself at that stage, and not to take action. Action was the one thing, since the end of the Palestine War in 1949, that the Security Council never had taken in the Middle East, not even on its own resolution condemning the Egyptian blockade of Israel in July 1951. Even since the Canal crisis began, constructive action had already been frustrated once by the Soviet veto of 13 October. The Anglo-French case for individual action was that the Security Council had already shown itself incapable of collective action and that action was essential. The United Nations was stimulated to undertake an active role in the Middle East as a direct result, but it was not the Security Council that played it.

The General Assembly was not the only legatee to the role of leadership which the Security Council had forfeited. It was too large for the role; and the Secretary-General was another claimant. The assumption of increased powers by the Secretary-General was not wholly welcome to the British Government, which viewed him primarily as an administrator. But an executive and initiative role was already implicit in the first Secretary-General's conduct in the Korean crisis, when it was welcome; and it was made much more explicit and emphatic by his successor, Dag Hammarskjöld. Hammarskjöld's first intervention in public diplomacy was when he undertook to fly to China in December 1954 to secure the release of a number of U.S. airmen held by the Chinese as spies. In the following month he offered the United Nations' mediation to arrange a cease-fire between the two Chinese Governments in their dispute over the offshore islands. In the Middle East crises of 1957–8, after the Anglo-French expedition against Egypt, he played an individual role of some importance on his own initiative. In May 1959 he took a mediating part in the preparation of the Foreign Ministers' conference at Geneva and publicly stressed, in a speech he made in that month at Copenhagen, the positive role which the U.N. had to play, even for instance, in the arrangement of a meeting at the Summit. Whether this elevation of the Secretary-General's role would come to be acceptable from the British point of view is an unsettled question, but it was an important innovation.

It illustrates one aspect of the United Nations' evolution which might be expected to appeal to the British, whose constitution bears the marks of a similar evolution. It has been an empirical and rather haphazard process, not unduly handicapped by pedantic adherence to a clumsily drafted Charter. In 1959 the organization was still at an early and some-what amorphous stage of its evolution, with conspicuously bad features but also some good ones. If one wanted an example of total failure on the part of the United Nations, none is more obvious or discouraging than the discussion of disarmament, the story of which from 1945 to 1959 has been recorded in detail elsewhere.[1] So complete was the frustration of this debate that after trying practically every other course it was decided in November 1958 to enlarge the Disarmament Commission to include the entire membership of the United Nations. It is not surprising that in consequence the four major powers decided in 1959 to take the question virtually out of the hands of the United Nations, and to form a new ten-power committee representative equally of the Soviet and Western Blocs. In this new attempt the U.N.'s role was merely to acquiesce and authorize it; and the new attempt failed in its turn in 1960. The one excuse for the U.N.'s failure over disarmament is that the Charter does not charge it with the task of reducing armaments but only of 'regulating' them. That does not alter the fact that nearly fifteen years have been wasted on the subject without tangible result.

When looking for the merits of the U.N., it is customary to point to the Specialized Agencies. This is just, and it corresponds to the British Government's experience, though their achievements are not uniform. To almost all of them Britain has been one of the largest contributors: second only to the U.S.A. in the case of U.N.R.R.A., the International Refugee Organization, the U.N. Works and Relief Agency for Palestine, and the Technical Assistance Programme since it was launched in 1949.

---

[1] Anthony Nutting, *Disarmament – an Outline of the Negotiations* (O.U.P. for R.I.I.A., 1959).

From 1957 Britain was actually the largest single supplier of technical experts to the U.N. Agencies. To some of them Britain has in her turn been particularly indebted – for instance, to the World Bank for helping to restore financial relations with Egypt in 1959. About others, such as U.N.E.S.C.O. and the Economic and Social Council itself, the British Government has sometimes felt reservations. Even the best of the Agencies can serve unwelcome political purposes: U.N.R.R.A., for instance, is believed to have helped to facilitate the illegal immigration of Jews into Palestine in 1946–7.

Among the most useful of the organs of the United Nations, though not themselves agencies, are the Economic Councils for various regions of the world: for Europe (E.C.E.) since 1947, the Far East (E.C.A.F.E.) since 1947, Latin America (E.C.L.A.) since 1948, and Africa (E.C.A.) since 1958. The value of these regional advisory organizations under the United Nations tends to bear out the general experience of the British Governments since the war, which has been that global organization is by contrast an expensive and time-consuming way of approaching specialized problems. It would be unthinkable for Britain to contract out of her responsibilities to the world-wide organs of the U.N., although these are always onerous and costly and often exasperating. But when it comes to getting things done, the main successes seem to have been achieved on a more limited basis: in defence, by N.A.T.O.; in economic aid, by the Colombo Plan and Point Four; in political evolution, by the Commonwealth. To this extent Churchill's original conception of regional responsibility has been vindicated.

11

Party Politics

FOREIGN policy is not normally a matter of controversy between the British political parties except when matters of defence are concerned; but that is nowadays a large exception. There are other occasional exceptions, as will be seen – for instance, when strongly held moral principles are at stake; but these also often involve questions of defence. Most of the cases since the Second World War when a government has been seriously handicapped by controversy in parliament, or in the country, have been cases involving, in the last analysis, matters of life and death for British citizens. As a general rule they have followed a fairly consistent pattern. When a Labour Government was in power, a 'strong' policy in defence of British interests was likely to command more support from the opposition than within the Government Party. When a Conservative Government was in power, exactly the opposite was the case. The post-war years therefore show examples of divisions on foreign policy along four different lines of cleavage: opposition by the Conservatives to the Labour Government's policy, and by the Labour Party to the Conservative Government's policy; and divisions within both parties, whether in or out of office.

When the Labour Party came to power in 1945, Bevin said in his first speech on foreign policy to the House of Commons on 20 August that 'the basis of the Government's policy was in keeping with that worked out by the Coalition Government'. The statement pleased the Opposition more than some Labour supporters, who wished to see the doctrine of continuity in foreign policy rejected and a distinctively Socialist foreign policy evolved. It was consistent with Bevin's statement that the Government continued to restrict Jewish immigration into Palestine, for instance; but it did not seem so consistent, to many Government supporters, with the policy put forward by the National Executive at the Labour Party conference in December 1944. Bevin was also criticized by his own side for not taking a stronger line against Spain under Franco, and for continuing the policy in Greece which he had inherited from the Coalition. He was attacked by Labour M.P.s in the House of Commons in February 1946 for his handling of the recent debates in the United Nations (when the presence and use of British troops in Greece, in the Levant states, and in Indonesia had been criticized); and again in June at the Labour Party conference, and in October at the Trade Union Congress. On each of these occasions the criticisms were directed generally at the Government's policy towards the United Nations, the Soviet Union and the U.S.A.; but its policy in Egypt and India was generally praised. The attitude of the Conservatives in opposition was exactly the reverse.

The examples quoted are typical in illustrating the basis of Bevin's disagreement with some of his followers. To the latter, a strong policy seemed to mean one of oppressing small nations or subject peoples. They therefore opposed those of the Government's policies which were most acceptable to the Opposition, who saw matters rather in terms of Britain's rights, prestige and power, and supported those which the Opposition most severely criticized. In particular, the Opposition criticized Attlee for starting negotiations for a new treaty with Egypt in May 1946 by announcing in advance that the Government would agree to withdraw all British troops; and in December Churchill explicitly dissociated the Opposition from the Government's policy for Indian independence. In both cases the Labour Party generally supported its leaders. But on other aspects of foreign policy, a vocal minority in the Party felt so strongly critical of Bevin that it moved a hostile amendment in the debate on the Address in November 1946, which was overwhelmingly defeated. Bevin, who was in New York at the time, spoke of the attack as a 'stab in the back'.

The next major issue on which the Labour Party split in the House of Commons was the Conscription Bill, against which seventy-two Labour M.P.s voted on its second reading in April 1947. Immediately after it was passed, the Government announced the reduction of National Service to one year, for which it was criticized by the Opposition in its turn. As the Defence White Papers show, conscription was an essential element in the Government's defence planning, but there was a strong pacifist element in the Labour Party to which such planning was itself repugnant. With growing fear of Soviet aggression, however, defence became increasingly a matter of bi-partisan policy. The North Atlantic Treaty had a wide basis of support. Churchill, Eden and the Government leaders spoke with one voice in support of the defence plans and against the Communist danger. The unanimity of Government and Opposition became even more emphatic when the Korean War broke out in 1950. But there was not the same unanimity among the Government's supporters. In July 1950 a motion was tabled in the House of Commons by twenty-three Labour M.P.s urging mediation in Korea, the withdrawal of U.S. troops from Formosa, and the admission of the Chinese Communist Government to the United Nations. In November another motion by Labour M.P.s called again for the end of the Korean War. A strong feeling has also long persisted in a section of the Labour Party against British participation in N.A.T.O.

Two other consequences of the fear of general war in 1949–50 also split the Labour Party during its second period of office. One was the cost of the British rearmament programme, which appeared to some Labour supporters likely to imperil the Welfare State. Some support for this view could be found in the melancholy arguments of the Defence White Paper for 1951; and in April of that year, after certain Health Service charges had been introduced for the first time, Aneurin Bevan and two other ministers resigned from the Government. The other controversy was about the need for German rearmament as a contribution to the defence of Europe. That issue was first debated in the House of Commons in February 1951, when a Labour amendment was moved against the Government. Attlee successfully argued that German rearmament was necessary, but misgivings remained in the Labour Party. A year later the Labour Party Executive proposed that a German contribution to the defence of Europe should not be decided upon until free elections throughout Germany had first been held.

In the second period of Labour Government (1950–1), during which the Korean War began, the Government could count on Conservative support for most of its foreign policy, especially in matters of defence. Such support was pledged soon after the Government took office, at the beginning of March 1950. It was an important factor, since the Labour majority was small. But it was not without exceptions, particularly in Europe and the Middle East, over which Conservative opposition was persistent throughout the years 1946–51. The principal case of disagreement in Europe was over the European Movement, in which Churchill played a leading part. In his famous speech at Zürich on 19 September 1946 he had first proposed 'a kind of United States of Europe'; and in 1947 he had founded a 'United Europe Committee'. He was one of the sponsors of the Congress of Europe at The Hague in May 1948, towards which the Government was cool: Labour M.P.s were advised by their Executive not to join the United Europe Committee. In June 1948 Churchill led an all-party delegation to the Prime Minister to seek support for a European Assembly; but although both

Attlee and Bevin had spoken in favour of unifying Europe, they felt that Churchill was going too far and too fast.

When the Council of Europe first met in August 1949 the Labour Government indicated its lukewarm interest by sending an unimpressive delegation to represent Britain. Churchill nevertheless persevered. In June 1950 he criticized the Government for its negative attitude towards the Schuman Plan, and in August he personally moved the resolution at the Council of Europe for the formation of a European army under a single Minister of Defence. Despite this vigorous championship of European union while in opposition, the policy pursued by Churchill when he returned to power in 1951 did not seem very different from that of Bevin. It was not obvious to most Europeans in 1950 that Churchill was advocating a European union in which Britain would not take part, though this was apparent from careful reading of his speech at Zürich in 1946.

The second area in which the Labour Government could not count on Conservative support was the Middle East. It was the Conservative conviction that a weak policy in the Middle East would be fatal to British interests, though there were exceptions to the rigidity with which that conviction was held. In the case of the Palestine mandate, for instance, Churchill was himself among the first to advocate surrendering it unless American support could be obtained. But there were no such reservations in the opposition to the Government's method of negotiation for a new treaty with Egypt in 1946, by declaring Britain's willingness to withdraw her troops in advance; nor to the Government's handling of the Palestine war when it broke out in 1948. In January 1949, after British aircraft had been shot down over Egypt by the Israelis, the Opposition moved a vote of censure on the Government's policy in the Middle East in general. A firm policy, on the other hand, could generally command Conservative support.

The Tripartite Declaration on the preservation of peace and the existing frontiers in the Middle East, made by the U.S., French and British Governments in May 1950, was an example of firm policy which was therefore also bi-partisan. The Anglo-Iranian oil crisis of 1951, after the Iranian Government had nationalized the oil industry, was a contrary example. When the Anglo-Iranian Oil Company was evicted from Abadan without resistance on the part of the Government, although preparations had been made for the use of force, the Opposition was indignantly critical. The issue only failed to stand out as a matter of contention between the two parties because it was merged in the issues of the General Election which immediately followed in October 1951. But if the Labour Government had used force against Iran, as the Opposition urged, then it would again have split its own party.

So far the conflicts considered were all either within the Labour Party in power or between the Labour Government and the Conservative Opposition. With the change of Government in 1951 the converse begins to appear: divisions within the Conservative Party in power, and criticisms of the Conservative Government by the Labour Opposition. But one of the earlier lines of cleavage does not disappear. Whereas the Conservatives in opposition were seldom seriously divided, the Labour Party in opposition was as deeply divided as when it was in power. The principal issues on which the Labour Party was divided were all concerned with defence: the rearmament of Germany, the formation of defence pacts, and the development of nuclear weapons. Those on which the Conservatives were divided were also concerned with defence, and particularly with the defence of the Middle East: the negotiations with Egypt leading to the new treaty of 1954, and the Suez Canal crisis in 1956. The issues on which the Labour Opposition criticized the Conservative Government included all the above and some more. They were principally the following: the negotiation of the Korean armistice, the rehabilitation and rearmament of Germany, the Cyprus dispute, the Middle East crises of 1956 and 1958, the policy towards China and the offshore islands, the policy concerning nuclear weapons and tests, and colonial policy in Africa. The motives behind the Opposition's criticisms were almost equally divided between moral disapproval and the fear of war.

The Korean War illustrated the latter of these two motives. At the beginning of 1952, when a truce had been precariously in force for six months, Churchill promised the Americans that Britain would support 'prompt, resolute and effective' action if the truce were broken. The Opposition, which had itself experienced in office the difficulty of restraining U.S. military leaders, sharply criticized Churchill's undertaking, and inferred that it constituted a new commitment. Churchill was able to show, speaking to the House of Commons at the end of February 1952, that his Government had undertaken no new commitments beyond what had been inherited from the Labour Government. It had in fact undertaken less than the U.S. Government desired.[1] Nevertheless the Opposition's anxiety was not entirely allayed, and the

[1] The details are given in Sir Anthony Eden's *Full Circle*, p. 18.

fear persisted throughout the protracted negotiations in Korea that the U.S. Government would carry the British Government with it into a new and rash adventure. The Opposition criticized the conduct of the negotiations in the House of Commons in May 1952, and again in June 1953 as they laboriously approached their climax: the main issue then being the Americans' insistence that prisoners of war should not be compulsorily repatriated. At last the Communist side gave way on this issue – which seemed to justify American persistence – and the armistice was signed on 27 July 1953. At the same time the sixteen nations which had fought for the United Nations in Korea issued a declaration implying that if the armistice were to be broken, the war might have to be extended beyond Korean territory. From this declaration the Labour Party expressly dissociated itself.

The case of Germany roused even deeper feelings within the Labour Party. German rearmament had been opposed by Labour M.P.s while the Party was in power, and the resistance to it grew in opposition. When the agreements relating to Germany consequent upon the signature of the E.D.C. Treaty on 27 May 1952 were presented to the House of Commons at the end of July, there were misgivings on both sides of the House, but particularly among the Opposition. Two years later, when the E.D.C. had collapsed and been replaced by W.E.U., the same misgivings still persisted. The objectors in the Labour Party were strongly supported by a section of the Trade Union movement; and although the official leadership had the majority behind it, the Labour Party conference in September 1954 only defeated a motion against German rearmament by 371,000 votes out of more than 6,000,000. When the House of Commons debated the new agreements in November, the Opposition abstained from the vote in order to avoid an open split. It was calculated that the leader of the Party could count on only 124 certain followers, against 72 certain dissidents. The suspicion of Germany persisted in some sections of the Labour Party after the restoration of sovereignty to the Federal Republic in 1955. Thereafter it merged into a general disquiet about the influence exercised by Chancellor Adenauer over allied policy towards the problems of European security.

The questions of European security, German reunification, disarmament and the development of nuclear weapons were all closely related, and the complexity of them stirred deep emotions in Britain. It was in April 1954 that these emotions first confusedly broke the surface, as a result of a conjunction of circumstances which came about by chance but not without real underlying connexions. The accident to a Japanese fishing-boat from an American nuclear test explosion in March; the curious proposal of the Soviet Government that it should join N.A.T.O.; the crisis of the war in Indo-China, which seemed about to engulf the major powers as well as France; the misunderstandings about allied policy between Dulles and Eden; and the imminence of final decisions on German rearmament: all these combined in the space of a few weeks to create an atmosphere of extraordinary tension both within and between the political parties in Britain. The Opposition urged the Government to give serious consideration to the Soviet approach to N.A.T.O., and Attlee urged the Government to convene a conference at the Summit on disarmament; but in both cases the Government ignored the Opposition's advice. The Opposition was itself divided on all the major issues at stake: the defence of S.E. Asia, the hydrogen-bomb, and German rearmament. After a confused debate in the House of Commons on 13 April, Aneurin Bevan resigned from the parliamentary committee of the Labour Party in disagreement with its official policy.

The immediate crisis passed, but the problems remained. Nuclear weapons and European security in particular continued to divide the parties, though Bevan was eventually converted to the policy of the Labour Party's official leadership. Gaitskell, who succeeded Attlee as leader of the Opposition in December 1955, tried to devise positive policies, distinct from those of the Government, which could command the support of all his party together with the Trade Union leaders. For European security, his policy was 'disengagement', which he first formulated in December 1956, as

'. . . the idea of a large neutral area, which would be guaranteed by a security pact and from which armed forces would be withdrawn, both on the Russian side and on our side'.

This idea, subject to modifications, became the official policy of the Labour Party. Neither it nor such variants as the Rapacki Plans (put forward by the Polish Government in 1957–8) were acceptable to the Government. The essential difference between the two views was whether the direct confrontation of the Soviet and Western armed forces across a clearly drawn line through Europe was a source of danger or a guarantee against risks.

On the other hand, the Government also had difficulty with its own supporters over defence policy, but of a different kind. As the Defence White Papers for 1957–9 show, it was proving impossible to afford both the cost of nuclear weapons and the full range of conventional forces. The Government argued that it was not only impossible but unnecessary to keep so large a number of men in the forces as well as to maintain the nuclear deterrent. Early in 1957, therefore, they announced plans for a considerable reduction of manpower, including the termination of National Service at the end of 1960 These decisions were believed not to have the undivided support of the service chiefs, and roused some criticism in the House of Commons on the Conservative side. In particular, it was doubted whether regular recruitment would raise sufficient forces in place of conscription; but on the whole pessimistic predictions were falsified, and the Conservative criticisms died down.

In the case of nuclear weapons, Gaitskell was less successful in winning the bulk of his followers to a single policy opposed to the Government's. The official policy adopted by the Labour Party was a unilateral renunciation of tests by Britain, but not a unilateral renunciation of the weapon itself. Attlee had in effect set out this dual policy while he was still Leader of the Opposition in March 1955. Bevan, who had then been a dissident, later strengthened Gaitskell's leadership by supporting both halves of the policy. But there remained a strong element in the Party, and also in the Trade Unions, which favoured complete unilateral renunciation of the hydrogen-bomb itself, not merely of tests. Gaitskell attempted a compromise in 1959 by putting forward the policy of a 'non-nuclear club', which was defined in terms of an agreement to be signed by every country except the U.S.A. and the U.S.S.R. 'not to test, manufacture or possess nuclear weapons', with a proviso for full and effective international controls. On these terms the Labour Party would be willing itself to renounce Britain's nuclear weapons.

The policy was naturally criticized from the side of the Government. For the Conservatives considered the retention of nuclear weapons by Britain to be a necessary part of the 'deterrent' against war; and they also argued that if Britain's commitments were to be maintained, the renunciation of nuclear weapons would add greatly to the cost of defence (since nuclear weapons are cheap in comparison with the equivalent conventional forces) and would necessitate the reintroduction of National Service. On the other hand, the project of a 'non-nuclear club' was also criticized from the opposite direction by some, though not all, of the Trade Union leaders, who adhered to the policy of complete unilateral renunciation. Not without difficulty, a sufficient measure of support for the official policy was secured to ensure that there would not be an adverse vote at the Labour Party Conference scheduled for October 1959. Owing to the General Election, the conference was not held as planned. But there remained some ambiguity about the effect that an adverse vote would have had on the Labour Party's policy if it had occurred, and the Party's electoral defeat left much re-thinking to be done.

By comparison with these contentious issues, the Labour Opposition was able to present a more united front against the Government on the problems of colonial policy and the Middle and Far East. There was still, however, a tendency for the rank and file of the Labour Party to run ahead of the official policy, which was noticeable particularly in the case of Cyprus. It had been a bi-partisan policy until 1954, affirmed more than once under the Labour Government as well as by its successors, that no change of sovereignty over Cyprus would be considered; but the Labour Party was quicker than the Conservatives to react to the strength and passion of the Greek claim. In July 1954, when a junior Minister for the Colonies used the unfortunate word 'never' in the context of questions on Cyprus (though not with explicit reference to Cyprus), he was violently attacked by the Opposition. The Conservative Party was not divided over Cyprus except when the Government showed signs of weakening towards the Greek claim. For instance, there was general support for the decision to deport Archbishop Makarios from Cyprus to the Seychelles Islands in March 1956, but the decision to release him a year later caused the resignation from the Government of Lord Salisbury.

On the other hand, the Opposition advocated a more sympathetic policy towards the Greeks. At successive Labour Party conferences resolutions were passed in favour of self-determination for Cyprus, and in October 1957 the resolution took the form of a commitment by the National Executive to try 'to complete the process of self-determination', without partition of the island, during the Party's next period of office. How far a Labour Government would have felt itself bound by that undertaking is an open question, which later events made unanswerable. In June 1958 the Opposition in parliament gave a modified blessing to the Government's latest new plan for Cyprus; and when this was superseded by the Zürich and London agreements early in 1959, the Opposition gave its support to the settlement, though not without some continuing criticisms.

The Cyprus dispute was naturally involved with the general issues of Middle Eastern policy, since after the British withdrawal from the Suez Canal Zone in 1954 the island became the Headquarters of British forces in the Middle East, and also, from 1955, the main base of British support for the Baghdad Pact (the Central Treaty Organization). In this part of its policy the Government found itself harassed almost equally by the Opposition, which disapproved of the Baghdad Pact, and by its own followers, some of whom disapproved of the decision to withdraw from the Canal Zone. The first rumblings of dissent among the Conservatives were heard in a debate on the negotiations with Egypt in December 1953. They broke into open revolt in July 1954, when the heads of agreement of the new treaty were announced. On both occasions the Opposition also criticized the Government. On the latter occasion, when the transfer of the Middle East Headquarters to Cyprus was discussed, Attlee told the House of Commons that when he had been Prime Minister 'the military' never thought Cyprus satisfactory as a base. The Government was in no danger from the sniping on either side at the time, but two years later, when Cyprus was in revolt and the Suez Canal crisis erupted, there was an uncomfortable number of M.P.s in a position to say, 'I told you so'.

The Canal crisis was the outstanding example since the Second World War of the extreme difficulty of carrying through a policy involving the use of force without a virtually united country behind the Government, which means also a united House of Commons. At first it appeared that the Government could count on such unity. In August 1956 the Leader of the Opposition approved the steps taken by the Government in reaction to the Egyptian nationalization of the Suez Canal Company, including the recall of reservists to the forces. But when the crisis reached its climax at the end of October, the Opposition's attitude turned to one of hostile criticism, directed particularly at the ultimatum of 30 October and the use of the veto in the Security Council on the same day. The allegation of collusion with the Israeli Government, which was denied (though not so categorically as it was made), became another point of criticism.[1]

Something of the same disquiet was felt by a minority on the Conservative side. Several members criticized the Government, some gave up the party whip, and two junior ministers resigned. On the other hand, there was even stronger feeling among the 'Suez rebels' of 1954, six of whom resigned the party whip in protest at the failure to carry

---

[1] There is no mention of this subject in Sir Anthony Eden's *Full Circle*.

the action against Egypt through to a successful conclusion. The latter class of critics of the Government were even more severe in blaming U.S. policy for what had happened. Over a hundred Conservative signatures were found for a motion which deplored the attitude of the U.S.A. towards the Anglo-French action as 'gravely endangering the Atlantic Alliance'. No doubt it was true that American opposition had been decisive in causing the British and French Governments to halt the operation in Egypt, but disunity in Britain had certainly played a contributory part.

The disarray at the end of 1956 was remedied with surprising rapidity. It was not repeated in 1957, when further eruptions of the Middle East crisis occurred in Jordan during April and between Syria and Turkey in the late summer; nor over the revolt of the Imam of Oman against the Sultan in July, which British troops helped to suppress. Even after the revolution in Iraq a year later, the atmosphere of debate on the Middle East in the House of Commons on 16 July 1958 (the day after American troops had landed at Beirut) was notably restrained. But in the following twenty-four hours the climate changed. British troops were flown to Jordan, from motives also connected with the Iraqi revolution, early on 17 July; and the Opposition declined to give the British action the same measure of acquiescence which it had given to the American action on the previous day. Two days later, however, when Khrushchev threatened disaster in the Middle East and demanded an immediate conference 'at the summit' on the situation, the Opposition approved the Prime Minister's response, which was to suggest that such a meeting might be held at the United Nations. Thereafter the crisis petered out in a surprising but welcome return to normality.

Its place as an issue of party contention was immediately taken by the Far Eastern crisis over the Chinese offshore islands in August 1958. While Quemoy was under Communist bombardment, the Labour Party leaders urged in September that British policy should be explicitly dissociated from U.S. policy, which appeared to be committed to fight for the islands. The Government refused to agree. It made clear that Britain was not committed to fight for the islands, but was in general support of the U.S. position. To the Opposition the distinction appeared to be one without a difference; but once again the crisis unexpectedly petered out in the following weeks. During the remainder of the Government's term no further issues arose in the Middle East or Far East to provoke open discussion between the two parties, though the Labour Opposition continued to press the Government to try harder to secure the admission of the Chinese Communist Government to the United Nations – a reversal of the position which it had taken up when in office in 1951.

Colonial policy, or at least a significant sector of it, remained the one irreconcilable issue between the parties. In Africa the Opposition's criticisms of the Government's colonial policy were strong, united and consistent. The Opposition did not feel itself encumbered by any share of the past responsibility for the crises in Africa, as it had elsewhere. It was therefore entirely free to criticize the Government. It did so particularly, first, over the treatment of former Mau Mau terrorists in Kenya, in the aftermath of the rebellion, which culminated in the death of eleven detainees at the Hola camp in March 1959. The Hola tragedy, which was bitterly debated in the House of Commons in July, coincided with the climax of a second fiercely contested issue in African colonial policy, that of the Central African Federation.

Again the Opposition was in a position to disclaim any responsibility inherited from the past, because although the Federation had been mooted during their second term of office, the decisive steps towards it had not been taken until 1952. In May 1953, two months before the Federation came into effect, Attlee had asked that it should be postponed; and in December 1953 a general motion of censure on the Government's policy in Africa was moved. Four years later, when the Federation was a going concern, a parliamentary delegation which had made a visit to Central Africa in August 1957 reported against the premature transfer of native affairs to the Federal Government, for which the Federal Prime Minister was pressing. As the last episode shows, there were also Conservatives who shared some of the Opposition's anxiety about some aspects of the Federation; but when the outbreak of violence in Nyasaland came in March 1959 the parties divided on a clear-cut line for and against the continuation of the Federation in principle. That principle was probably the essential issue on which the Government was unable to accept without reservation the Devlin Commission's report. The Commission's criticism of the principle of the Federation might eventually have to be accepted; but it could not be accepted out of hand, at the end of a parliamentary session, when no practicable alternative was in sight.

The issues discussed in the present chapter show that there were three types of question liable to provoke divisions between or within the parties: firstly, which policy is likely to preserve peace and which to lead to war? – secondly, which policy is morally right? – thirdly, what policy can the country's economy afford? The examples show that all three questions – of security, conscience and cost – might in particular cases cause divisions along all the possible lines of cleavage, though they seemed to do so more frequently and more deeply in the Labour Party than among the Conservatives. Practically every case, moreover, touched in some respect at least on Britain's relations and obligations towards allied or friendly countries. From every point of view, therefore, the study of party politics goes to support the conclusion that no British Government since the war has been the undivided master of its own foreign policy.

PART III

The Quest for New Relationships

12

Changing Patterns

THE lesson of Part II, seen against the background of Part I, is that Britain was no longer big enough to act alone in the world. Nor were any of the other traditional nation-states of Western Europe. The conditions of the middle of the twentieth century had put a heavy premium on size and resources. Quantitative factors were beginning to count for more than qualitative. A great power had to develop both, of course, but it was not enough to excel in qualitative factors alone. Indeed, it never had been, for the qualitative superiority of the nation-states of Western Europe was matched, in their heyday, by quantitative superiority as well, judged by the criteria of the nineteenth century. Now that the possibility of industrialization is open eventually to all, political units which have both a large population and easy access to raw materials have the advantage. Whereas the nineteenth century was dominated by countries with a high level of skill and populations of the order of 30–40,000,000, the world is now dominated by countries with a high degree of self-sufficiency in raw materials and populations of over 100,000,000. Britain has neither advantage.

There are only four countries in the world today whose populations run into nine figures – that is, are in excess of 100,000,000. These are, in order of magnitude, China, India, the U.S.S.R. and the U.S.A. They contain respectively $22\frac{1}{2}$ per cent, 14 per cent, $7\frac{1}{2}$ per cent, and 6 per cent of the population of the world. It is interesting that for the present the most powerful of the four are the two smallest, the U.S.S.R. and the U.S.A., but neither of them probably expects that precedence to last. Of the next four powers in order of size, below the 100,000,000 mark, three are Asian (Japan, Indonesia, Pakistan); only one is European (Germany), and that only if reunited. Britain comes tenth, after Brazil, around the 50,000,000 mark, with no likely prospect of entering the nine-figure class in the present century. Practically no other powers have any prospect of entering the top class in terms of size, though if the United Arab Republic could fulfil all its ambitions its prospects would be good. As the last example shows, size of population is not the only criterion: geographical extent and location are also important, and so is access to raw materials, particularly to the principal sources of energy, among which oil is now replacing coal and is almost simultaneously being caught up by nuclear power. The human capacity to exploit such advantages is also vital, but only very short-sighted people imagine that that is now confined to the Anglo-Saxon or West European stocks.

The advantages of sheer size make themselves felt in a number of ways. Militarily, they make it possible to mobilize larger homogeneous forces with uniform equipment, a common staff structure, and a relatively cheaper 'infrastructure' (as it is called in N.A.T.O.). Even an alliance such as N.A.T.O. does not gain the full benefit of such economies of scale, for many differences of equipment, language, and national idiosyncrasy still prevail. The 250,000,000 of Western Europe could presumably produce larger effective forces if they were citizens of one country instead of a dozen. They could also afford collectively the cost of the whole apparatus of modern war, including nuclear weapons, which at present is beyond the unaided capacity of any of them.

So far as Britain is concerned, these facts have been admitted in the Defence White Papers since 1957, and what is true of Britain is true *a fortiori* of the rest of Western Europe, not excepting even Germany and France. Moreover, the same is true of the scientific and technological development which lies behind defence as well as much else. The disproportion between the British output of scientists and engineers and those of the U.S.A. and the U.S.S.R. is well known, the latter being respectively 40 per cent and 160 per cent higher than Britain's as a proportion of the population. Will and habit are important in this context as well as size, but it is reasonable to suppose that if the populations were more nearly equal, the proportionate as well as the absolute difference would be smaller.

In the economic context size of population has even more evident advantages. Apart from economies of scale in production, what has most forcibly struck West European observers about the economic predominance of the U.S.A. since the Second World War is the importance to it of a very large domestic market uninterrupted by trade barriers. British thinking has been so much, and so necessarily, directed towards export trade that it is easy to overlook the striking growth of domestic markets over international markets. For instance, Britain's own domestic trade is three times as large as her overseas trade, and the internal trade of the U.S.A. is three and a half times as large as the whole world's international trade. The significance of the U.S.A.'s advantage in having an internal market more than three times as large as Britain's may be measured by the fact that in one single post-war year (1950–1) the mere *increase* in output of the U.S.A. exceeded the *total* output of Britain. The U.S.A. has become a jealously observed model illustrating the value of size in the economic context, just as the U.S.S.R. has been in the military, scientific and technological contexts.

From one point of view, therefore, it can be seen as one of the principal objects of post-war policy of the West European Powers to try to produce for themselves the advantages and the status which size, coupled with human capacity and material resources, conferred on the two biggest powers of the middle of the century; bearing in mind at the same time that those two might in their turn have been superseded by the end of the century. The puzzle was one to which different European countries had different approaches, some of them (particularly France) being also divided among themselves. The smaller powers, not unreasonably, tended to stand aside from the argument and await its outcome.

There is much interest in all their points of view, but since this book is a study of British foreign policy and since the British position was the most distinct of all, the present chapter will be concerned with Britain's attempt to work out a new pattern of relations in a world dominated by powers of a new order of magnitude. The possibility of reaching a comparable order of magnitude for herself turned inevitably on her relations with three other groups of powers: Western Europe, the Commonwealth, and the Atlantic community. The crucial question of the 1950s seemed to be, with which of these three did Britain's most important reciprocal advantages lie?

United Europe

What appeared from the British point of view to be the characteristically continental approach to the problem outlined above was the movement for a United Europe. It was not unanimously supported even within the so-called Six (France, the German Federal Republic, Italy, Belgium, the Netherlands and Luxembourg). There were many reservations and backslidings, particularly in France, though much less so in Germany under the strong and continuous guidance of Chancellor Adenauer. There was also a desire, particularly on the part of the smaller partners, to retain as much individuality as possible. But United Europe remained, broadly speaking, the goal and inspiration of the major continental nations as a whole. It was also liberally encouraged by the U.S.A., as well as inspired by Churchill, whom many looked upon as its spiritual progenitor. But it commanded little real support from Britain under either a Labour or a Conservative Government. Since the idea appeared to offer a solution in theory to the problems from which Britain suffered as much as the continental nations, it is important to see why this was so.

First it will be convenient to summarize the continental developments in the direction of union, before illustrating the British reaction to them. They took place separately, though closely interrelated, on the political, the economic and the military planes; and they fell into five periods. The first period, from the end of the war to the spring of 1948, was one of development chiefly on the economic plane: it was the period dominated by the European Recovery Programme. General Marshall's speech at Harvard on 5 June 1947 was the first major step towards the economic union of Europe, though it had been preceded by earlier ventures on a smaller scale, such as the 'Benelux' union of Belgium, the Netherlands and Luxembourg, which had been signed in 1946, and nominally came into effect on 1 January 1948. To administer 'Marshall Aid', the Organization for European Economic Co-operation (O.E.E.C.) was set up in April 1948, but an attempt to form a customs union of the thirteen participants proved abortive. During this first period the significant events on the political and military planes were Churchill's speech at Zürich on 19 September 1946, which had given impetus to the whole conception of unification; and the signature of the Treaties of Dunkirk in March 1947 and Brussels in March 1948, which were distant harbingers of integrated defence.

In the second period, covering the rest of 1948 and 1949, progress was transferred to the political and military planes. The Congress of Europe was held at The Hague in May 1948, again under Churchill's impulse. In July, at a meeting of the Foreign Ministers of the Treaty of Brussels, the French proposed that they should create a European Assembly and a customs union. Bevin's reaction was cool. Early in 1949, however, the Hague Congress bore fruit in a conference in Paris on the creation of a Council of Europe, and in June the statute of the Council was promulgated. Meanwhile defence had begun to command increased attention, as a result of events in Eastern and Central Europe. The project of a 'North Atlantic Regional Pact' was first discussed in Washington in July 1948. In October the Brussels Treaty Powers agreed upon a collective approach to the U.S.A. to negotiate such a pact. On 4 April 1949 the North Atlantic Treaty was signed and N.A.T.O. was created. No comparable event took place on the economic plane during this period, though some new ventures were tried: a Franco-Italian treaty of customs union was signed in March 1949, but never ratified, and the Benelux 'pre-union' came into effect.

The third period, from the beginning of 1950 to the middle of 1951, was also one of experiment on the economic plane, culminating in a major success. Britain herself played a part in the early stages: for instance, the 'Uniscan' Treaty was signed between Britain and the Scandinavian Powers in January 1950, with the initial effect of removing various currency restrictions between the four countries; and Britain was also a participant in the creation of the European Payments Union (E.P.U.) by the O.E.E.C. in June. But neither of these was a 'supranational' development involving a real surrender of national sovereignty, as was the 'Schuman Plan' put forward in May. Schuman, the French Foreign Minister of the day, expressly said that his intention was 'to make war between France and Germany impossible' by merging their coal and steel industries, together with those of Benelux and Italy. Britain expressed interest and a wish to be kept informed, but none to participate. The Treaty of the Six creating the European Coal and Steel Community was signed on 18 April 1951, and came into effect in July 1952. Meanwhile, encouraged by success, the French had put forward two new ventures: on the economic plane, the 'Pflimlin Plan' for concerting European agricultural policies in January 1951; and on the military plane, the 'Pleven Plan', to create a European army, including German troops, in October 1950. Britain supported the proposed rearmament of Germany, as did the U.S.A., and both proposed in July 1951 to end the state of war with Germany. But there was no question of Britain's participation in the European Defence Community (E.D.C.), which grew out of the Pleven Plan.

The fourth period, from the middle of 1951 to the end of 1954, was that of the long-drawn-out struggle to give substance to E.D.C. The treaty creating it was signed on 27 May 1952, but nothing could bring the French Assembly to ratify it: neither the acceptance by the other five powers of French amendments in March 1953, nor the agreement of association with it by Britain in April 1954, nor the alternate encouragement and objurgation of the Americans. The treaty lapsed for want of French ratification in August 1954. Its place was rather inadequately taken in October by an enlargement of the Brussels Treaty, which already included Britain as well as France, Belgium, the Netherlands and Luxembourg, to include Italy and West Germany also. But Western European Union (W.E.U.), as it was called, involved no real surrender of national sovereignty.

Meanwhile more solid but less spectacular developments were taking place on an economic plane. The negotiations on the Pflimlin Plan proved too difficult, and the co-ordination of agricultural policy was transferred to O.E.E.C. The High Authority of E.C.S.C. came into operation, with a British delegation in attendance, whose position was formalized by the creation of a Council of Association in December 1954. A European Productivity Agency was established by O.E.E.C. in May 1953; a convention establishing a European Organization for Nuclear Research was signed in July; and a protocol establishing a European Conference of Ministers of Transport in October. Britain was a party only to those of the above ventures which came under the auspices of O.E.E.C. But two significant, though abortive, attempts were made to facilitate Britain's deeper participation in the unifying process. In March 1952 Eden put forward a plan for merging the European agencies (O.E.E.C., E.C.S.C. and E.D.C.) within the general framework of the Council of Europe. In September of the same year the Council of Europe adopted a plan for a preferential tariff area including Europe, the Commonwealth and European overseas dependencies. That nothing came of the latter, the first comprehensive plan for something like a Free Trade Area, was particularly regrettable.

Economic developments again dominated the fifth period, from the beginning of 1955 to the spring of 1957. A number of special committees were set up by O.E.E.C., including one on agriculture in succession to the Pflimlin Plan. In August 1955 the O.E.E.C. countries signed the European MonetaryAgreement in anticipation of convertibility, though it was not until the end of 1958 that it became effective. The principal development, however, was again one in which Britain could not be included. In June 1955 representatives of the Six met at Messina to work out the idea of a 'common market' which had been implicit in E.C.S.C. On the same occasion the first suggestion of a similar association for nuclear energy was put forward. A small committee was appointed under the chairmanship of the Belgian Foreign Minister, Spaak, which presented its report in April 1956. In May the Six met in Venice to approve the Spaak report. The resultant treaty, by which the European Economic Community (or Common Market) and Euratom were created, was signed in Rome on 25 March 1957.

Lest so far-reaching a step should divide Western Europe irremediably, O.E.E.C. had already begun to explore the possibility, which was first put forward by Macmillan as Chancellor of the Exchequer in October 1956, that a Free Trade Area should be created to include both the Common Market and any other members of O.E.E.C. which wished to join. Unlike the Common Market, which would have common internal and external tariffs, the Free Trade Area would have only a common internal tariff system, thus safeguarding Britain's system of preferential tariffs with the Commonwealth. The complicated details of this possibility were exhaustively debated in O.E.E.C. throughout 1957 and 1958. At times it was thought that the differences, which lay essentially between the French and British Governments, were fairly narrow. The West German Government in particular worked hard to bring about a reconciliation of ideas. But on 14 November 1958 the French Government announced that it could not take part in a Free Trade Area on the lines proposed at all. Meanwhile the first tariff cuts under the Treaty of Rome were to take effect on 1 January 1959, but the Six made the conciliatory gesture of offering corresponding cuts to the other members of O.E.E.C. The door was thus closed on Britain, but not bolted.

The problem of devising a new economic relation with the Six had still to be solved, for it was impossible to go on behaving as if the Common Market did not exist. Even if it had still a margin of fifteen years to come into full effect, it might well take much less. One suggestion that was put forward early in 1959 was that Britain should reopen the negotiations in association with the Commonwealth countries, many of which were bound to be affected by the new Common Market; another was that Britain should herself join the Common Market. Neither idea commended itself to the Government, which chose instead to form a new association, the European Free Trade Association by name, comprising what were called the 'Outer Seven': Britain, Sweden, Norway, Denmark, Austria, Switzerland and Portugal. In July 1959, the month in which the association of the Outer Seven was formed, two new developments occurred: Greece sought to join the Six in the Common Market; and Finland hinted at the possibility of joining the Outer Seven, but yielded to Soviet pressure against doing so. Europe was thus becoming more sharply divided into separate economic leagues – the Soviet Bloc, the European Economic Community, and the European Free Trade Association – from which practically no country, except Yugoslavia and Spain, stood entirely aloof. Whether the barriers between them would grow more rigid or more permeable in the next stage of evolution was an unanswered question at the end of 1959; but it was arguable that the Outer Seven had made it harder rather than easier to enlarge the association of the Six by forming their own association outside it.

The attitude of Britain to these developments has been implied throughout the foregoing account. There has never been any sentiment in favour of Britain's participation in European union, except among a few enthusiasts. But it was an ideal which no one would wish to speak openly against, so that if ministers spoke of it at all they tended to be vaguely non-committal, or unfortunately to express more warmth than they really felt. It was easier, however, for the Opposition to espouse such ideas than for the Government. Churchill's oratory at Zürich in 1946, at The Hague in 1948 and at the Council of Europe in 1950 may have given the impression that a Conservative Government would go farther towards integration with Europe than a Labour Government. So might the insistence of the Opposition in May 1950 that Britain ought to attend the first conference on the Schuman Plan. But in fact the statements made on the Conservative side went no farther and meant no more than much that had been said by Bevin and Attlee.

Bevin spoke in January 1948 of 'a consolidation of Western Europe' and of 'Europe as a unit'; and a year later he spoke of 'a practical organism in Europe, in which we shall cease to be English and French, cease to be English and Italian, cease to be English and Belgian, but will be European'. Attlee was more prosaic, but the 'Federation of Europe' of which he spoke in the House of Commons in May 1948 did not sound very different from the 'United States of Europe' of which Churchill had spoken in Zürich in September 1946. Europeans were inclined to read too much into both of them.

Although the two parties were in general, with individual exceptions, almost equally cautious about joining a European union, the reasons were different. On the Labour Party's side, economic integration would only have been acceptable provided that it did not compromise the Socialist experiment in Britain, including such cardinal features as full employment, the standard of social services and the system of controls. This point of view was expressed in June 1950 in a publication by the Labour Party's National Executive on *European Policy*, which implied that co-operation between Britain and Europe must be limited until all European Governments were Socialist. The Conservative view was expressed by Churchill and Eden in the House of Commons on 26–7 June, when they argued that national sovereignty should not be regarded as inviolable, that concessions ought to be made to the French initiative, but that there could be no question of Britain joining a purely European federation. The basic obstacle was the priority of obligations to the Commonwealth, which the Socialists also invoked, though Churchill denied them the right to do so.

The essential continuity in practice of Conservative with Labour policy towards Europe became clear at the Council of Europe in November 1951. Thereafter all fresh ventures in the direction of unification had the same reception in Britain. Britain was sympathetic towards them, and would like to be associated with them in some way, but could not join them. The proposal of a Free Trade Area to supplement the Common Market was only an application of the same principle, though an unusually elaborate one. It was represented to the Europeans as a decisive and in some way a radical innovation in British policy, but it was not so seen by them: 'too little and too late' was the European verdict on it. Even when the British ministers were seeking to emphasize the boldness of the step that Britain was willing to take towards Europe, they seemed only to damn it with faint praise. Early in 1957 the President of the Board of Trade told the Ministerial Council of O.E.E.C. that:

'Bringing the insular British to the edge of the European continent has not been easy. We are obstinate people of strong habits . . .'

and then he went on to add:

'Our wish to join is not a case of political fascination. We are not dreaming of a third force or of a European bloc endowed with supranational institutions and anxious to rival Russia or the United States. We are more prosaic, and I trust, more practical.'

These words seemed practically an invitation to the Europeans to close the door, as in due course they did.

Although the Government perhaps underestimated the strength of European feeling for unity, it correctly assessed the British people's feelings against 'continental entanglements'. The interesting question is not why ordinarily the British do not want to become Europeans, but why exceptionally they sometimes talk and behave as if they do. If the history of world events is looked at as a whole during the years of progressive unification, it can be seen that the periods in which the

European idea made some progress in British political thinking are those of disappointments, alarms and setbacks in other parts of the world. The period 1946–8 was one of impending economic disaster, and the period 1948–50 one of fear of imminent war. During those five years, in consequence, Britain drew close to Europe, in O.E.E.C. and N.A.T.O., to an extent unexampled in history.

So well did the treatment work in the next two years that it seemed unnecessary to carry it any farther. Besides, in 1953 Stalin died and the Korean War ended. So far as Britain was concerned, Europe receded into the background in comparison with the problems of the Middle East, the Far East and Africa. War in Europe seemed to have been made impossible by nuclear weapons, and by 1955 co-existence seemed to have come to stay. Moreover, the period 1953–5 was one of great prosperity in Britain, the inflationary basis of which was not universally realized. It looked as if Britain had no need of Europe either militarily or economically, and the European idea faded.

The bubble was pricked in 1956–7. The halting of the Anglo-French expedition against Egypt and the financial crisis of 1957 were sharp warnings against complacency. The first in particular brought on an anti-American reaction, and even a measure of disillusionment with the Commonwealth. On the other hand, relations with the French, who were after all the leaders of the European movement, survived the setback in the Middle East remarkably well. As the impossibility of total independence became clearer, and the idea of interdependence came to birth, the most natural direction in which to turn in order to give it substance seemed, in the immediate circumstances, to be Europe; but only in the immediate circumstances, which were exceptional. Looked at again in the cold light of reason a year or two later, it appeared that there were many respects in which Europe could not provide what Britain needed if she were to enter into a larger association on a permanent and deeply committed basis.

Militarily, Europe could provide little help in guarding Britain's world-wide commercial interests. Economically, though a merger with Europe would provide Britain with the opportunity of that large domestic market which was such an advantage to the U.S.A., it would not also contain within it, as the U.S.A. came near to doing, all the raw materials needed by a manufacturing nation. Politically, the problem of belonging simultaneously to a federation and a Commonwealth was a baffling one, in which the position of the Crown was only one of the intractable elements. From all these points of view, it looked as if

Europe could not provide the vehicle on which Britain might rise to the new order of magnitude and the new level of sovereignty which the U.S.A. and the U.S.S.R. had established. If such a vehicle were really desired, however, it looked from the very same points of view as if the Commonwealth might perhaps provide it instead.

The Commonwealth

A unified Commonwealth, functioning as a single political, economic, strategic and even cultural unit, has been the dream of many idealists. The dream has become more modest since the end of the last century, when imperial federation under a single parliament was actively canvassed, particularly in Australia and New Zealand, as well as in Britain. Yet even during the Second World War, the British Ambassador to the U.S.A. was heard speaking to a Canadian audience of the British Empire as 'a fourth Great Power' in the post-war world, though his words were not well received. Smuts had something of the same vision. Churchill would go no farther than to say that he had 'not become the King's First Minister in order to preside over the liquidation of the British Empire'. Liquidation would certainly be too strong a word to describe what has in fact happened since the war. The Commonwealth has greatly expanded; but the members of the expanding Commonwealth, like the heavenly bodies of the expanding universe, in growing seem to have grown apart. The question is whether they any longer have sufficient cohesion to play the role of a single power, if such a role were to be chosen by them. This leads on to the tantalizing questions: What is it, if anything, that still holds the Commonwealth together? Is there in fact any single bond that is both comprehensive and exclusive?

Certainly there is no longer any political bond. The measure of political devolution can be seen in the most concrete test of sovereignty, the declaration of war. In 1914 the King declared war on behalf of the whole British Empire at a stroke. In 1939 the King declared war on behalf of the United Kingdom, the Indian Empire and the colonies, but Canada, Australia, New Zealand and South Africa each declared war separately. South Africa did so only after a change of Government; and the Republic of Ireland remained neutral throughout. In any future war the Queen would declare war only on behalf of the United Kingdom and the remaining colonies; and some at least of the new countries of the Commonwealth would probably declare their neutrality. That is the essence of independence, and it serves to emphasize the fact that there are not eleven members of the Commonwealth plus Britain:

there are twelve members of the Commonwealth, of which Britain is one. The principle remains even as the numbers grow.

The fact that the Queen is recognized as Head of the Commonwealth does not diminish the political distinctness of the members of the association, but rather emphasizes it. She is Queen of several countries besides Britain, but not of all. The Commonwealth of which she is Head includes three republics (India, Pakistan and Ghana) and some others which have declared more or less definitely their intention to become republics. It also includes an elective monarchy (Malaya). It includes, too, a number of countries which have, in different ways, deviated from the political tradition bequeathed to them by British rule. That tradition consisted essentially of parliamentary democracy based on universal adult suffrage and normally operated by a party-system. Universal adult suffrage has never been the practice in South Africa, where the vote is not now possessed by native Africans at all; and in the Central African Federation it is possessed only by a small minority of them. Racial problems are at the root of this discrimination, yet in the Federation of the West Indies, another multi-racial society, there is no such discrimination in the franchise. In New Zealand, on the other hand, the pre-European population, the Maoris, not only enjoy full adult suffrage but have four seats in parliament reserved for them; and this constitutes discrimination in their favour, especially as the even division between the two principal parties can easily give them the balance of power.

Experience has shown that political systems cannot be exported ready-made: they have to grow in their environment. Although all members of the Commonwealth set out upon independence with an essentially British system of government by parliamentary democracy, most have departed from the British model. In Pakistan a revolution abolished the constitution in 1958; and if it were to be restored, many Pakistanis expected it to take the presidential form, modelled on the U.S. constitution, rather than the British form. Some South African Nationalists favour a similar recasting of their constitution. Elsewhere the two-party system has failed to take root. In India and Ghana, where the Government party came to power in the first instance as the spearhead of Nationalist revolt against colonial rule, it was natural that a one-party system with practically no parliamentary Opposition should prevail. If there is a real Opposition in such cases, it is more likely to be within the ruling party, which may therefore eventually split and thus create a party system out of itself. But there are also other possibilities, such as an authoritarian régime, as in Pakistan; or parties may grow round personalities rather than principles, as in the West Indies; or there may be a multiplicity of splinter parties, especially where there has been no real struggle for independence to give an initial coherence to political life, as in Ceylon.

It is useless, therefore, to look for any political uniformity in the contemporary Commonwealth. There are certain common aspirations, of which perhaps the rule of law is the most important that has survived from the British imperial system; and perhaps even universal adult suffrage would be claimed as the goal of all, even if some are clearly much farther from it than others. Politically, the Commonwealth can only be defined as that group of countries with which Britain conducts her relations through the Commonwealth Relations Office instead of the Foreign Office. The definition serves to emphasize the great import-ance and value of the C.R.O. in the Commonwealth system; but it is unsatisfactory, on major as well as minor grounds. One minor ground is that the Republic of Ireland, though no longer a member of the Commonwealth, is still a country with which Britain conducts her relations through the C.R.O. A major ground is that the survival of the C.R.O., to which there is no counterpart in any other Common-wealth country, appears to give Britain a central and even a dominant position which she does not seek. It is a constant theme of discussions of the Commonwealth in Britain that there ought to be more traffic and intercourse between the other Commonwealth countries and not only between each of them and Britain. Yet for virtually all of them what the Commonwealth relation means is their own relation with Britain, rather than with each other; and now that London is no longer an imperial capital, this does not make for real cohesion.

As political links are weakened, however, it may well happen that economic links remain as strong as ever, if not stronger. It is natural that this should have happened as the British Empire evolved into the Commonwealth, since the Empire was founded on trade. Trade flows where it is natural for it to flow, unless it is artificially prevented: that is no doubt why, for instance, there are more British businessmen in India since independence than ever before. The fact that Britain is still the best customer of most members of the Commonwealth, the survival of Imperial Preference, and the strength and cohesion of the Sterling Area, are all evidence of the foundation of the association on solid and mutual economic interest. But it would be a mistake to regard their future with complacency, or to suppose that any of them constitutes a permanent bond. None of them except Imperial Preference passes the test of being both comprehensive and exclusive to the Commonwealth; and Imperial Preference has itself been largely whittled away in the post-war years.

The Sterling Area is a good example of the rule that if economic factors alone counted, the Commonwealth would continue to exist only so long as it suited members to belong to it. While some non-members of the Commonwealth also belong to the Sterling Area, Canada does not and South Africa is half in and half out. How much advantage other Commonwealth countries draw from membership of the Sterling Area varies from case to case, and the newest members are those which have most cause to question the advantages. For instance, privileged access to the London money market to raise loans is much emphasized as an advantage of membership of the Sterling Area; but Indians would point out that this advantage is in practice more effectively enjoyed by the old members of the Commonwealth, particularly Australia and South Africa, than by themselves. India's future source of capital as she runs down her wartime sterling balances is likely to be the U.S.A.: and the U.S.A. is also investing substantially in other parts of the Commonwealth, though not yet on a scale approaching that of Britain.

The accumulation of sterling balances is itself another matter in which the newer countries see the advantages of the system to the older members rather than themselves. The colonies were the principal dollar-earners of the Sterling Area in the post-war period, and in effect their surplus was compulsorily borrowed by Britain in exchange for a rise in their sterling balances. If they had not been subject to British Exchange Control, and if the opportunities had offered as they now do, these colonies might well have preferred to spend their surpluses on imports rather than lend them to London. Chief among such colonies were Malaya, Ghana and Nigeria, all three of which achieved independence within fifteen years after the end of the war. They might well come to see their economic advantage in a different light from that of the Sterling Area as a whole.

It has not been in any case an object of post-war British policy to make the Sterling Area, or the Commonwealth, a closed and exclusive economic association. That is precisely why it was not possible to bring the Commonwealth into the Common Market as a single unit. If it had been possible, the result would have been to frustrate the industrialization of many of the new Commonwealth countries, and to turn them into hewers of wood and drawers of water for the more developed countries of Europe indefinitely; and that would have been intolerable to them. All the Commonwealth countries have trading interests with countries outside the Sterling Area – Canada with the U.S.A., Australia and New Zealand with S.E. Asia and the Far East, and all of them with Europe. These interests are not regarded as incompatible with intra-Commonwealth trade: on the contrary, the more the one expands, the more the other is likely to do so. Even if this were not recognized, however, as it was at the Commonwealth Economic Conference at Montreal in 1958, and even if Britain wished the Commonwealth to operate as a closed economic unit, it would have been impossible to make it do so. In the economic context the Commonwealth is an intricate system of reciprocal relations and mutual benefits within a larger world-wide system. It functions as such for just so long as its members find advantage in it. If they ceased to do so, no kind of economic constraint could continue to hold them together.

What is true potentially in the economic context is already true actually in the strategic context. Whatever else may hold the Commonwealth together, certainly no common policy on defence does so. This may seem strange at first sight, when it is recalled how large a part strategy played in the creation of the British Empire. Even today the head of the British Army is still called Chief of the Imperial General Staff. Although economic motives played the leading part in the acquisition of most major British possessions, many other territories had nothing more to commend them than their strategic location. But with the transition of the larger territories into independent countries, there has not been developed any corresponding sense that such outposts as Gibraltar, Malta, Cyprus, Aden and so on are part of a Commonwealth system of defence. They remain a purely British responsibility. No future war would be fought by the Commonwealth as a single defence unit.

That much is common ground to all the independent member-states. But many go farther. Perhaps as many as half of them would declare themselves neutral if a Third World War were to break out. The Prime Minister of Ceylon declared, at the time when he was seeking the removal of the British base in 1956, that Ceylon would be free to offer facilities to any power, even to enemies of Britain. At the other extreme, those that reject a neutral policy have in some cases gone even beyond their alliances with Britain to make treaties with other powers to which Britain is not a party: Australia, New Zealand and Pakistan are examples. In each case the other party to the treaty is the U.S.A.; and no one could conceivably interpret such alliances as anti-British. But they are symptomatic of a changed world, in which the U.S.A. holds a stronger position to protect some parts of the Commonwealth than Britain herself.

Certain important links still remain. The presence of Australian forces in Malaya is an example of a sense of joint responsibility for defence. British officers continue to hold senior commands in the forces of the newer countries; and the appointments of an Indian Deputy G.O.C. in the Malayan Federation Army and of an Australian Commander-in-Chief of its Navy are interesting extensions of the same principle. Commonwealth countries have the privilege of sending officers to military and staff training colleges in Britain, though it is sometimes argued that the presence of those from professedly neutral countries acts as an inhibiting factor on the usefulness of such courses for the others. So long as these interchanges survive, there will remain a common body of tradition and doctrine among the armed services of the Commonwealth. That may be valuable in more ways than in the conduct of war. Quite possibly, for instance, it has been a factor in preventing war between India and Pakistan. But it is a long way from constituting a binding link of defence policy over the whole Commonwealth.

The impossibility of defining strong and tangible links in terms of politics, economics or defence has led enthusiasts for the Commonwealth to seek the real links in the intangible sphere of culture. The idea is not absurd. When a great imperial power withdraws from its sovereignty over other peoples, it is likely nevertheless to leave enduring traces of its cultural tradition behind. That is what the Romans and the Arabs did in Western Europe, the Portuguese and the Spanish in Latin America, the Turks and the French in the Middle East. All the more was it likely to happen in the British Empire, since English is not just the language of the British or even of the Commonwealth: it is a world language, which has already overtaken French as the normal second language of most countries. Where English is the language of higher education, international communication, and even of the central administration, as it is almost universally in the Commonwealth, it cannot help carrying with it powerful influences of British thought and practice. The conferences of the Commonwealth Prime Ministers are perhaps the keystone of the whole system; and it would be unthinkable that they should be conducted through interpreters.

Where English is the language of higher education, it is likely that people will wish to send their sons and daughters to British universities. Many Commonwealth ministers have had a British university education, and the consequences have been important. At lower levels, too, British practice tends to set the standard throughout the Commonwealth, not least in Asia and Africa: for university degrees, for professional qualifications, and even for academic dress, regardless of the climate. Associations of lawyers, journalists, parliamentarians and other professional people constitute an important link. So does English literature, which is at least as likely to be quoted at an international conference by an Indian or a Nigerian as by an Englishman. The Press and broadcasting are influences in the same general sense, and so are the intra-Commonwealth systems of communications, such as postal and telegraphic services, Reuter's News Agency, the British Overseas Airways Corporation, and many others. Cumulatively, these are far from negligible factors, but they must not be thought to add up to a massive total, nor should too great a strain be put upon them. There is no general answer to the question of their strength and durability that will hold good universally for so diverse a collection of peoples as the Commonwealth.

The situation differs as between two kinds of Commonwealth countries: those which are now of mainly British, or at least European descent, because they were virtually uninhabited when Europeans first arrived, or were inhabited only by extremely primitive peoples; and those which had considerable indigenous populations with a culture and history of their own before the Europeans came. In the first category are Canada, Australia, New Zealand and South Africa; in the second India, Pakistan, Malaya, Ceylon, Ghana, Nigeria and the West Indies. The countries of the first category are in effect part of European civilization. In those of the second category it may prove difficult in the long run for the British cultural tradition, or even the English language, to survive. In no case can the British afford to take anything for granted. Even in Canada and South Africa, for instance, English is in competition with other European languages, and in the latter case at least it looks like losing the competition. In India, Pakistan and Malaya, where English is still an official language because there is no other common to all educated people, steps are already being taken to remove it from that position. If these steps are eventually successful, English will not disappear altogether, but it may be relegated to the status of a widely spoken second language, as it is, for instance, in Norway or the Netherlands today.

In any case, English has never been more than the language of a small educated class in the thickly populated countries of Asia and Africa. It may be the language of higher education, but primary education – which is all that most Asians and Africans ever receive – has to be given in the vernacular; and that may mean hundreds of different vernaculars. Even in New Zealand and Australia, where English could never be displaced, there is already a strong and growing sentiment of belonging to a distinct nationality, not simply of being Englishmen living in the Antipodes; and the majority of immigrants into Australia are no longer of British stock. On all the races and peoples included in the Commonwealth, moreover, one of the first and strongest cultural influences that they become aware of once they have mastered English is that of the U.S.A. Another foreign influence of a very different kind that also uses the English language in the Commonwealth is Communism. In fact, it is not so much the British cultural link that is being preserved, except incidentally and in a diluted form. It is the English language as an international medium of communication; and that is neither exclusive to the Commonwealth nor universal within it.

Thus all the formal links dissolve under close inspection. The Commonwealth Relations Office alone seems to remain; and even the C.R.O. is the point of exchange for grievances and disputes as well as for agreements. The most notorious disputes, of course, have been those between India and Pakistan over Kashmir and the Indus waters; but there are others. The treatment of Asians and native Africans in South Africa, and Australia's alleged discrimination against Asian immigrants, are grievances felt deeply by the Afro-Asian members of the Commonwealth. Britain's action against Egypt in 1956, and the question of the recognition of Communist China, are other cases that split the Commonwealth more or less seriously. Colonialism and race relations are two issues that are bound to provoke continuing dissension, however misconceived. Yet none of these points of friction has ever in fact caused the Commonwealth to split irremediably, or driven any member-country to leave it. It does seem possible to speak of a sense of solidarity, and even of a common outlook on world problems, if not of a sentiment of unity. At least it is unthinkable that members of the Commonwealth should go to war against each other; and that is more than can be said for the United Nations.

In all other respects the advantages of belonging to the Commonwealth are diffused and variegated. Some members enjoy one advantage, some another, but probably none enjoys all and the advantages that each enjoys are different. In one respect, however, the advantage offered by membership of the Commonwealth is uniform and unique. It may be called the sense of secure status in a disordered world. What has made the world disordered is that two contrary things are going on in it at the same time. One is the trend towards larger aggregations of power, because the traditional nation-state is no longer large enough for modern conditions: the U.S.A. and the U.S.S.R. having set the new standard, amalgamations like United Europe and the United Arab Republic are attempts to measure up to it. On the other hand, simultaneously, more and more nations are struggling into independent existence, sometimes even smaller than the traditional nation-states, and pressing forward to achieve the very status of national sovereignty which the older nations are finding obsolete. Most members of the Commonwealth today fall into the category either of new nations or of small states by modern standards. In the contradictory pattern of the world today all of them, even the least new and least small, find that the Commonwealth provides a satisfactory half-way house between standing alone in a harsh world and being absorbed into some larger unit of sovereignty. That is the essential justification of the twentieth-century Commonwealth. But of course it means, *ex hypothesi*, that the Commonwealth cannot itself be that larger unit of sovereignty within which, if at all, Britain must find the possibility of standing on equal terms with the twentieth-century giants.

The Atlantic Community

The last possible candidate for the role described is the so-called Atlantic Community. The term has been current for at least a decade, but it has acquired little precision or definition. It has been used with approval by British Governments of both parties, but more particularly perhaps by enthusiasts outside the Government. Attlee spoke as early as June 1950 of entering 'a formative and decisive phase in the organization of the Atlantic Community', which would require 'the surrender in an unprecedented degree by each country of the ability to do as it pleases'. Two and a half years later the Conservative Government, explaining its policy to the Council of Europe, emphasized that the Atlantic Community did not mean, in British eyes, 'a federation embracing the countries of the North Atlantic Treaty Organization'. The Opposition would no doubt have broadly agreed. But there was an awkward ambiguity about the negative in the last quotation: undoubtedly it governed the idea of a federation, but whether it also governed the countries of N.A.T.O. was not clear. In other words, although it was certain that the Atlantic Community was not to be a federation, it was less certain whether or not the membership of the Atlantic Community was coextensive with that of N.A.T.O.

The North Atlantic Treaty contains, in Article II, express provisions for non-military co-operation, but attempts to apply them have had only limited success. Political co-operation has been a matter of frequent discussion, especially since the Suez Canal crisis of 1956, when the rest of the N.A.T.O. powers were shocked by the failure of Britain and France to consult them. But there were obvious limitations to the possibility of political consultation about matters outside the N.A.T.O. area; and even in the case of Cyprus, which was discussed in the North Atlantic Council in 1958, it is doubtful whether N.A.T.O.'s intervention made any real contribution towards a settlement. Economic co-operation was hardly more successful as an application of Article II. The idea of N.A.T.O. collectively administering aid to underdeveloped countries did not appeal to the U.S.A. as a method of channelling American funds, nor to the underdeveloped countries, most of which wished to have nothing to do with a military alliance. Nor could it be overlooked that one or two members of N.A.T.O. were themselves underdeveloped countries, in no position to contribute to the development of others. The problems of non-military co-operation were in fact so intractable that in May 1956 the North Atlantic Council appointed a special committee of 'three wise men' to advise them on the subject. But the results remained meagre.

It is not hard to see why. A community formed for any other purpose except defence out of the fifteen countries composing N.A.T.O. would be a curious entity. It is true that only twelve out of the fifteen were members of N.A.T.O. in 1950, and that the fifteenth had not yet adhered by the end of 1952, but that only enhances the curiosity. None of the last three adherents – Greece, Turkey and the German Federal Republic – is in the strict sense an Atlantic power at all, nor were they the first members of N.A.T.O. of which that is true. But irrespective of the facts of geography, the essential point about N.A.T.O. is that it consists simply and solely of those fifteen powers which were both able and willing to come together for a common defensive purpose against a potential aggressor, and which were mutually acceptable to each other. Other powers were willing but not universally acceptable, such as Spain; others would have been acceptable but not willing, such as Switzerland.

But for the particular purpose in view at the time, the fifteen members of N.A.T.O. were both the maximum and the minimum. They could not be increased without promoting dissension and even secession; they could not be reduced without prejudicing defensive capability.

From any other point of view, however, they were not a natural grouping. Even from the point of view of strategy, the boundaries of N.A.T.O. are inconvenient. It is impossible to call 'natural' boundaries which divide Scandinavia, which split Germany down the middle, and which leave Portugal, Greece and Turkey separated from their allies by the exclusion of intervening countries. The N.A.T.O. front is further almost split in half by the intruding wedge of neutral Switzerland and Austria; and some of the U.S.A.'s most important air-bases for the defence of Western Europe are not on N.A.T.O. territory at all. The only truly distinctive feature about N.A.T.O. is that it is the first alliance in history from which it is impossible for any power to contract out of its obligations if the test of war comes, because the physical intermingling, particularly in the integrated H.Q. (S.H.A.P.E.), has been carried so far that an attack on one power would be an attack on all in fact and not merely on paper.

From any other point of view than the strategic, it is plain that the fifteen powers would not be an association uniquely dictated by the circumstances. Economically, the natural groupings of Europe have proved to be either wider than N.A.T.O. (for instance, O.E.E.C.) or narrower (for instance, E.C.S.C. and the Common Market). Politically, if N.A.T.O. is looked upon as a bulwark of Western democracy, the inclusion of Turkey and Portugal is an anomaly; and so is the absence of Sweden and Switzerland, well known though the reasons are. Looked upon as a community embodying a cultural heritage, it is as curious to find Turkey included in it as to find Spain excluded from it. From all these points of view it is difficult to identify the Atlantic Community, if such a thing exists at all, with the membership of N.A.T.O.

The Community, to become a reality, would evidently have to be in some respects narrower and in others wider than N.A.T.O. It is easy, though invidious, to suggest where it would have to be pruned; but the extensions of its limits in the other direction is more problematical. Most members of N.A.T.O. have close connexions in other parts of the world outside the alliance. Some have other alliances: Britain and Turkey belong to the Central Treaty Organization (formerly the Baghdad Pact), Britain and France to S.E.A.T.O. Some have special relations with other countries which divide loyalties and distract their attention. The Scandinavian members have a special relation with Sweden and Finland, which all but prevented them from joining N.A.T.O. at all. France has a special relation with Tunisia and Morocco, the latter of which is certainly an Atlantic state though not a member of N.A.T.O.; and Portugal has a special relation with Brazil, which is as much an Atlantic state as the U.S.A. Turkey and Greece have a treaty with Cyprus, which was expressly excluded from N.A.T.O. while it was a British colony. The German Federal Republic (West Germany) has a peculiarly vital relation with, as well as a separation from, the German Democratic Republic (East Germany). Both the last two examples show that such special relations can be the cause of dissension and even potential wars as well as of a distraction of interest. Finally, five members of N.A.T.O. (Britain, France, Portugal, Belgium,[1] the Netherlands) were still colonial powers, a fact which presented the same kind of difficulties to an Atlantic Community as to a Common Market.

It is not surprising that it has never been possible to give precision to the idea of the Atlantic Community. British attempts to do so have given the appearance of being half-hearted and fumbling: for instance, the so-called 'Grand Design' presented by the Foreign Secretary to the Council of Europe in the summer of 1957, which sought to merge a number of European organs of co-operation with U.S. and Canadian participation. It was ill received by the European representatives, among whom the Six in particular were anxious to complete the process of giving form and substance to their own supranational institutions without blurring the edges and confusing the objective by tacking on to them accretions from across the Atlantic or even, by that time, from across the Channel. The failure in 1957 was decisive: perhaps success had not even been expected. By 1959, when N.A.T.O.'s tenth anniversary was celebrated in a number of influential and splendid gatherings, the emphasis was laid entirely on solidarity and not at all on merger. The idea that in the Atlantic Community Britain could find a new kind of sovereign political unit, belonging to a new order of magnitude, was as much an idle dream as the same conception of the Commonwealth.

Interdependence

The larger unit, into which British sovereignty would have to be merged in order to achieve equality with the U.S.S.R. and the U.S.A.,

[1] Belgium ceased to be a colonial power in 1960, when the Congo became independent.

has thus proved to be a will-o'-the-wisp, at least in the period under review. That was indeed probably the wish of the majority of people in Britain, and in such matters democracy can work decisively. The place of the larger unit was taken by 'interdependence', which was applied in the economic, political and strategic contexts alike, so far as the circumstances of each allowed. Interdependence had two advantages over integration or full union. Firstly, it did not involve more than a minimum abdication of sovereignty. Secondly, it was possible to form different patterns in different contexts: to be economically interdependent with one group of powers and strategically interdependent with another. From both points of view it appealed to the British instinct in foreign affairs, which was for caution and flexibility, and against permanent and comprehensive ¦commitments. It meant forgoing the advantages of scale which were enjoyed by the U.S.A. and the U.S.S.R., and probably even by the Six, but it was still not obvious in 1959 how great a sacrifice that meant. It seemed probable that in any case any British Government would have followed the same course, and that any change would be slow to command popularity.

The one change of circumstances which could certainly alter the compromise implied in 'interdependence' would be war. War, or at least coercion by the threat of force, has hitherto been the usual, if not the invariable, catalyst of the process by which the upward change is made from smaller-scale to larger-scale units of sovereignty. The mediaeval state superseded the city-state by force, and the nation-state the mediaeval. The process is not always complete and all-embracing, as the survival of Luxembourg or even San Marino shows to this day, but it is generally thorough and effective, as it was in Germany and the U.S.A. There is perhaps no other means by which a real merger of Britain's sovereignty into some larger unit could be brought about except in the course of war, as it well might have been in 1940 if the French Government had accepted Churchill's offer, or of course if Hitler had won. It is clearly futile to speculate what would be the consequences of such a war, but it is relevant to consider what were the chances of it breaking out, as seen at the end of the 1950s. If they were non-existent, then there was probably no serious threat to the course which Britain had chosen.

Wars may begin, it is said, not only by design but by accident. In 1959 people's fears, at least in Britain, appeared to be of accident rather than design. But it is difficult in fact to find any war in history that ever broke out by accident in the strict sense. What is probably meant by 'accident' is miscalculation. The distinction is important. A war could be said to break out by miscalculation if the initial act were deliberate but the consequences were not intended: this may well have been true in 1914. It could be said to break out by accident only if the initial act as well as its consequences were unintended; but no example comes readily to mind. In fact such a thing is exceedingly unlikely to happen. Guns do not go off by themselves. Nuclear weapons are even harder to set off: it seems almost inconceivable that a nuclear weapon should be set off against a potential enemy by mere accident. This view is borne out by several cases in which nuclear bombs have been dropped by accident without causing nuclear explosions. Those who fear a war breaking out by accident in the strict sense are postulating a unique event, unprecedented in human history. Miscalculation, however, is another matter, and a rather less improbable one. The arguments against war by miscalculation are today much the same as against war by design. They rest partly on the nature of modern weapons, both nuclear and conventional, and partly on the changed psychological climate of international affairs.

In the field of weapons there is still an important distinction between the conventional and the nuclear. But since, as it is commonly argued nowadays, small nuclear weapons have almost reached the status of being conventional, the distinction which is more important is that between powers which have nuclear capability and those which have not. At the end of the period under review, the only three powers in the first category were the U.S.A., the U.S.S.R. and Britain, with France approaching the threshold. These powers were all conscious of the fatal consequences that would follow, for themselves as well as for their enemies, from the use of nuclear weapons. They were all determined therefore that nuclear weapons should never be used: that was the meaning of the deterrent. The Conservative Government in Britain also believed that the confrontation of the nuclear powers across a clear-cut line in Europe was an additional guarantee that the risks which might lead to nuclear war would never be taken.

It further believed that the possession of nuclear weapons by Britain added significantly to the power of the deterrent, at least in three respects. Firstly, the British component in the first stage of an Anglo-American use of the deterrent, if it became necessary, would, according to expert opinion, be proportionally very considerable. This was the case because of the development of an experienced and powerful Bomber Command in the Second World War; and therefore the same argument did not apply to France, which had not that experience. Secondly, British nuclear weapons added to the allied deterrent in the event that the U.S.A. might not be willing to use its own nuclear weapons unless U.S. territory were directly subjected to nuclear attack, a reluctance which seemed increasingly probable in the late 1950s. Thirdly, the possibility that Britain could use nuclear weapons on her own, even without the U.S.A., if her vital interests required it, constituted an important influence on allied policy, and also presumably on Soviet policy.

The force of the last points may be illustrated in two ways. Firstly, situations have arisen in the last decade (in Korea and Indo-China, for instance) in which the U.S. Government appeared to be on the brink of risking total war with nuclear weapons. The British Government then wished to restrain the U.S. Government from doing so. When reaching a decision whether to allow themselves to be restrained, the Americans could well be influenced by the knowledge that sooner or later a situation might arise in which the British Government might seek to drag them into similar risks, and they might wish to restrain the British. If the British possessed nuclear weapons, as the Americans knew that they either would or already did, the force of British persuasion on the Americans in such a case would be greatly enhanced. Secondly, the existence of British nuclear weapons would reduce the danger that the U.S.A. might contract out of the risks involved in a Soviet attack on Europe which did not extend to the U.S.A. The 1958 White Paper was no doubt addressed both to the U.S. Government and to the Soviet Government when it declared that if the latter 'were to launch an attack . . . even with conventional forces only', the Western Allies 'would have to hit back with strategic nuclear weapons'. From these conceptions, however, most of the Labour Party in opposition recoiled.

There were further arguments against the surrender of nuclear weapons by Britain, whether unilaterally or in agreement with others as members of a 'non-nuclear club'; and these lead straight to the crucial point. If Britain made such a gesture of renunciation, then either the two chief nuclear powers would follow suit, or (much more probably) they would not. In the latter case Britain would merely have weakened her international standing: she would automatically have been excluded, for instance, from conferences such as that which began at Geneva in November 1958 on nuclear tests. But in the other case, if the U.S.A. and the U.S.S.R. were likewise to renounce nuclear weapons, then it was arguable that European security would be reduced rather than enhanced. For then the powers would be confronting each other across a line through Europe no longer armed with weapons which they all regarded as too terrible to use, but armed only with weapons which they did not so regard. In other words, the pre-war situation would be restored. In those circumstances, as experience had proved, war would be more likely, not less likely; and in the course of such a 'conventional' war, if it broke out, nuclear weapons would presumably be reintroduced, since unlike the weapons themselves the scientific knowledge lying behind them could not be abolished. It did not appear that the risk could be significantly reduced by expanding the dividing line through Europe into a 'neutral zone', in other words, by 'disengagement'; for that too had been tried before. It was 'disengagement', and not a close confrontation of the rival powers, that led to the Korean War in 1950.

Although it was impossible to predict with certainty the consequences of dispositions other than those actually prevailing, there was a presumption for the *status quo* in preference to risky readjustments, at least until a mutually satisfactory system of disarmament could be devised. The *status quo* had in fact kept the peace in Europe for five years between the achievement of approximate nuclear parity and the end of 1959. There seemed to be no reason why it should not continue to do so, since all parties to it found the stakes too high to justify risks. As has been pointed out earlier, all the crises of recent years have shown that none of the major powers wishes to risk a war of mutual suicide. But they have also shown something even more important: that it is possible not only for the nuclear powers to avoid war with each other, but also to prevent lesser powers from starting local wars which would eventually engulf them all. Crises like those of 1956–9 in the Middle East or the Far East would almost infallibly have led to local war, and perhaps then to global war, a generation ago. Today they do not do so.

The reason again lies partly in the nature of modern weapons. Even the so-called conventional weapons today are so intricate, so highly skilled in use and expensive in production, that no small power can afford to produce for itself a full array. Small powers therefore buy them from big powers, and with their weapons they also buy a commitment just as binding as a formal treaty. For the continuing need for technicians, spare parts and ammunition is so great that no small power can thereafter go seriously to war for any length of time without the acquiescence of the great power which supplies them. Given that the great powers obviously want war to be avoided, they have the power to prevent it locally as well as globally. The supply of weapons to small powers like Iraq and Indonesia (whose armed forces are in any case usually instruments of internal security rather than war) can therefore be a contribution to the guarantee of peace. If several great powers supply weapons to the same small power, the guarantee is even stronger, because the weapons will all be different; and no country can fight a war for long if its weapons come from many different sources, any of which could be cut off at will. The fact that in 1958–9 Indonesia bought military equipment from the U.S.S.R., Italy, Britain and the U.S.A. is therefore comforting rather than the reverse; and so is the fact that the United Arab Republic and Iraq have military equipment from both sides of the Iron Curtain.

With the last examples the argument passes over from the domain of weapons to the domain of international psychology. The impact of modern weapons is only one of many illustrations of the fact that a change of climate has come about in international relations. It may be best summed up as a loosening, if not a dissolution, of the patterns which seemed so fixed and rigid only a few years ago. When or how the process began is not easy to say. But it is possible to point to an accumulation of significant events early in 1955: a partial *rapprochement* between the Soviet and Yugoslav Governments; the Bandung Conference of the Afro-Asian Powers; the signature of an Austrian Peace Treaty; conciliatory words addressed by Chou En-Lai, the Chinese Communist Foreign Minister, towards the Americans; the appointment of a member of Eisenhower's cabinet in charge of disarmament negotiations; a renewal of discussions about a Summit Conference.

None of these things came out of a clear sky: all had a history behind them. But from that period onwards it was possible to detect a trend towards flexibility, and away from rigidity, which on the whole gathered strength despite much faltering and many setbacks in the next five years. There was a great increase in two-way traffic – political, commercial and individual – even across the Iron Curtain; though it was still made much harder for ideas to cross it from West to East, and people from East to West, than vice versa; and the traffic was often suspended by grim events. The exchange of visits between Western and Soviet heads of Governments in 1959, and the circumspect approach to the Summit at the same time, although they produced no immediate changes of substance, nevertheless suggested that coexistence between the two opposing blocs had come to stay. But it was perhaps no longer the relation between the two blocs alone that mattered.

At the beginning of 1955 international events had seemed to revolve round two irreconcilable poles, embodied in Dulles and Molotov. Five years later both had gone, and the man in the street could hardly have named their successors. But that was not so much because the leading roles had passed to their principals, Eisenhower and Khrushchev: it was rather because the two poles had lost a good deal of their magnetic force. Many more names now counted in international affairs as men without whom great decisions could not be sealed: Macmillan, de Gaulle, Adenauer, Nehru, Diefenbaker, Menzies, Chou En-Lai, Rapacki, Nkrumah, Nasser, Tito, Sukarno, and others farther down the list. Nor was it possible to put all these names into ready-made groups, for or against this side or that. They had views and policies of their own, which might carry them into one group in one context and another in another. Poland and China joined Yugoslavia in marching now in step, now out of step with the Soviet Bloc; France and Germany were sometimes the only members of the Western Alliance in step at all; India and Egypt and Ghana marched as they pleased, and they even had Eisenhower's word for it that they were entitled to do so.

As the rigid patterns relaxed it became possible to take a new look at old patterns in a new light. Many of them were none the easier to solve for all that, and with many it might be necessary to learn to live for a long time: Berlin and divided Germany, for instance; or the two Chinas; or divided Korea and Vietnam; or the relations of Israel and the Arab states. These problems were not soluble in the ordinary sense of the word 'solution', implying a settlement which all concerned can be persuaded to accept by mere reason. But they might come to be tolerated, however intolerable they seemed, when it became apparent that there was no way of changing them. Where changes were both possible and necessary, on the other hand, the prospects were at least improved by the changing atmosphere. In Africa, for instance, behind the sombre foreground, there were encouraging factors in the background. One was that the African leaders were in most cases, apart from exceptions like Kenyatta and Lumumba, men of moderation and good will. Another was that the European Powers, no longer looking on each other as colonial rivals, were not only moving generally in the same direction, but were more willing to move in concert, for instance in recognizing the need to redraw the boundaries of Africa. It was also a matter for relief that the possibility of war between the great powers over Africa was virtually non-existent.

Yet other problems of a familiar kind might never arise again at all.

For instance, the dependence of Western Europe on oil from the Middle East might eventually cease to be so burning a problem, as the development of atomic energy decreased its seriousness and the emergence of a buyer's market in oil induced the producing countries to take a more reasonable view of their relation with the customers than they did in the days of a seller's market. There were already signs of this possibility in 1958: in Iraq, as also in Venezuela in that year, a revolutionary change of Government took place without interrupting the flow of oil for a single day, since the revolutionaries knew as well as their predecessors that it was their country's life-blood. This was a sharp and welcome contrast to what happened in Iran in 1951; and it was a sign of the times. At the same time, the Western oil companies and Governments were learning from experience the salutary lesson that their dealings with oil-producing countries must not only be economically fair but politically equal; and this too was a sign of the times.

The dissolution of the set patterns of the past also coincided with the emergence of problems which could only be tackled by abandoning old conceptions and formulating new ones. Such problems happened to come almost simultaneously on sea, land and in the air (or rather, space) in ascending order of importance. At sea the old problem of territorial waters took on a new acuteness as one power after another sought unilaterally to extend its reach: Communist China, for instance, made a claim which would embrace the offshore islands geographically, whoever held sovereignty over them. On land, there was a great stimulation of interest in Antarctica as a result of the International Geophysical Year in 1958. There the nations faced the problem that seven of them had claims, in five cases mutually recognized, on the only uninhabited continent; and that the U.S.A. and the U.S.S.R., which were not among the seven, would recognize no claims. Finally, beyond the earth the advent of space-rockets and earth-satellites raised problems to which traditional concepts of human affairs seemed to have small relevance.

Men could find the new concepts to tackle such problems, if they had to. A beginning was made, for instance, in the case of Antarctica, with the International Geophysical Year of 1958, in which thirteen powers took part, including the U.S.A. and the U.S.S.R. in addition to those claiming territory. Co-operation on a practical and scientific basis proved so successful that the idea gained ground of attempting to solve the problem of sovereignty by an international 'functional approach'. A twelve-power treaty regulating the peaceful development of

Antarctica was signed in Washington before the end of 1959 with an almost unexampled readiness and unanimity, which seemed an encouraging omen for the future. Whatever might come of this, there was apparent in 1959 a new readiness among the nations to discuss such problems in an imaginative and flexible spirit, in contrast with the rigidity of earlier years.

The improved international atmosphere of 1959 sprang not so much from a hope that things were changing as from a recognition that in some important ways they had changed, and the changes were irreversible. The prospect was therefore better than the false dawn of 1955, because it was based on recognized realities. For Britain in particular the outlook was encouraging, since Britain was not a power that wished to bring about radical changes in the world but to live with the world as it was. British policy, as was said in the Introduction, is not to achieve objectives but to protect interests. The protection of British interests overseas, which are fundamentally peaceful and commercial, is hardly likely to be seriously, still less to be fatally, threatened in the calmer and more reasonable atmosphere of international relations which seemed likely to follow the gradual elimination of the danger of major war and the great reduction of the danger of local war.

There still remain very grave problems for British foreign policy, but none which need reduce policy-makers to despair. Britain is no longer capable of an entirely independent foreign policy; but nor is any other power. Britain's relations with the rest of Western Europe gave rise to great uneasiness in 1959; but even if Western Europe was united in its coldness towards Britain, this was at least an improvement on the past, when Western Europe was perpetually disunited by war or the threat of war. National wars between the states of Western Europe are now as much a matter of past history as between Britain and the U.S.A.: and that is no small gain to set against the temporary disturbance of inter-allied relations. Nor is Europe the only area of the world where the problems of the future, grave and difficult though they remain, are relatively much less severe in comparison with what was to be expected a generation or even a decade ago.

There were grounds for cautious optimism not only about the state of the world fifteen years after the war, but also about Britain's position in it. Although no longer in the top category of great powers, Britain was the most indispensable and influential of the next category: indispensable to the U.S.A. and the Western Alliance, influential not only with them but also with the rival bloc and with the neutrals. The strength of Britain's standing in the world can be best measured by two examples which are frequently quoted (generally by domestic critics) to prove the exact opposite: the consequences of the Suez intervention, and colonial policy in Africa.

In neither case is there any real basis abroad for the belief expressed by critics at home that they have damaged Britain's reputation in the world. Both political parties deserve credit for this fact. In the case of the Suez intervention, foreign sentiment was almost equally divided between sympathy for the Conservative Government and admiration for the Socialist Opposition – two incompatible but equally pro-British sentiments. In the case of colonial policy, the most pertinent fact is that so large a number of Africans – in Nyasaland, the Cameroons and the High Commission Territories, for instance – should look to London rather than anywhere else for fair treatment, whether under a Conservative or a Labour Government. Such confidence in Britain abroad, however deplorable it may seem to critics at home, augurs well for the foreseeable future.

Apart from being desirable in itself, it provided the essential basis for the two most important tasks of British policy in the long run. One was to remain a great commercial power; for a strong and favourable balance of payments was recognized as the one indispensable condition of prosperity at home, as well as of the capacity to promote prosperity abroad in underdeveloped areas. The other was to maintain the English language, with the cultural tradition and educational system that flowed from it, in its place as the first in the world. This was not a foregone conclusion, though its chances were good, English having already outstripped Spanish and French as a world-language, and not yet been rivalled by Russian or Chinese. Compared with these challenges to Britain's leadership, problems of defence and colonial rule, though still inescapable, were mercifully becoming secondary.

A case might be made out, then, for believing in 1959 that the world was cooling down. It was rather like a dying volcano, not yet extinct but unlikely to have another major eruption. The crater of such a volcano is a pool of molten lava, from which boiling gobbets are thrown up into the air from time to time, some to a considerable height, some hardly breaking the surface. Until the molten lava solidifies and cools, the process can be alarming to watch, and people are always uneasy watching it. The possibility cannot be ruled out for a long time that a massive quantity of lava will boil up and overflow; but on the whole it seems unlikely that anything worse will happen than a very large, very hot gobbet being thrown up to a greater height than normal – by the Chinese Communists, for instance. The other powers have learned their lesson – the lesson taught by Hitler, by Stalin, by the Japanese militarists. Such men belonged to the pre-nuclear age, and are unlikely to be repeated in the countries that produced them. The present-day Chinese Communists also belong to the pre-nuclear age, but it is reasonable to hope that before long they may enter it. By then there is a good chance that the volcano will be extinct. Until then, we must be constantly ready for the worst, which has seemed imminent for the last ten years; but if we are ready, it may never happen.

Index

Index

Note—References to the following are too numerous to be indexed:
Europe, Great Britain, the U.S.A. and the U.S.S.R.

249